2000 EDITION

THE OFFICIAL LOCOMOTIVE ROSTERS & NEWS

ISBN 0-919295-32-0

PLEASE READ

SPECIAL REWARD

Copyright offences historically have been swiftly dealt with, resulting in substantial monetary awards. We encourage anyone who knows of any contravention of the above paragraph to communicate in confidence at once with us concerning proof of violation. The first person to provide us with the satisfactory proof resulting in prosecution will be entitled to the substantial reward totaling one-half of the successful settlement after legal expenses.

PRINTE[

DPA-LTA L.

D0711648

PO BOX 100 STATION "R"   PO BOX 300[
MONTREAL QC CANADA H2S 3K6   CHAMPLAIN NY 12[

PRICE $26.95

ACKNOWLEDGMENTS

Acknowledgments of appreciation are extended to the following
contributors, in varying degrees, listed alphabetically below,
in addition to the mechanical and operational staff of the
railroads.

Keith Baker	William W Joly Jr
Stan Bolton	James B Kerr
Felix R Brunot	George Kovacs Jr
Ed Capen Jr	Stephen A Mayotte
Sam Carlson	Mike Murray
Bruce Douglas	James L Paty
Anthony Fernandez	Dave Read
Pat Frangella	Wayne Slayton
Brent Holt	Herbert E Snook
Fred James	George Stefanics

Craig Walker

EDITORIAL LAYOUT AND COMPOSITION

Mrs Olga M Kerr Beloved wonderful wife of the editor

COVER PHOTOGRAPH

SD90MAC Model 6000hp Courtesy of Electro-Motive Division -
General Motors Corporation. This particular demonstrator is in
operation on the Union Pacific Railroad, and is still owned
by EMD-GM.

PUBLISHER'S FOREWORD

The 2000 Edition now has consolidated roster fleets, featuring
heritage railroads, of the four largest Continental Systems -
BNSF CSX NS and UP. This edition features 24 pages of full color
builders photographs showing the most recent deliveries, as well
as the most popular surviving older models, as we started last
year.

As always, your comments and personal observations are welcomed.
Do not be shy! Even a single postcard will do. Any information
used from a contributor will be acknowledged with your name in
our next edition.

Respectfully submitted,

Jim Kerr - Editor & Publisher
October 31, 1999

RENTAL LOCOMOTIVES ID

PRIVATE LESSORS

CECX HELM LOCOMOTIVE LEASING
EMDX ELECTRO-MOTIVE DIVN-GM
GACX GENERAL AMERICAN TRANSP
GATX GENERAL AMERICAN TRANSP
GCFX ALSTOM-CONNELL
GEAX TRANSCISCO LEASING
GECX GENERAL ELECTRIC
GFSX GENERAL AMERICAN CAPITAL
GLCX GLC LEASING - GATX
GSCX GATX-GLC LEASING
GWRX OMNITRAX
HATX HELM ATLANTIC LEASING
HELM HELM LOCOMOTIVE LEASING
HJVX HELM LOCOMOTIVE LEASING
HLCX HELM LOCOMOTIVE LEASING
HLMX HELM FINANCIAL
HPIX HELM PACIFIC LEASING
HPJX HELM PACIFIC LEASING
ILSX INDEPENDENT LOCOM SVCES
LLPX LOCOMOTIVE LEASING PARTN
LLWS LAVACOT
LMS GENERAL ELECTRIC LEASING
LMX GENERAL ELECTRIC LEASING
LRCX LIVINGSTON REBUILD CTR
MCHX TRANSCISCO LEASING
MKCX HELM LOCOMOTIVE LEASING
MPEX MOTIVEPOWER INDUSTRIES
MPI MOTIVEPOWER BOISE LOCOM
MWRX MIDWEST RAIL
NDYX USL CAPITAL RAIL SVCES
NREX NATIONAL RY EQUIPMENT
OWY OAKWAY LEASING EMD-GM
PNC PRECISION NATIONAL
RUSX USL CAPITAL RAIL SVCES
TILX TRINITY INDUSTRIES LSG

PROMINENT LEASING RAILROADS

AMTK AMTRAK
ATSF ATCHISON TOPEKA & S F (BNSF)
BCOL BRITISH COLUMBIA RY
BN   BURLINGTON NORTHERN
BNSF BURLINGTON NORTHERN SANTA FE
CCP CHICAGO CENTRAL & PACIFIC (IC)
CN   CANADIAN NATIONAL
CNW CHICAGO & NORTHWESTERN (UP)
CP   CANADIAN PACIFIC
CR   CONRAIL-CONSOLIDATED RAIL
CSX CSX RAIL TRANSPORTATION
CW   COLORADO & WYOMING
DMIR DULUTH MISSABE & IRON RANGE
DRGW DENVER & RIO GRANDE WEST (UP)
GTW GRAND TRUNK WESTERN (CN)
IC   ILLINOIS CENTRAL
IMAL I&M RAIL LINK
KCS KANSAS CITY SOUTHERN
MKT MISSOURI-KANSAS-TEXAS (UP)
MNCW METRO NORTH
MP   MISSOURI PACIFIC (UP)
MRL MONTANA RAIL LINK
NS   NORFOLK SOUTHERN
SOO SOO LINE (CP)
SP   SOUTHERN PACIFIC LINES (UP)
ST   GUILFORD RAIL SYSTEM
STLH ST LAWRENCE & HUDSON (CP)
UP   UNION PACIFIC
VIA VIA RAIL CANADA
WS   WISCONSIN & SOUTHERN

PROMINENT LEASING RAILROADS

These locomotives are listed in the Rosters. But locomotives rented-out are not shown as such since it would reflect duplication of data of major lines leasing locomotives between themselves.

STANDARD GAUGE

North American railroads, like European railways, are Standard Gauge with few exceptions. Standard Gauge is 4'-8½" or 1435mm between the rails. Gauge exceptions are listed after the railroad name. Most Narrow Gauge railroads are 3'-0".

HOW TO USE THIS ROSTER BOOK

COLUMN 1   Is the locomotive road number group, or road number. Exceptions or notes may follow roster.

COLUMN 2   Is the actual number of operational units in the road number group.

COLUMN 3   Is the locomotive builder. The two major current builders representing almost all locomotives built in North America now, are GE-General Electric, and GM-General Motors (GM Canada in London, ON and Electro-Motive Division in La Grange IL) other builders are listed below with * indicating current builder.

*ADT	ABB-Daimler Benz (ASEA)	IC	Illinois Central
ALCO	American Locomotive	LIMA	Lima Locomotive (LH)
*ALST	Alstom (AMFT)	MLW	Montreal Locomotive (ALCO)
BALD	Baldwin (BLH,BW)	*PLYM	Plymouth Locomotive
B-AL	Bombardier - Alstom	PORT	Porter Locomotive
*BBD	Bombardier	*REP	Republic Locomotive
*BL	Boise Locomotives (MK)	*VMV	Paducahbilt (KY)
DAV	Davenport Locomotive	VULC	Vulcan Locomotive
FM	Fairbanks-Morse (CLC)	WHIT	Whitcomb (Baldwin)
*GEII	Generation II (MINN)		

COLUMN 4   Is the original builders model - or in the case of major rebuild or remanufacture, or upgrading, the latest changes will be reflected in the originals builder model since significant physical/powerful changes have occurred.

COLUMN 5   Is the original builders model horsepower, unless altered by rebuild, remanufacture or re-rating. Steam locomotives are shown by Whyte wheel arrangement. Electric locomotives are shown either by model, horsepower or weight in tons.

COLUMN 6   Is the original builders year date, except in the event of rebuild or remanufacture the latest date because of the significant upgrading in operating life and valuation.

E&OE

A&R LINE   Winamac IN

7302	1 GM	SD18	1800	1963

ABERDEEN & ROCKFISH RR AR   Aberdeen NC

205	1 GM	GP7	1500	1951
210	1 GM	GP7U	1750	1953
300	1 GM	GP18	1800	1963
400	1 GM	GP38	2000	1968
	4			

ABERDEEN CAROLINA & WESTERN RY ACWR   Star NC

18	1 GM	GP18	1800	1960
71,896	2 GM	GP7	1500	1950
699,900	2 GM	GP9	1750	1954
1132	1 GM	SW7	1200	1950
1600-1608	9 GM	GP16	1600	1980-1982
3800-3803	4 GM	GP38	2000	1967
	19			

ABILENE & SMOKY VALLEY RR   Abilene KS

4	1 ALCO	S1	660	1945
93	1 GE	44-TON	300	1940
381	1 WHIT	45-TON	360	1943
3415	1 BALD	STEAM	4-6-2	1919
	4			

ACADIANA RY AKDN   Opelousas LA

50-52	3 GM	NW2	1200	
101	1 GM	NW2	1000	1950-1952
701,3018	2 GM	GP30	2250	1963
703,4128,1610	3 GM	GP7	1500	1952
	9			

ADIRONDACK SCENIC RR ADCR   Thendara NY

105	1 GE	44-TON	380	1942
705	1 GM	SW1	600	1941
1508	1 GM	F7A	1500	1953
2064	1 ALCO	C420	2000	1964
8223	1 ALCO	RS3	1600	1950
	5			

ADRIAN & BLISSFIELD RR ADBF   Blissfield MI

1751-1752	2 GM	GP9	1750	1976-1984

AGENCE METROPOLITAIN TRANSPORTATION AMT   Montreal QC

1301-1306	6 GM	FP7A	1500	1951-1952
1310-1313	4 ALST	GP9RM	1800	1990
1314-1320	7 GM	F59PHI	3000	2000
	17			

AGE OF STEAM RR MUSEUM   Dallas TX

7-DUT	1 BALD	STEAM	0-6-0	1923
1107-C&W	1 BLW	VO1000	1000	1943
1625-SLSF	1 ALCO	STEAM	2-10-0	1918
2379-SP	1 FM	H-12-44	1200	1956
4018-UP	1 ALCO	STEAM	4-8-8-4	1942
4501-SLSF	1 BALD	STEAM	4-8-4	1942

AGE Cont

4903-PRR		1 PRR	ELECTRIC*	4620	1940
6913-UP		1 GM	DDA40X	6600	1969
		8	* GG1 MODEL	ACQUIRING F9A MODEL	

AKRON BARBERTON CLUSTER RY AB Barberton OH

1203	1 GM	SW1200	1200	1953
1501-1502	2 GM	SW1500	1500	1966-1967
	3			

ALABAMA & FLORIDA RY AF Opp AL

903-905	3 GM	GP9	1750	
1610-1612,1614	4 GM	GP16	1600	1980
	7			

ALABAMA & GULF COAST RY Fountain AL

2175-2184	10 GM	GP30M	2000	1981-1983
2202,2238	2 GM	GP30	2250	1963
	12			

ALABAMA RR ALAB Monroeville AL

1600-1601	2 GM	GP16	1600	1980

ALAMO GULF COAST RR San Antonio TX

2253,2282	2 GM	SW1500	1500	
2664	1 GM	SW1001	1000	
	3			

ALASKA RR ARR Anchorage AK

1503		1 GM	F7B	1500	1952
1551-1554		4 GM	MP15	1500	1976-1980
1802		1 GM	GP9	1750	1951
2001-2008	A	8 GM	GP38-2	2000	1978-1986
2501-2502,2504	B	3 GM	GP35	2500	1963-1964
2801-2809		9 GM	GP49	2800	1983-1985
3001-3016	C	16 GM	GP40-2	3000	1972-1983
3017,3019-3020		3 GM	GP40	3000	1970
4001-4008		8 GM	SD70MAC	4000	1999
4009-4016		8 GM	SD70MAC	4000	2000
		61 A	2003-2008 BUILT AS GP40		
		B	2501 BUILT AS GP30	C	IS GP40

RENTALS

505		1 GM	GP38-2	2000	
3873-3874		2 GM	GP40-2	3000	
4400-4405,4408-					
4411,4413-					
4414	HLCX	9 GM	GP40-3	3000	1990
		12			

ALBANY PORT RR ALBY Albany NY

12-13	2 GM	SW9	1200	1953

ALBERTA PRAIRIE EXCURSIONS APST Stettler AB

41-MSR	1 BALD STEAM	2-8-0	1920
6060-CNR	1 MLW STEAM	4-8-2	1944
	2		

ALBERTA RY MUSEUM APRY Edmonton AB

73-NAR	1	CLC	STEAM	2-8-0	1927
1392-CNR	1	MLW	STEAM	4-6-0	1913
7944-CNR	1	GM	NW2	1000	1946
9000-CNR	1	GM	F3A	1500	1948
	4				

ALEXANDER RR ARC Taylorsville NC

3	1	GE	44-TON	400	1951
6-7	2	ALCO	S3	660	1953-1950
8	1	GM	SW9	1200	1952
	4				

ALGERS WINSLOW & WESTERN RY AWW Oakland City IN

203-206	4	GM	SD9	1750	1955

ALGOMA CENTRAL RY Sault Ste Marie ON

1501-1504	4	GM	GP7LM	1500	1978
1505-1508	4	GM	GP7M	1500	1978
1750-1756	6	GM	FP9AR	1750	1958
1761-1762	2	GM	FP9BR	1750	1958
2001-2006	6	GM	GP38-2	2000	1981
3026-3027	2	GM	GP40	3000	1967
6001-6006	6	GM	SD40-2	3000	1973
	30				

ALIQUIPPA & SOUTHERN RR ALQS Aliquippa PA

1202,1204-1205	3	GM	SW1200	1200	1954-1955

ALLEGHENY & EASTERN RR ALY Warren PA

301-302	2	GM	GP40	3000	1968
305-306	2	GM	GP35	2500	1964
	4				

ALLEGHENY VALLEY RR Columbus OH

7559	1	GM	GP10	1850	1976

ALMANOR RR Chester CA

166	1	GE	70-TON	600	1955

ALTON & SOUTHERN RY ALS East St Louis IL

1500-1517	18	GM	SW1500	1500	1969-1971
1522	1	GM	MP15	1500	1980
2000-2001	2	GM	GP38-2	2000	
	21				

ALTOONA RAILROADERS MEMORIAL MUSEUM Altoona PA

121-C&BL	1	GM	SW9	1200	1951
1361-PRR	1	JUNI	STEAM	4-6-2	1918
2681-ROYH	1	BRKV	3-TON	60	1941
2826-BWC	1	VULC	STEAM	0-4-0	1918
4913-PRR	1	JUNI	ELECTRIC*	4620	1942
6712-SS	1	BALD	VO660	660	1940
	6	* GG1 MODEL			

AMADOR FOOTHILLS RR Martell CA

10	1	BLH	S12	1200	1952

AMTRAK AMTK - NATIONAL RR PASSENGER CORP

1-20		20	GE	DASH9-P42B	4200	1996
21-120	*	100	GE	DASH9-P42B	4200	1997
151,159		2	ROHR	TURBO	1600	1976
192-199		5	GM	GP40-H	3000	1993
200-415		139	GM	F40PH	3000	1976-1981
450-470		21	GM	F59PHI	3200	1998
485-486	A	2	GM	FL9A-DM	1750	1979-1980
500-519		20	GE	DSH8-P32BWH	3200	1991
530-539		10	GM	MP15	1500	1993
550-567		15	GM	SW1200M	1200	1953
582-590		5	GM	CF7	1500	1976
600-610	B	11	GE	ELECTRIC	6000	1975
620-621	B	2	GE	ELECTRIC	6000	1975
650-652	E	3	B-AL	ELECTRIC*	8000	1998
653-664	E	12	B-AL	ELECTRIC*	8000	1999
700-709	A	10	GE	DSH9-32ACDM	3200	1995
710-717	A	8	GE	DSH9-P32ACDM	3200	1998
720-724		5	GM	GP38	2000	1995
736-742		4	GM	SW1	600	1947-1950
760,781		2	GM	GP7	1500	1950-1953
764-775		10	GM	GP9	1750	1954
790-799		10	NRE	SW1000	1000	1994
800-843	C	43	GE	DASH8-P40B	4000	1993
901-953	D	52	GM-A	ELECTRIC	7000	1980-1988
2000	E	1	B-AL	ELECTRIC*	6000	1998
2001-2039	E	39	B-AL	ELECTRIC*	6000	1999
2001-2009	F	9	GM	F59PHI	3200	1994
2010-2029		20	GM	F59PHI	3200	1997
2051-2052		2	GE	DSH8-P32BWH	3200	1991
90200-90368		15	AMT	CCB-UNIT	0	1996-1999
		582				

EXCLUDING CCB-UNITS LOCOMOTIVES NOW
DIVIDED INTO NORTHEAST CORRIDOR AND
WEST LINES * 2 REPLACEMENTS EXPECTED

A DM SUFFIX MEANS DUAL MODE - OPERATED, EITHER AS DIESEL-
ELECTRIC OR STRAIGHT ELECTRIC B E60CP MODEL
C EXCEPT 819 D EXCEPT 900,903 AEM7 MODEL BUILT BY
GM/EMD/ABB-ASEA BROWN BOVERI E B-AL IS BOMBARDIER-ALSTOM
F OWNED BY CALTRANS CALIFORNIA DEPT OF TRANSPORTATION

ANGELINA & NECHES RIVER RR ANR Lufkin TX

12	1	ALCO	S4	1000	1958
1500	1	GM	SW1500	1500	1972
2000	1	GM	GP38-2	2000	1980
	3				

ANN ARBOR RR AA Howell MI

7771,7791,7802	3	GM	GP38	2000	1969

APACHE RY APA Snowflake AZ

81-84	4	ALCO	C420	2000	1965
97-99	3	MLW	C424	2400	1966
700,800,900	3	ALCO	RS36	1800	1962
	10				

APALACHICOLA NORTHERN RR AN Port St Joe FL

712,714-715	3 GM	SW1500	1500	1968-1969
720-722	3 GM	GP15T	1500	1983
	6			

APPANOOSE COUNTY COMMUNITY RR APNC Centerville IA

116	1 GM	GP9	1750	1953
973	1 GM	GP7	1500	1951
	2			

ARCADE & ATTICA RR ARA Arcade NY

14	1 BALD	STEAM	4-6-0	1917
18	1 ALCO	STEAM	2-8-0	1920
110-111	2 GE	44-TON	380	1941-1947
112	1 GE	65-TON	400	1945
	5			

ARIZONA & CALIFORNIA RR ARZC Parker AZ

3001-3004	4 GM	GP30	2250	1983
3501-3503	3 GM	GP35	2250	1968
3801,3803-3804*	3 GM	GP38	2000	1969-1970
	10	* 3804 IS GP38-2 BUILT 1972		

ARIZONA CENTRAL RR Clarksdale AZ

2278	1 GM	GP9	1750	1979
2279	1 GM	GP7	1500	1953
3413	1 GM	GP10	1800	1981
	3			

ARIZONA EASTERN RY AZER Claypool AZ

23	1 GM	SW9	1200	1951
24-25	2 GM	SW1200	1200	1964
1309	1 GM	SW12M	1300	
1501	1 GM	SW1500	1500	1964
2045,2170-2171	3 GM	GP20	2000	1977-1960
2501-2503	3 GM	GP35	2500	1977-1980
	11			

ARIZONA RY MUSEUM Chandler AZ

1-USA	1 PLYM	30-TON	200	1943
10-MA	1 BALD	DRS66-1500	1500	1950
2562-SP	1 BALD	STEAM	2-8-0	1906
	3			

ARKANSAS & MISSOURI RR AM Springdale AR

12,14-18	6 ALCO	T6	1000	1959
20,22	2 ALCO	RS1	1000	1951-1943
42	1 ALCO	RS32	2000	1961
44-68	12 ALCO	C420	2000	1963-1966
4500	1 MLW	M630	3000	
	22			

ARKANSAS LOUISIANA & MISSISSIPPI RY Monroe LA

1513-1514	2 GM	CF7	1500	1974-1972
1812,1815-1816	3 GM	GP28	1800	1964
	5			

ARKANSAS MIDLAND RR AMR   Jones Mill AR

493		1 GM	CF7	1500	1951
700,703,707,722					
726,728,850,908					
918		9 GM	GP8	1600	1973-1978
		10			

ARKANSAS-OKLAHOMA RR   Wilburton OK

365	1 ALCO	C420	2000	1967
2010	1 GM	SW8	800	1976
	2			

ARKANSAS RR MUSEUM   Pine Bluff AR

336-SLSW	1 BALD	STEAM	2-6-0	1909
819-SLSW	1 SLSW	STEAM	4-8-4	1942
5006-SLSW	1 GM	GP30	2250	1963
	3			

ARNAUD RY   Pointe Noire QC

901-902,904-906	5 MLW	RS18	1800	1964

ASHLAND RY - OHIO DIVISION ASOH   Mansfield OH

32-33	2 GM	GP9	1750	1952
65	1 GM	NW2M	1200	1948
2912	1 GM	GP35	2500	1964
	4			

ASHTABULA CARSON JEFFERSON RR ACJR   Jefferson OH

107,518	2 ALCO	S2	1000	1950

AT&L RR ATL   Watonga OK

1127	1 GM	SW1200	1200	1964
1948	1 GM	GP9	1750	1958
2165,2169	2 GM	GP7	1500	1979
2491	1 GM	CF7	1500	1974
8102	1 GM	GP10	1750	
	6			

ATCHISON TOPEKA & SANTA FE (SEE BURLINGTON NORTHERN SANTA FE)

ATLANTIC & WESTERN RY ATW   Sanford NC

100-101	2 GE	70-TON	600	1948-1950
202,1219	2 GM	SW1200	1200	1954
	4			

AUSTIN & TEXAS CENTRAL RR   Cedar Park TX

786	1 ALCO	STEAM	2-8-2	1916

BAD WATER RR   Bonneville WY

BTI-1,BDW-1001	2 GM	SW1500	1500	1975

BALLARD TERMINAL RR   Seattle WA

78,99	2 GM	SW1	600	1940-1954

BANGOR & AROOSTOOK RR BAR   Bangor ME

20-24		5 GM	GP7R	1500	1952
60,68,70,75		4 GM	GP7	1500	1950-1952
79		1 GM	GP9	1750	1954
175-176	HATX	2 GM	GP38	2000	
301-303		3 GM	GP38	2000	1966-1969
350-366		17 GM	GP38R	2000	1996-1997
411-419	HATX	4 GM	GP40	3000	
4301-4305	HELM	5 BL	GP40	3000	1968-1971
		41			

B & O RR MUSEUM Baltimore MD

B&O-TOM THUMB	1	B&O	STEAM REP	0-4-0	1830
B&O-A JACKSON	1	B&O	STEAM	2-2-0	1832
B&O-JOHN HANCOCK	1	G&W	STEAM	0-4-0	1836
1-CC&O	1	CC&O	STEAM	4-6-0	1882
1-GC&E	1	LIMA	STEAM	3-TRUCK	1905
4-SEH	1	PORT	STEAM	0-4-0T	1950
10-B&O	1	GE	ELECTRIC	10-TON	1909
11-PM	1	GM	SW1	600	1942
13-B&O LAFAYETTE	1	B&O	STEAM REP	4-2-0	1837
19-B&O	1	GE	44-TON	400	1950
25-B&O WM MASON	1	MMW	STEAM	4-4-0	1856
32-CTN	1	BALD	VO1000	1000	1944
36-B&O	1	GM	E9A	2400	1955
50-B&A	1	GE	70-TON	600	1950
51-B&O	1	GM	EA	1800	1937
57-B&O MENNON	1	NCM	STEAM	0-8-0	1848
81-WM	1	GM	BL2	1500	1948
92-B&O	1	GM	E8A	2250	1950
117-B&O PERKINS	1	B&O	STEAM	4-6-0	1863
138T-WM	1	ALCO	SLUG	0	1962
195-WM	1	ALCO	RS3	1600	1953
217-B&O	1	B&O	STEAM	4-6-0	1869
236-WM	1	GM	F7A	1500	1952
377-C&O	1	BALD	STEAM	4-6-0	1902
490-C&O	1	C&O	STEAM	4-6-4	1946
545-B&O CROMWELL	1	B&O	STEAM	2-8-0	1888
592-CNJ	1	ALCO	STEAM	4-4-2	1901
600-B&O JC DAVIS	1	B&O	STEAM	2-6-0	1875
633-B&O	1	GM	SW900	900	1955
802-CSSSB	1	GE	ELECTRIC	2-D-D-2	1949
919-NC&SL	1	GM	F7B	1500	1950
1000-CNJ	1	A-GE	BOXCAB	300	1925
1309-C&O	1	BALD	STEAM	2-6-6-2	1949
1604-C&O	1	LIMA	STEAM	2-6-6-6	1941
1616-L&N	1	GE	U25B	2500	1964
2101-RDG AFT#1	1	RDG	STEAM	4-8-4	1945
2705-C&O	1	ALCO	STEAM	2-8-4	1943
3684-B&O	1	GM	GP40	3000	1966
4500-B&O	1	BALD	STEAM	2-8-2	1918
4876-PRR	1	PRR	ELECTRIC	2-C-C-2	1940
X5000-C&O	1	GE	ELECTRIC	12-TON	1917
5300-B&O WASH'G'N	1	BALD	STEAM	4-6-2	1927
5605-B&O	1	GM	GP7	1500	1953
6607-B&O	1	GM	GP9	1750	1956
6944-B&O	1	GM	GP30	2250	1962
7402-B&O	1	GM	SD35	2500	1964
9063-B&O	1	ALCO	S2	1000	1948
9733-B&O RRM	1	FM	H12-44	1200	1955

47 EXCLUDES SLUG

BARRIE COLLINGWOOD RY CCGX Barrie ON

1000-1001	2	GM	GP9	1750	1959

BATTEN KILL RR BKRR Greenwich NY

605,4116	2	ALCO	RS3	1600	1950-1952

BAUXITE & NORTHERN RY BXN Bauxite AR

15-16	2	GM	MP15	1500	1974

BAY AREA RAPID TRANSIT BART Oakland CA

5000,5013	2	PLYM	50-TON	670	1970-1979
5002	1	PLYM	15-TON	125	1963
	3				

BAY COLONY RR BCLR Lexington MA

1702-1703,1751	3	GM	GP9	1750	1955-1957
1750	1	GM	GP8	1750	1996
2443	1	GM	CF7	1500	1977
2501	1	ALCO	C425	2500	
	6				

BAY LINE RR BAYL Panama City Beach FL

500-507	8	GM	GP38	2000	1969-1968
508-510	3	GM	GP38-2	2000	1973-1975
511	1	GM	GP38	2000	1969
512	1	GM	GP9	1750	1956
	13				

BC RAIL BCOL North Vancouver BC

401-410		10	MLW	SLUGS	0	1981-1987
601-630	A	27	BCR	CRS20-CAT	2000	1990-1999
743-767	B	23	GM	SD40-2	3000	1979-1985
2860		1	MLW	STEAM	4-6-4	1940
3601-3615	C	15	GE	B36-7	3600	1980
3621-3626		6	GE	C36-7E	3600	1998
3716		1	MLW	STEAM	2-8-0	1912
3901-3903		3	GE	DASH8-39B	3900	1987
4601-4622	D	22	GE	DASH8-40CM	4000*	1990
4623-4626		4	GE	DASH8-40CM	4000*	1993
4641-4644		4	GE	DASH9-44CWL	4400	1995
6001-6007	E	7	GM	ELECTRIC	6000	1983-1984
		113				

9 NEW LOCMOTIVES FOR 2000 DELIVERY
4300-4500HP - 6 MLW/ALCO 420 UNITS FOR SALE
EXCLUDES SLUGS   LATE 1999.

A   EXCEPT 616,618,625
B   EXCEPT 755,760   C EX-ATSF 7484-7496, 7498-7499
D   *UPGRADED TO 4400HP - 4601,4603-4604,4606,4609-4612
4615-4618,4620-4622 COMPLETED
1996-1998.
E   GF6C MODEL AT TUMBLER RIDGE, BC

BEAUFORT & MOREHEAD RY BMH Morehead City NC

1686	1	GE	80-TON	500	1953
1852,1860	2	FM	H16-44	1600	1953
	3				

BEECH MOUNTAIN RR BEEM Elkins WV

113	1	ALCO	S2	1000	1954

BELFAST & MOOSEHEAD LAKE RR BML Unity ME

50,53-54	3	GE	70-TON	600	1948-1952
1149	1	SWED	STEAM	4-6-0	1913
	4				

BELTON GRANDVIEW & KANSAS CITY RR Belton MO

5	1	ALCO	STEAM	2-8-0	1923
102	1	GM	GP9	1750	1956-1957
1632	1	BALD	STEAM	2-10-0	1918
	3				

BELT RY CO OF CHICAGO BRC Chicago IL

480-481	2	GM	GP9	1750	1956
490-495	6	GM	GP38-2	2000	1972
500	1	GM	TR2A	1200	1949
502-505	4	GM	TR4A	1200	1950
511	1	GM	TR2B	1200	1949
513-515	3	GM	TR4B	1200	1950
524-526	3	GM	SW1200	1200	1963
530-532	3	GM	SW1500	1500	1967-1968
533-536	4	GM	MP15	1500	1975-1980
537-539	3	GM	SW1500	1500	1968-1970
560-566,570-575	13	GM	SD40	3000	1966
	43				

BELVIDERE & DELAWARE RIVER RY Ringoes NJ

780,782	2	GM	GP7	1500	1950
1848-1849	2	GM	GP9	1750	1955
8142,8159	2	GM	SW1200RS	1200	1959-1960
	6				

BERKSHIRE SCENIC RY MUSEUM BCRY Lenox MA

67	1	GE	50-TON	400	1957
954	1	ALCO	S1	660	1945
8619	1	GM	SW8	800	1953
	3				

BESSEMER & LAKE ERIE RR BLE Greenville PA

150-153	4	GM	SW1500	1500	1972
454	1	GM	SD7	1500	1953
658	1	GM	SD38-2	2000	1974
715A-722A	3	GM	F7A	1500	1952
715B	1	GM	F7B	1500	1952
821-847	9	GM	SD9	1750	1956-1958
853-856,858-859	6	GM	SD18	1750	1962
862	1	GM	SD38	2000	1967
865-869	4	GM	SD38AC	2000	1971
870-890	18	GM	SD38-2	2000	1973-1975
900-910	11	GM	SD40T-3	3000	1999-2000
	59				

BHP NEVADA RR NN/MAA Ely NV

13	1	ALCO	RS3	1600	1951
201-205	5	GM	SD9	1750	1952-1976
	6				

BIG SOUTH FORK SCENIC RY KT Stearns KY

102	1	ALCO	S2	1000	1944-1949
105	1	ALCO	S1	660	1942
	2				

BIRMINGHAM SOUTHERN RR BS Fairfield AL

210,212-213	3	GM	SW1000	1000	1967-1969
218-226	9	GM	SW1001	1000	1972-1975
260-261	2	GM	MP15	1500	1976
302	1	GM	SW7	1200	1981
303	1	LTRR	SLUG	0	1993
370	1	GM	MP15	1500	1976
574-575.588	3	GM	SW9C	1200	1977-1983
601-603	3	GM	SW1001	1000	1976
629,634,639-					
640,644,649-650					
652,657-658	10	GM	SD9	1750	1957-1958
700-702,704	4	GM	GP38-2	2000	1972-1973
	36	EXCLUDES SLUG			

BLACK HILLS CENTRAL RR BHCR Hill City SD

7,103-104	3	BALD	STEAM	2-6-2	1919-1926
6657	1	WHIT	80-TON	650	1942
	4				

BLACK MESA & LAKE POWELL RR Page AZ

5301	1	BL	MP1600	1600	1975
6001-6006	6	GE	ELECTRIC*	6000	1972-1976
6007-6014	8	GE	ELECTRIC*	6000	1982-1983
	15	* E60C MODEL			

BLACK RIVER & WESTERN RR BRW Ringoes NJ

60	1	ALCO	STEAM	2-8-0	1937
752	1	GM	GP9	1750	1956
820	1	GM	NW2	1000	1949
1523	1	GM	GP7	1500	1952
	4				

BLOOMER LINE BLOL Gibson City IL

7549,7561	2	GM	GP10	1850	1991-1990

BLUEGRASS RR MUSEUM BRRM Versailles KY

63-TRRA	1	ALCO	STEAM	0-6-0	1940
717-USA	1	PORT	STEAM	0-6-0T	1947
1849	1	FM	H12-44	1200	1953
2043,2074,2086	3	ALCO	MRS1	1600	1953
	6				

BLUE MOUNTAIN RR BLMR Walla Walla WA

784.790.792,799	4	GM	GP35L	2500	1980
2606	1	GM	CF7	1500	
	5				

BOONE & SCENIC VALLEY RR BSVR Boone IA

17-CO&E	1 CLC	STEAM	2-8-0		1940
205-LS&I	1 ALCO	RS1	1000		1945
1003,1103-C&NW	2 GM	NW2	1000		1949
1031-RE	1 ALCO	S2	1000		1943
1858-USA	1 GE	44-TON	520		1943
2254-USAF	1 GE	80-TON	600		1943
8419-B&SV	1 SINO	STEAM	2-8-2		1989
	8				

BOOTHBAY RY BRYV (2'Gauge) Boothbay ME

1-2	2 BALD	STEAM	0-4-0T		1895
281-KT	1 PLYM	4-TON CBL	35		1929
5-7,13	4 HENS	STEAM	0-4-0T		1913-1938
	7				

BORDER PACIFIC RR BOP Rio Grande City TX

96	1 GM	GP7	1500		1973

BRANDON CORP BRAN Omaha NE

427	1 GM	NW2	1000	
4198	1 GM	GP7	1500	
	2			

BRANDYWINE VALLEY RR BVRY Coatesville PA

8201	1 GM	NW2	1000		1949-1942
8202,9007	2 GM	SW9	1200		1956-1961
8203	1 GM	SW7	1200		1950
8204-8205,9008	3 GM	SW1200	1200		1957-1964
8206-8209	4 GM	SW7	1200		1950
	11				

BRANFORD ELECTRIC RY BERY East Haven CT

-Q&BSR	1 WAS	ELECTRIC	150		1917
4-SBRY	1 SBRY	ELECTRIC	800		1905
12-CSR	1 B-W	ELECTRIC	800		1917
5002-MTC	1 MTC	ELECTRIC	400		1918
	4				

BRANSON SCENIC RY BSRY Branson MO

98-B&O	1 GM	F9PH	1750		1998
99-CSX	1 GM	GP30M	2000		1982
2912-2913	2 GM	GP35	2500		
	4				

BRITISH COLUMBIA FOREST MUSEUM (3'Gauge) Duncan BC

1-WP&Y	1 GE	25-TON	150		
1-BS&W	1 LIMA	STEAM	2-TRUCK		1911
1-HLC	1 LIMA	STEAM	2-TRUCK		1920
2-SLL	1 CLIM	STEAM	2-TRUCK		1910
3-MLC	1 LIMA	STEAM	2-TRUCK		1924
9-FC	1 WHIT	85-TON	900		
9-HLC	1 CLIM	STEAM	2-TRUCK		1915
22-23	2 PLYM	8-TON			
24-ERC	1 VULC	STEAM	0-4-0T		1898
25-GW	1 VULC	STEAM	0-4-0T		1910
26-NM	1 PLYM	11-TON	260		1940
4210-JI	1 VULC				1937
	13				

BROWNSVILLE & RIO GRANDE INTERNATIONAL RR BRG   Brownsville TX

237,1130,1145	3	GM	SW1200	1200	1962-1964
8463	1	ICG	GP10	1750	1980
	4				

BUCKEYE CENTRAL SCENIC RR BCRR   Hebron OH

8599	1	GM	SW1	600	1948

BUCKINGHAM BRANCH RR BB   Dillwyn VA

1,101	2	GM	GP7	1500	1953-1951
2-3	2	GM	GP16	1600	1981
87001	1	BALD	60-TON-CAT	500	1987
	5	INCLUDES SHENANDOAH VALLEY RR			

BUFFALO & PITTSBURGH RR BPRR   Leicester NY

40,42	2	GM	SW1500	1500	1970
46	1	GM	MP15DC	1500	1960
50-51	2	GM	GP38	2000	1969
101-106	6	GM	GP40	3000	1967
450-457	8	GM	SD45-2	3600	1986
626,874,886	3	GM	GP9	1750	1955-1958
1510	1	GM	SW1500	1500	1970
2000-2003	4	GM	GP38	2000	1967-1971
3000-3001,3100					
3102,3106-3107					
3111,3119,6673	9	GM	GP40	3000	1966-1971
7803,7822	2	GM	GP38	2000	1969
	38	EXPECTING 5 - SW1500 MODELS			

BUFFALO SOUTHERN RR BUFF   Eden NY

29	1	WHIT	35-TON	300	1941
30, -	2	GE	44-TON	400	1946
81,93,105-107,					
2010	5	ALCO	S2	1000	1943-1948
423	1	ALCO	C415	1500	1966
5010	1	ALCO	RS11	1800	1961
	10				

BURLINGTON JUNCTION RY BJRY   Burlington IA

9	1	BLH	BLN 65-TON	600	1991
21,701-702	3	ALCO	C415	1500	1966-1968
44	1	GE	44-TON	300	1941
	5				

BURLINGTON NORTHERN (MANITOBA) BNML   Winnipeg MB

1685	1	GM	GP9	1750	1957

BURLINGTON NORTHERN & SANTA FE RAILWAY SYSTEM CONSOLIDATED ROSTER

HERITAGE	BN SF (ATSF)		BNSF			+ RENTALS
5	BN	1 GM	NW12	1200		1975
20-65	BN	5 GM	SW1500	1500 A		1968-1973
70	BN	1 GM	SW1	600		1941
90-97	SF	3 GM	SDFP45	3600 B		1982-1967
100-157	BNSF	26 GM	GP60M	3800 C		1990
104-162	SF	34 GM	GP60M	3800 D		1990
163-253	BN	8 GM	SW1200	1200 E		1955-1965
318,324	BN	2 GM	SW1500	1500		1973
325-347	SF	22 GM	GP60	3800 F		1991
342	BNSF	1 GM	GP60	3800		1991
380-441	BN	4 GM	SW1000	1000 G		1970-1972
500-559	SF	48 GE	DASH8-40BW	4000 H		1990
505-558	BNSF	11 GE	DASH8-40BW	4000 I		1990
560-581	BNSF	6 GE	DASH8-40BW	4000 J		1992
561-582	SF	16 GE	DASH8-40BW	4000 K		1992
600-699	SF	99 GE	DASH9-44CW	4400 L		1994
601-602	BN	2 GM	GP9	1750		1957
684	BNSF	1 GE	DASH9-44CW	4400		1994
700-799	BNSF	100 GE	DASH9-44CW	4400		1997
800-866	SF	62 GE	DASH8-40CW	4135 M		1992
808-826	BNSF	5 GE	DASH8-40CW	4135 N		1992
867-951	SF	85 GE	DASH8-40CW	4135		1993
960-1012	BNSF	53 GE	DASH9-44CW	4400 O		1994*
1001,1004	BN	2 GM	MP15	1500		1975
1013-1098	BNSF	86 GE	DASH9-44CW	4400		1996
1099-1123	BNSF	25 GE	DASH9-44CW	4400		1997
1103-1128	SF	11 GM	SLUG	0 P		1941-1979
1200-1201	BNSF	2 BL	MK1200G	1200		1994
1299-1375	BNSF	37 GM	GP7	1500 Q		1973-1981
1312-1329	SF	10 GM	GP7	1500 R		1980-1981
1375-1399	BN	13 GM	GP15-1	1500 S		1977
1400-1438	BN	14 GM	GP10	1750 T		1974-1976
1408	BNSF	1 GM	GP10	1750		1975
1460	SF	1 GM	SW-BLW	1500		1970
1477-1498	BNSF	12 GM	GP15-1	1500 U		1977
1500-1531	BN	31 BL	GP28M	1800 V		1992
1525	BNSF	1 BL	GP28M	1800		1992
1532-1539	BN	8 BL	GP28M	1800		1993,1992
1559-1574	SF	8 GM	SD39	2500 W		1985-1986
1590-1599	BN	10 VMV	GP28P	1800		1993
1600-1601	BNSF	2 GM	GP9	1750		1954-1955
1603-1607	BNSF	4 GM	GP9	1750 X		1957-1958
1609-1623	BNSF	11 GM	GP9	1750 Y		1954-1956
1625-1629	BNSF	5 GM	GP9	1750		1957-1958
1633-1634	BNSF	2 GM	GP9	1750		1954-1956
1636-1674	BNSF	6 GM	GP9	1750 Z		1978-1980
1685-1703	BNSF	3 GM	GP9	1750 AA		1954-1958
1711-1956	BN	6 GM	GP9	1750 AB		1954-1958
1991	BN	1 GM	SD60M	3800		1991

2002-2050	BNSF	33	GM	GP20	2000 AC	1977-1981
2010-2236	SF	38	GM	GP7	1500 AD	1977-1981
2051-2053	BNSF	3	GM	GP20	2000	1960-1961
2054,2057	BN	2	GM	GP20	2000	1961
2075-2077	BN	3	GM	GP38-2	2000	1970
2078-2087	BN	9	GM	GP38-2	2000 AE	1972
2081-2103	BNSF	4	GM	GP38-2	2000 AF	1972-1974
2088-2109	BN	18	GM	GP38-2	2000 AG	1974
2110-2129	BNSF	5	GM	GP38	2000 AH	1971
2111-2138	BN	23	GM	GP38	2000 AI	1971
2139-2177	BNSF	9	GM	GP38	2000 AJ	1970
2150-2153	BN	3	GM	GP38-2	2000 AK	1980
2155-2176	BN	16	GM	GP38	2000 AL	1970
2178-2189	BN	9	GM	GP38X	2000 AM	1970
2179-2181	BNSF	3	GM	GP38X	2000	1970
2192-2248	BNSF	23	GM	GP38	2000 AN	1982-1985
2244-2299	SF	43	GM	GP9	1750 A0	1978-1980
2256-2280	BN	16	GM	GP38-2	2000 AP	1973
2257-2278	BNSF	7	GM	GP38-2	2000 AQ	1973
2281-2300	BN	9	GM	GP38-2	2000 AR	1974
2282-2298	BNSF	8	GM	GP38-2	2000 AS	1974
2300-2359	SF	35	GM	GP38	2000 AT	1983-1985
2302-2313	BN	11	GM	GP38-2	2000 AU	1975
2305-2332	BNSF	3	GM	GP38-2	2000 AV	1975-1976
2314-2333	BN	17	GM	GP38-2	2000 AW	1976
2334-2369	BN	26	GM	GP38-2	2000 AX	1972
2341-2366	BNSF	9	GM	GP38-2	2000 AY	1972
2373,2375	BNSF	2	GM	GP38-2	2000	1980
2374	SF	1	GM	GP38-2	2000	1977
2377-2382	BNSF	6	GM	GP38-2	2000	1978
2400-2649	BNSF	116	GM	GP35	2500 AZ	1978-1985
2601	BN	1	GM	GP38-2	2000	1976
2700-2739	BN	38	GM	GP39-2	2300 BA	1981
2703-2780	SF	34	GM	GP30	2500 BB	1980-1984
2705	BNSF	1	GM	GP39-2	2300	1981
2740-2746	BNSF	5	GM	GP39E	2300 BC	1989
2748	BNSF	1	BL	GP39M	2300	1989
2749-2766	BNSF	10	GM	GP39E	2300 BD	1991
2751-2757	BN	3	GM	GP39E	2300 BE	1989
2760-2778	BN	10	GM	GP39E	2300 BF	1991
2772-2852	BNSF	21	GM	GP39-2*	2300 BG	1986-1989
2800-2805	BN	6	BL	GP39M	2300	1988
2804-2859	SF	78	GM	GP35	2500 BH	1979-1985
2806-2832	BN	26	BL	GP39M	2300 BI	1989
2833-2834	BN	2	BL	GP39M	2300	1990
2854	BNSF	1	GM	GP39-2	2300	1975
2855-2868	BNSF	10	GM	GP39-2	2300 BJ	1977
2870-2874	BN	5	BL	GP39M	2300	1991
2875-2878	BN	4	BL	GP39M	2300	1988
2879-2880	BN	2	BL	GP39M	2300	1989

BNSF Cont

2881-2884	BN	4	BL	GP39M	2300	1990
2885-2899	BN	15	BL	GP39M	2300	1991
2900-2924	BN	24	GM	GP39E	2300 BK	1990
2911,2931	BNSF	2	GM	GP39E	2300	1990-1989
2925-2934	BN	9	GM	GP39E	2300 BL	1989
2935-2984	BN	30	VMV	GP39V	2300 BM	1990
2941-2948	BNSF	7	GM	GP39-2	2300 BN	1979
2950-2958	BNSF	7	GM	GP39-2	2300 BO	1980
2966	BNSF	1	VMV	GP39V	2300	1990
3000-3007	BNSF	6	BL	GP40M	3000 BP	1988
3000-3069	SF	16	GM	GP20	2000 BQ	1977-1981
3011-3020	BNSF	6	BL	GP40M	3000 BR	1989
3025-3028	BNSF	4	GM	GP40E	3000	1989
3030-3039	BNSF	10	GM	GP40X	3600	1978
3110-3162	BN	49	GM	GP50L	3000 BS	1985
3138-3161	BNSF	4	GM	GP50L	3000 BT	1985
3163-3192	BNSF	30	GM	GP50	3600	1981
3193-3207	BNSF	14	GM	GP50	3600 BU	1985
3400-3705	SF	40	GM	GP39-2	2300 BV	1975-1988
3401-3415	BNSF	15	GM	SW15000	1500	1968
3416-3425	BNSF	9	GM	SW1500	1500 BW	1969
3426-3431	BNSF	5	GM	SW1500	1500 BX	1970
3432-3437	BNSF	5	GM	SW1500	1500 BY	1972
3438-3444	BNSF	7	GM	SD1500	1500	1973
3446-3455	BNSF	10	GM	SW1500	1500	1967
3456-3469	BNSF	13	GM	SW1500	1500 BZ	1973
3500-3502	BNSF	3	GM	SW1200	1200	1957-1958
3503-3504	BN	2	BL	GP40M	3000	1988
3503-3505	BNSF	3	GM	SW1200	1200	1955
3509-3518	BNSF	10	GM	SW1200	1200	1965
3509-3523	BN	9	BL	GP40M	3000 CA	1989
3519-3523	BNSF	4	GM	SW1200	1200 CB	1959
3525-3529	BNSF	5	GM	SW1200	1200	1958,1957
3530-3539	BNSF	9	GM	SW1200	1200 CC	1956,1955
3540-3547	BNSF	7	GM	SW1200	1200 CD	1957
3554	BN	1	GM	GP40E	3000	1989
3600-3618	BNSF	18	GM	SW1000	1000 CE	1972
3620-3627	BNSF	8	GM	SW1000	1000	1971
3628-3638	BNSF	9	GM	SW1000	1000 CF	1970
3640-3642	BNSF	3	GM	SW1000	1000	1971
3643-3653	BNSF	11	GM	SW1000	1000	1966
3700-3703	BNSF	3	GM	MP15	1500 CG	1975
3820-3821	BNSF	2	GM	GP7	1500	1973
3824-3837	BNSF	7	GM	GP7	1500 CH	1981,1980
3900-3982	BNSF	83	GE	DASH9-44CW	4400	2000
3950-3951	BNSF	2	GM	SLUG	0	1972
3958-3959	BNSF	2	GM	SLUG	0	1983,1981
3961-3968	BNSF	5	GM	SLUG	0 CI	1943-1944
3970	BNSF	1	GM	SLUG	0	1979
3971	BNSF	1	GM	SLUG	0	1970

3972-3974	BNSF	3	GM	SLUG	0	1987
3975	BNSF	1	GM	SLUG	0	1943
3976-3977	BNSF	2	GM	SLUG	0	1976
4011	BN	1	GE	B30-7	3000	1983
4022,4033	BN	2	GE	B30-7A	3000	1982
4053-4119	BN	65	GE	B30-7A	3000 CJ	1983
4200-4205	BNSF	5	GE	B23-7	2300 CK	1977
4227-4231	BNSF	3	GE	B23-7	2250 CL	1979
4247,4252	BNSF	2	GE	B23-7	2250	1980
4263-4275	BNSF	6	GE	B23-7	2250 CM	1984
4300-4605	BNSF	306	GE	DASH9-44CW	4400	1999
4606-4699	BNSF	94	GE	DASH9-44CW	4400	2000
4700-4719	BNSF	20	GE	DASH9-44CW	4400	1997
4720-4988	BNSF	289	GE	DASH9-44CW	4400	1998
4989-4999	BNSF	11	GE	DASH9-44CW	4400	1999
5000-5044	BN	17	GE	C30-7	3000 CN	1979
5002-5018	SF	6	GM	SD40	3000 CO	1980-1981
5020-5057	SF	22	GM	SD40-2	3000 CP	1988
5047-5126	BN	76	GE	C30-7	3000 CQ	1980
5058-5212	SF	55	GM	SD40-2	3000 CR	1978-1981
5127-5141	BN	14	GE	C30-7	3000 CS	1981
5143-5208	BNSF	32	GE	C30-7A*	3000 CT	1983
5220	BNSF	1	GE	SF30C	3000	1986
5250-5257	SF	4	GM	SDF40-2	3000 CU	1985
5326-5502	SF	10	GM	SD45	3600 CV	1982-1985
5375,5384	BN	2	GE	U30C	3000	1974
5492-5508	BN	8	GE	C30-7	3000 CW	1977
5510-5868	SF	39	GM	SD45-2	3600 CX	1986-1988
5545-5566	BN	21	GE	C30-7	3000 CY	1978
5567-5599	BN	29	GE	C30-7	3000 CZ	1979
5600-5624	BNSF	25	GE	AC4400CW	4400	2000
5979-5987	SF	5	GM	SDF45	3600 DA	1983
6100-6136	BNSF	15	GM	SD9	1750 DB	1954-1959
6102-6103	BN	2	GM	SD9	1750	1954
6107-6110	BN	3	GM	SD9	1750 DC	1956
6113-6114	BN	2	GM	SD9	1750	1957
6117-6126	BN	8	GM	SD9	1750 DD	1958
6127-6145	BN	6	GM	SD9	1750 DE	1954
6137	BNSF	1	GM	SD9	1750	1989
6140-6158	BNSF	3	GM	SD9	1750 DF	1955-1957
6150-6164	BN	9	GM	SD9	1750 DG	1955
6176,6199	BNSF	2	GM	SD9-3	1750	1955-1957
6177-6198	BN	14	GM	SD9	1750 DH	1957
6200-6210	BNSF	8	GM	SD39	2500 DI	1985
6212-6219	BNSF	4	GM	SD39	2500 DJ	1986
6217-6218	BN	2	GM	SD9	1750	1956
6226-6241	BN	4	GM	SD9	1750 DK	1959
6242-6246	BN	4	GM	SD9	1750 DL	1957
6260-6263	BN	4	VMV	SD38P	2000	1979
6264-6266	BN	3	VMV	SD38P	2000	1992
6267-6270	BN	4	VMV	SD38P	2000	1993

BNSF Cont

6289-6291 BN	3	GM	SLUG	0		1992
6292-6299 BN	8	GM	SLUG	0		1993
6300-6317 BNSF	12	GM	SD40	3000	DM	1981,1980
6318-6322 BNSF	4	GM	SD40	3000	DN	1971
6318-6323 BN	3	GM	SD40	3000	DO	1971
6325-6327 BNSF	3	GM	SD40	3000		1966
6329-6330 BNSF	2	GM	SD40-2	3000		1972
6330-6365 BN	8	GM	SD40-2	3000	DP	1972
6338-6362 BNSF	14	GM	SD40-2	3000	DQ	1988
6350-6363 SF	14	GE	B23-7	2250		1978
6364-6389 SF	23	GE	B23-7	2250	DR	1979
6366-6707 BN	21	GM	SD40-2	3000	DS	1974
6367 BNSF	1	GM	SD40	3000		1968
6374-6399 BNSF	18	GM	SD40-2	3000	DT	1972
6391-6404 SF	13	GE	B23-7	2250	DU	1980
6400-6414 BNSF	8	GM	SD45	3600	DV	1985-1982
6405-6417 SF	8	GE	B23-7	2250	DW	1984
6416-6418 BNSF	3	GM	SD45	3500		1982
6419 SF	1	GE	B23-7	2250		1987
6450-6498 BNSF	27	GM	SD45-2	3600	DX	1986
6499-6513 BNSF	6	GM	SD45-2	3600	DY	1987
6514-6515 BNSF	2	GM	SD45-2	3600		1988
6550-6552 BNSF	3	GM	SDF45	3600		1982
6700,6705 BNSF	2	GM	SD40-2	3000		1974
6715 BNSF	1	GM	SD40-2	3000		1988
6718-6806 BNSF	51	GM	SD40-2	3000	DZ	1979
6773-6797 BN	19	GM	SD40-2	3000	EA	1977
6802-6835 BN	26	GM	SD40-2	3000	EB	1973
6809-6848 BNSF	10	GM	SD40-2	3000	EC	1973*
6840-6846 BN	7	GM	SD40-2	3000		1978
6850-6851 BN	2	GM	SD40-2	3000		1974
6854-6896 BNSF	25	GM	SD40-2	3000	ED	1980
6898-6904 BNSF	6	GM	SD40-2	3000	EE	1981
6906-6910 BN	4	GM	SD40-2	3000	EF	1973
6909-6925 BNSF	7	GM	SD40-2	3000	EG	1973*
6912-6916 BN	3	GM	SD40-2	3000	EH	1972
6917-6928 BN	9	GM	SD40-2	3000	EI	1973
6929 BNSF	1	GM	SD40-2	3000		1974
6932-6944 BNSF	7	GM	SD40-2	3000	EJ	1981
6946-6958 BNSF	9	GM	SD40-2	3000	EK	1978
6963-6977 BNSF	13	GM	SDF40-2	3000	EL	1985
7000-7028 BN	26	GM	SD40-2	3000	EM	1977
7001,7016 BNSF	2	GM	SD40-2	3000		1977
7029-7125 BN	81	GM	SD40-2	3000	EN	1978
7040-7122 BNSF	12	GM	SD40-2	3000	EO	1978
7126-7185 BN	37	GM	SD40-2	3000	EP	1979
7150-7165 BNSF	4	GM	SD40-2	3000	EQ	1979
7206-7291 BN	79	GM	SD40-2	3000	ER	1980
7223-7288 BNSF	5	GM	SD40-2	3000	ES	1980
7300-7339 BNSF	40	ALST	SD40-2	3000		1999

BNSF Cont

7410-7429	SF	20	GE	DASH8-40B	4000	1988
7430-7449	SF	18	GE	DASH8-40B	4000 ET	1989
7500-7502	BN	3	GM	SD40-2	3000	1972-1980
7505	BNSF	1	GM	SD45-2	3600	1987
7800-7919	BN	19	GM	SD40-2	3000 EU	1977
7814	BNSF	1	GM	SD40-2	3000	1977
7821-7829	BN	9	GM	SD40-2	3000	1974
7830-7831	BN	2	GM	SD40-2	3000	1977
7832-7868	BN	31	GM	SD40-2	3000 EV	1978
7834-7867	BNSF	6	GM	SD40-2	3000 EW	1978
7869-7923	BN	48	GM	SD40-2	3000 EX	1979
7890-7906	BNSF	4	GM	SD40-2	3000 EY	1979
7924-7940	BN	16	GM	SD40-2	3000 EZ	1980
7938	BNSF	1	GM	SD40-2	3000	1980
8000-8008	BN	9	GM	SD40-2	3000	1977
8010-8028	BN	14	GM	SD40-2	3000 FA	1978
8014-8029	BNSF	6	GM	SD40-2	3000 FB	1978
8030-8089	BN	51	GM	SD40-2	3000 FC	1979
8032-8087	BNSF	7	GM	SD40-2	3000 FD	1979
8090-8181	BN	85	GM	SD40-2	3000 FE	1980
8104-8166	BNSF	7	GM	SD40-2	3000 FF	1980
8137-8142	SF	3	GE	C30-7A	3000 FG	1983
8155-8166	SF	9	GE	C30-7	3000 FH	1983
8200-8275	BNSF	76	GM	SD75M*	4300*FI	1995
8276-8301	BNSF	26	GM	SD75M	4300	1991
8500-8599	LMX*	95	GE	DASH8-39B	3900 FJ	1987
8700-8719	BNSF	20	GM	GP60	3800	1988
8720-8739	BNSF	19	GM	GP60	3800 FK	1989
8800-8958	BNSF	159	GM	SD70MAC	4000	1999
8959-8984	BNSF	26	GM	SD70MAC	4000	2000
9000-9099	EMD*	99	GM	SD60	3800 FL	1986
9200-9208	BN	9	GM	SD60M	3800	1989
9209-9267	BN	59	GM	SD60M	3800	1990
9268-9298	BN	29	GM	SD60M	3800 FM	1991
9277	BNSF	1	GM	SD60M	3800	1991
9297	BNSF	1	GM	SD60M	3800	1993
9400-9412	BN	13	GM	SD70MAC	4000	1993
9413-9519	BN	103	GM	SD70MAC	4000 FN	1994*
9520-9541	BN	22	GM	SD70MAC	4000	1995
9542-9569	BN	28	GM	SD70MAC	4000	1994
9546	SF	1	GE	SF30C	3000	1974
9570-9716	BN	144	GM	SD70MAC	4000 FO	1995
9647	BNSF	1	GM	SD70MAC	4000	1995
9711-9712	BNSF	2	GM	SD70MAC	4000	1996
9717	BNSF	1	GM	SD70MAC	4000	1993
9718	BNSF	1	GM	SD70MAC	4000	1996
9719-9731	BNSF	13	GM	SD70MAC	4000	1993
9732-9775	BNSF	44	GM	SD70MAC	4000	1996

BNSF Cont

9776-9865	BNSF	90 GM	SD70MAC	4000	1997
9866-9998	BNSF	133 GM	SD70MAC	4000	1998
9999	BNSF	1 GM	SD70MAC	4000	1999
		5,736	EXCLUDES SLUGS		

RENTALS DURING THE YEAR

3	EMDX	1 GM	SD60	3800	1984
741-838	EMDX	38 GM	GP38E	2000	1967-1996
1237-1245	GATX	9 GM	SD38-2	2000	1970
2000	EMDX	1 GM	SD40	3000	1973
2009	LLPX	1 GM	GP38	2000	
2801-2809	LLPX	8 GM	SD38-2	2000	1970
3621-4291	HLCX	3 GM	GP38	2000	
5978-5989	MPEX	4 GM	SDF45	3600	1982
6040-6048					
6300-6314					
6345-6348					
6381-6382	LLPX	30 GM	SD40-2	3000	1991-1997
8102-8119	LRCX	16 GE	C30-7	3000	
9502,9532	MPEX	2 GM	SD45	3200	1968
9625-9632	HBT	8 GM	MK1500D	1500	1996
		121			

NOTES

A ACTUAL 20,44,48,53,65   B ACTUAL 90,95,97
C EXCEPT 104,106,111-112,115-121,125,127,130,133,135-136
138,141-152,154,156   D EXCEPT 105,107-110,113-114
122-124,126,128-129,131-132,134,137,139-140,144
148,152-153,155,157   E ACTUAL 163,171,183,212,236
238-239,253   F EXCEPT 342   G ACTUAL 380,394,436.441
H EXCEPT 505,517,519,521,529,531-533,539,548,557-558
I ACTUAL ALL NUMBERS IN H ABOVE   J ACTUAL 560,566,570,577-578
581   K EXCEPT ALL NUMBERS IN J   L EXCEPT 684
M EXCEPT 808,811-812,814,826   N ACTUAL 808,811-812,814,826
0 * 970,973 BOTH BUILT 1996
P ACTUAL 1103-1108,1116,1118,1126,1128
Q EXCEPT 1301,1303-1308,1319,1321,1323,1326,1328-1329,1332
1334-1335,1337-1340,1344-1346,1351-1353,1355-1359
1361,1363-1365,1367-1368,1370-1372
R EXCEPT 1314,1317,1320,1323,1325-1328
S EXCEPT 1377-1378,1381,1383-1385,1388,1391,1394,1396-1398
T ACTUAL 1400,1402-1403,1406-1407,1409,1411,1413-1414
1418-1419,1422,1436,1438
U EXCEPT 1479-1480,1482,1486-1487,1489-1490,1492-1493,1495
V EXCEPT 1525   W ACTUAL 1559,1564-1567,1569-1571,1574
X EXCEPT 1606   Y EXCEPT 1612,1614-1615,1620
Z ACTUAL 1636,1639,1659,1663,1665,1674
AA ACTUAL 1685,1700,1703   AB ACTUAL 1711,1800,1804,1819,1841,1956
AC EXCEPT 2004,2007,2009,2014,2020-2023,2027-2028,2030
2033,2037,2043-2044,2048

BNSF NOTES Cont

```
AD  ACTUAL  2010,2012,2019-2020,2026,2055,2104,2108,2113
                2120,2122,2125,2132,2135,2137-2138,2141-2142
                2148-2149,2159,2193-2195,2204,2208-2209,2212-2213
                2216,2218,2220-2221,2224,2228,2231,2235-2237
AE  EXCEPT  2081  AF ACTUAL 2081,2094,2099,2103
AG  EXCEPT  2094-2095,2099,2103  AH ACTUAL 2110,2115,2119,2123,2129
AI  EXCEPT  2115,2119,2123,2126,2129    AJ ACTUAL 2139-2141,2157-
                2158,2167,2170,2175,2177    AK EXCEPT 2152
AL  EXCEPT  2157-2158,2165,2167,2170,2175    AM EXCEPT 2179-2181
AN  ACTUAL  2192-2193,2195,2201-2203,2206,2209,2217-2219
                2226,2229-2231,2237-2238,2240,2243-2246,2248
AO  ACTUAL  2244,2246-2247,2251-2263,2265,2267-2270,2272-2274
                2276,2279-2283,2285-2287,2289,2291-2299
AP  EXCEPT  2257,2259,2262,2264,2267,2274-2275,2277-2278
AQ  ACTUAL  ALL NUMBERS IN AP ABOVE  AR EXCEPT 2282-2283,2287-2289
                2291,2294-2298  AS ACTUAL 2282,2288,2291,2294-2298
AT  EXCEPT  2302-2303,2305,2311-2313,2316,2319,2323,2328-2330
                2336,2339-2341,2347-2349,2351-2352,2355-2358
AU  EXCEPT  2305  AV ACTUAL 2305,2324,2332  AW EXCEPT 2315,2324,233
AX  EXCEPT  2341,2346,2349,2351,2353,2355,2357,2359-2360,2366
AY  ACTUAL  ALL NUMBERS IN AX ABOVE
AZ  EXCEPT  2403-2408,2412,2415,2417,2422-2424,2427-2429,2434-2435
                2437,2439-2442,2446,2450,2453,2455,2457,2461,2465,2468
                2473-2476,2478-2500,2503-2504,2507,2513,2519,2521-2524
                2528,2530-2531,2534,2538-2539,2541-2543,2545-2546,2548-
                2550,2553-2554,2557,2559,2561,2565-2569,2573-2574,2576-
                2577,2581-2582,2584-2585,2587,2591,2594-2598,2601,2604-
                2607,2609-2610,2613-2614,2616-2617,2619,2623,2625,2639
                2641-2642,2644,2647  BA EXCEPT 2705,2729
BB  ACTUAL  2703-2705,2707-2708,2712,2715.2717,2722-2724,2727-2729
                2734-2735,2737,2739-2742,2746,2750,2755,2757,2762,2767
                2770,2775-2778,2780    BC EXCEPT 2741,2743
BD  EXCEPT  2750-2751,2755,2758-2760,2762,2764
BE  ACTUAL  2751,2753,2757
BF  EXCEPT  2762-2764,2766-2767,2769,2773,2775-2776
BG  ACTUAL  2772-2773,2783,2788,2791,2794-2799,2829,2835-2839
                2841-2842,2844,2852  * 2829 IS GP38H
BH  ACTUAL  2804,2807,2813,2819,2821-2824,2828,2830-2831,2834
                2838-2839,2841-2843,2845,2848-2850,2853-2854,2857
                2859,2861,2865-2869,2873-2874,2876-2877,2882,2884-
                2885,2887,2891,2894,2896,2897-2898,2901,2904-2907
                2909-2910,2913-2914,2916-2917,2919,2923,2925,2927-
                2936,2938,2941-2942,2944,2947,2951-2953,2955,2958-2959
BI  EXCEPT  2829    BJ EXCEPT 2858-2859,2864,2867  BK EXCEPT 2911
BL  EXCEPT  2931  BM EXCEPT 2941-2959,2966  BN EXCEPT 2947
BO  ACTUAL  2950,2952,2954-2958    BP EXCEPT 3002-3003
BQ  ACTUAL  3000-3001,3006,3009,3012,3023,3030-3032,3043,3046,3048
                3054,3060,3062,3069  BR ACTUAL 3011,3013,3014,3018-3020
BS  EXCEPT  3138,3144,3151,3161  BT ACTUAL 3138,3144,3151,3161
BU  EXCEPT  3206
```

BV	ACTUAL	3400-3402,3405-3413,3415-3418,3420-3421,3423-3424
		3436,3439,3441-3447,3449,3673,3678,3681,3683-3684
		3695,3697,3699,3705 BW EXCEPT 3724 BX EXCEPT 3428
BY	EXCEPT	3433 BZ EXCEPT 3564 CA EXCEPT 3512,3514-3515,3519-
		3521 CB EXCEPT 3521 CC EXCEPT 3521
CD	EXCEPT	3544 CE EXCEPT 3605 CF EXCEPT 3629,3634
CG	EXCEPT	3701 CH ACTUAL 3824,3827,3830,3833,3835-3837
CI	EXCEPT	3962,3964,3967 CJ EXCEPT 4054,4058 CK EXCEPT 4204
CL	EXCEPT	4228-4229 CM EXCEPT 4267-4272,4274
CN	ACTUAL	5000-5004,5006-5012,5025,5037-5038,5042,5044
CO	ACTUAL	5002-5003,5005,5010,5016,5018
CP	EXCEPT	5023-5026,5029,5031-5032,5034,5036-5037,5039,5043-
		5045,5048,5056 CQ EXCEPT 5049,5051,5057,5078
CR	ACTUAL	5058,5062-5063,5057,5070,5077,5082,5087,5090,5096-
		5097,5100,5104,5107-5108,5113,5116.5120-5124,5126-
		5127,5129,5132,5135-5137,5141,5143,5145-5146,5153-
		5155,5157,5159,5163,5167,5169,5172,5177-5179,5183
		5186-5187,5189-5190,5200,5204,5207,5212
CS	EXCEPT	5136 CT EXCEPT 5145-5147,5149-5151,5153-5160
		5162-5164,5180-5181,5185-5186,5190-5192,5195,5197-
		5202,5205-5207 6-C30-7 MODELS ARE 5165,5173-5174
		5183,5203-5204 CU EXCEPT 5253-5256
CV	ACTUAL	5326,5330,5333,5356,5378,5398,5401,5403,5434,5502
CW	EXCEPT	5493-5499.5501,5506 CX ACTUAL 5510,5512-5517,5802
		5804,5814-5819,5821,5823-5826,5828-5829,5832,5834-
		5836,5838,5842,5844,5851,5853,5856-5859,5862-5864
		5868 CY EXCEPT 5564 CZ EXCEPT 5568,5570,5574,5576
DA	ACTUAL	5979,5983,5985-5987 DB ACTUAL 6100-6101,6106,6108
		6111,6115-6116,6124-6125,6128-6129,6131-6132,6135-
		6136 DC EXCEPT 6108 DD EXCEPT 6124-6125
DE	ACTUAL	6127,6133-6134,6141-6142,6145 DF ACTUAL 6140,6147-
		6148 DG EXCEPT 6151,6155,6158-6159,6161,6163
DH	EXCEPT	6180,6182,6186-6189,6193,6197 DI EXCEPT 6203,6208-
		6209 DJ ACTUAL 6212,6216-6217,6219
DK	ACTUAL	6226,6233-6234,6241 DL EXCEPT 6243
DM	ACTUAL	6300-6301,6304,6306-6309,6311-6313,6315,6317
DN	EXCEPT	6321 DO ACTUAL 6318,6321,6323 DP EXCEPT 6335-6362
DQ	EXCEPT	6342-6343,6345,6348,6350,6352,6354-6356,6360-6361
DR	EXCEPT	6370,6373-6374 DS ACTUAL 6366,6368-6373,6378-6385
		6701-6704,6706-6707 DT EXCEPT 6378-6385
DU	EXCEPT	6395 DV ACTUAL 6400,6404-6405,6407-6410,6414
DW	EXCEPT	6406-6409,6416 DX ACTUAL 6450-6451,6453,6455-6463
		6470,6472,6477,6480-6481,6483,6487,6489-6491,6493
		6495-6498 DY ACTUAL 6499-6500,6502,6504,6509,6513
DZ	EXCEPT	6721-6722,6726,6729,6736,6744,6746,6749,6755-6756
		6759,6761,6763,6766-6767,6772-6780,6782,6784-6785
		6787-6789,6791-6793,6796-6797.6800.6804-6805
EA	EXCEPT	6781,6783,6786,6790,6794-6795
EB	EXCEPT	6803,6805,6809-6810,6812,6828-6829,6832

BNSF NOTES Cont

EC	ACTUAL	6809-6810,6812,6828-6829,6832,6836,6838,6847-6848
		* 6847 BUILT 1978 ED EXCEPT 6855-6856,6858,6861
		6864-6866,6869,6871,6873-6874,6881-6883,6885,6887
		6891,6895 EE EXCEPT 6901 EF EXCEPT 6909
EG	EXCEPT	6910,6912-6913,6916-6920,6923-6924 *6915 BUILT 1972
EH	EXCEPT	6914-6915 EI EXCEPT 6921-6922,6925
EJ	ACTUAL	6932,6934,6936-6937,6940,6943-6944
EK	ACTUAL	6946-6948,6950-6951,6954-6956,6958 EL EXCEPT 6967,6973
EM	EXCEPT	7001,7016,7019 EN EXCEPT 7040,7043,7047,7069,7079
		7081,7085-7086,7088,7094-7097,7107,7121-7122
EO	ACTUAL	NUMBERS AS IN EN EP EXCEPT 7149-7150,7155-7156
		7159,7165,7167-7183 EQ ACTUAL 7150,7155,7159,7165
ER	EXCEPT	7221,7223-7224,7241,7256,7265,7272,7288
ES	ACTUAL	7223-7224,7256,7265,7288 ET EXCEPT 7434,7441
EU	EXCEPT	7814 EV EXCEPT 7834,7839,7841,7844,7860,7867
EW	ACTUAL	7834,7839,7841,7844,7860,7867
EX	EXCEPT	7890,7892,7899,7901,7906-7907,7917
EY	ACTUAL	7890,7892,7901,7906 EZ EXCEPT 7938
FA	EXCEPT	8014,8016-8017,8022,8027
FB	ACTUAL	8014,8016-8017,8022,8027,8029
FC	EXCEPT	8032,8043,8046-8048,8050,8053,8074,8077
FD	ACTUAL	8032,8046-8048,8050,8053,8087
FE	EXCEPT	8104,8115,8120,8142,8145,8160,8166
FF	ACTUAL	NUMBERS AS FE ABOVE FG ACTUAL 8137,8140,8142
FH	EXCEPT	8160-8161,8165
FI		* 7 UNITS RERATED TO 4500HP 8225,8227,8239,8244
		8247-8248,8250
FJ	EXCEPT	8518-8519,8568,8575,8593 ALL UNITS LONG TERM
		LEASED FROM GE FK EXCEPT 8731
FL	EXCEPT	9062 ALL UNITS LONG TERMED LEASED FROM EMD-GM OAKWAY
FM	EXCEPT	9277,9297
FN	EXCEPT	9500-9503 * 9614,9616 BUILT 1995
FO	EXCEPT	9647,9711-9712

CADDO ANTOINE & LITTLE MISSOURI RR

306	1	ALCO	RS20M	2000	1956
319-321	3	ALCO	C424	2400	1963
	4				

CALDWELL COUNTY RR Morgantown NC

1747,1811	2	GM	GP16	1600	1980

CALIFORNIA NORTHERN RR CNRR Napa CA

103-113	11	GM	GP15-1	1500	1976

CALIFORNIA STATE RR MUSEUM CSRM South Sacramento CA

-TC	1	PLYM	2'GAUGE		
1-CPRR	1	NORR	STEAM	4-4-0	1862
1-SP	1	COOK	STEAM	4-2-4T	1863
1-NSL	1	BALD	STEAM*	2-6-0	1879
1-2-SCPC	2	BALD	ELECTRIC*	18-TON	1914
3-ST&E	1	BALD	STEAM	2-6-2	1922
5-ATSF	1	BALD	STEAM	0-4-0	1899
8-HT	1	WHIT	45-TON	300	1943
10-GR, 10-KRM	2	PORT	STEAM	0-6-0ST	1942
12-V&T	1	BALD	STEAM	4-4-0	1873
12-NPC	1	BALD	STEAM*	4-4-0	1876
13-V&T	1	BALD	STEAM	2-6-0	1873
21-V&T	1	BALD	STEAM	2-4-0	1875
65-534,545-USN	2	ALCO	MRS1	1000	1953
112-NWP	1	ALCO	STEAM	4-6-0	1908
206-KN	1	BLH	DIESEL-HY	300	1954
347B-ATSF	1	GM	F3B	1350	1949
347C-ATSF	1	GM	F7A	1500	1949
402-SN	1	GM	SW1	600	1939
543,608-ATSF	2	FM	H12-44TS	1200	1956-1951
913A-WP	1	GM	F7A	1500	1950
1010-ATSF	1	BALD	STEAM	2-6-2	1901
1240-USAF	1	GE	44-TON	380	1953
1605,1655-USAF	2	GE	80-TON	500	1953-1952
1771-SP	1	BALD	STEAM	2-6-0	1902
2030-USA	1	GM	SW8	800	1951
2085-USA	1	WHIT	20-TON	150	1941
2260-ATSF	1	BLW	DS44-10	1000	1948
2381-ATSF	1	ALCO	S2	1000	1949
2394-ATSF	1	ALCO	RS1	1000	1950
2404-ATSF	1	GM	NW2	1000	1939
2925-ATSF	1	BALD	STEAM	4-8-4	1944
4294-SP	1	BALD	STEAM	4-8-8-2	1944
4466-UP	1	LIMA	STEAM	0-6-0	1920
5021-ATSF	1	BALD	STEAM	2-10-4	1944
5208-SP	1	BLW	DRS66-15	1500	1949
6051-SP	1	GM	E9A	2400	1954
6402-SP	1	GM	F7A	1500	1952
7367-USAF	1	GE	80-TON	500	1952
8219-SP	1	GM	F7B	1500	1949
8799-SP	1	KRAU	DIESEL-HY	4000	1963
9820-ATSF	1	ALCO	RSD15	1500	1959
	47	* 3'GAUGE INCLUDES SACRAMENTO SOUTHERN			

CALIFORNIA WESTERN RR CWR   Fort Bragg CA

14		1	BALD	STEAM	2-6-2	1924
45		1	BALD	STEAM	2-8-2	1924
64-66		3	GM	GP9	1750	1955
		5				

CALTRAIN-PENINSULA CORRIDOR JOINT POWERS BOARD CALT
San Carlos CA

900-919		20	ALST	F40PH-2	3000	1999
920-922		3	BL	F40PH-2	3000	1998
		23				

CAMAS PRAIRIE RAILNET   Lewiston ID

1-6		6	GE	B23-7	2250	
143		1	GM	SW1000	1000	
		7				

CAMP CHASE INDUSTRIAL RR   Columbus OH

1855		1	GM	GP16	1600	1982

CANADIAN AMERICAN RR CDAC   Bangor ME

40		1	GM	GP40	3000	
266-397	AMTK	10	GM	F40PH	3000	
401-420	HELM	8	GM	GP40	3000	
450-453		4	GM	F40PH	3000	
500-518	NREX	19	GM	GP35R	2000	
3610,3612,3616						
3680	HELM	4	GM	GP38	2000	1968-1971
		46				

CANADIAN MUSEUM OF RAIL TRAVEL   Cranbrook BC

1409-CPR		1	GM	FP9A	1750	1954
1901-CPR		1	GM	F9B	1750	1954
4090-CPR		1	MLW	FA2	1600	1953
4469-CPR		1	MLW	FB2	1600	1953
		4				

CANADIAN NATIONAL RY (CN NORTH AMERICA) + RENTALS

102-103	2	GMBN	E8A	2400	1977
200-207	8	GM	SLUGS	0	1985-1986
211-281	71	ALST	SLUGS	0	1986-1993
500-526	27	GM	SLUGS	0	1978-1980
1063	1	GM	GMD1	1200	1985
1150-1182 A	16	GM	GMD1M	1200	1958-1960
1339-1396	15	GM	SW1200RS	1200	1959-1960
1400-1444	37	ALST	GMD1BRB	1200	1989
1600-1601	2	ALST	GMD1A	1200	1988
1650-1653	4	GM	SD38-2	2000	1976
2400-2429	30	GE	DASH8-40CW	4000	1990
2430-2454	25	GE	DASH8-40CW	4000	1992
2500-2522	23	GE	DASH9-44CW	4400	1994
2523-2562	40	GE	DASH9-44CW	4400	1997
2563-2602	40	GE	DASH9-44CW	4400	1998
2603-2642	40	GE	DASH9-44CW	4400	2001
4000-4010	6	ALST	GP9RM	1800	1981-1982
4033,4036	2	ALST	GP9RM	1800	1984
4100-4116	16	ALST	GP9RM	1800	1984
4117-4128	11	ALST	GP9RM	1800	1989-1990
4129-4143	15	ALST	GP9RM	1800	1991
4700-4732	33	GM	GP38-2	2000	1972
4760-4810	46	GM	GP38-2	2000	1973-1974
5000-5001	2	GM	SD40	3000	1967
5018-5074	17	GM	SD40	3000	1967-1968
5078-5116	7	GM	SD40	3000	1969
5129-5154	13	GM	SD40	3000	1969-1971
5201-5233	12	GM	SD40	3000	1971
5241-5277	36	GM	SD40-2W	3000	1975
5279-5293	15	GM	SD40-2W	3000	1976
5294-5313 B	19	GM	SD40-2W	3000	1978
5314-5323	10	GM	SD40-2W	3000	1979
5324-5363	40	GM	SD40-2W	3000	1980
5364-5387 C	24	ALST	SD40-2U	3000	1994-1995
5388-5398	11	GM	SD40-2	3000	1978-1999
5400-5439	40	GM	SD50F	3600	1985-1986
5440-5459	20	GM	SD50F	3600	1987
5500-5503 D	4	GM	SD50F	3800	1986
5504-5563 E	59	GM	SD60F	3800	1989
5600-5625	26	GM	SD70I	4000	1995
5626-5730	104	GM	SD75I	4300	1996
5731-5765	35	GM	SD75I	4300	1997
5766-5800	35	GM	SD75I	4300	1999

C N Cont

6000-6009		10	ALST SD40QRM	3000	1992-1993
6010-6028		19	ALST SD40QRM	3000	1995-1996
6030-6079 GCFX		50	ALST SD40-3	3000	1997-1998
7000-7013		14	ALST GP9RM	1800	1985
7014-7043		28	ALST GP9RM	1800	1991
7044-7078		35	ALST GP9RM	1800	1992
7079-7083		5	ALST GP9RM	1800	1993
7100-7101		2	ALST SW1200RM	1350	1986
7102-7107		6	ALST SW1200RM	1350	1987
7200-7213		14	ALST GP9RM	1800	1985-1986
7214-7231		18	ALST GP9RM	1800	1986
7232-7240 F		8	ALST GP9RM	1800	1987
7241-7248		8	ALST GP9RM	1800	1988
7249-7270		22	ALST GP9RM	1800	1990
7271-7280		10	ALST GP9RM	1800	1993
7300-7317 G		17	ALST SW1200RSM	1200	1987
7500-7532		27	GM GP38-2	2000	1977-1985
9400-9530		107	GM GP40-2L	3000	1974
9531-9631		61	GM GP40-2L	3000	1975
9632-9667		33	GM GP40-2L	3000	1977
9668-9673 H		6	GM GP40-2L	3000	1974
9674-9677		4	GM GP40-2L	3000	1975
		1,437	EXCLUDES SLUGS		

RENTALS DURING THE YEAR

700-739*	LMSX	25	GE DASH8-40CW	4000	1994
869-892	NREX	8	VMV SD40-1	3000	
		33	* SPLIT-SHARED ANNUALLY WITH NS		

NOTES

A		1150-1182 RETRUCKED FROM A1A-A1A TO B-B
B	EXCEPT	5300
C		5364-5387 ACQUIRED 1994 FROM UNION PACIFIC RR
D		5500-5503 RENUMBERED FROM 9900-9903
E	EXCEPT	5514
F	EXCEPT	7234
G	EXCEPT	7315
H		9668-9677 ACQUIRED FROM GO TRANSIT

MODEL SUFFIX RB MEANS REBUILT, RM MEANS REMANUFACTURED
GENERAL NOTE: CN TWENTY-FIVE YEARS AGO PIONEERED THE DELUXE
SAFETY CAB AND CANADIAN WIDE NOSE AS WELL AS CARBODY DESIGN
WITH TAPERED FRONT SIDE DESIGN FOR BETTER VISIBILITY. CN
DOES NOT GENERALLY SUFFIX MODELS WITH M OR W.

CANADIAN PACIFIC RY (SEE SOO LINE ALSO ST LAWRENCE & HUDSON)

740-752	4 GM	SD40	3000	1969-1971
760-787	12 GM	SD40-2	3000	1972-1993
1001-1025	15 GM	SLUG	0	1984-1996
1100-1151	11 GM	SLUG	0	1995-1997
1202-1203	2 GM	SW9	1200	1982-1983
1204-1251	16 GM	SW1200RS	1200	1981-1985
1400-1401	2 GM	F7AU	1750	1998-1999
1404-1437 A	10 GM	MP15DC	1500	1975
1503-1507	3 GM	GP7	1500	1981-1984
1510-1546	29 GM	GP9	1750	1980-1983
1550-1652	80 GM	GP9	1750	1984-1987
1683-1686	3 GM	GP7	1750	1980-1985
1689-1696	8 GM	GP9	1750	1980-1988
1900	1 GM	F7BU	1750	1999
3000-3020	13 GM	GP38	2000	1970-1971
3021-3135	107 GM	GP38-2	2000	1983-1986
5415-5431	14 GM	SD40-2	3000	1975-1976
5475-5485	2 GM	SD40-2	3000	1975
5490-5499	10 GM	SD40-2	3000	1995
5500-5562	23 GM	SD40	3000	1966-1967
5564	1 GM	SD40-2	3000	1972
5677-5717	30 GM	SD40-2	3000	1974-1975
5718-5798	35 GM	SD40-2	3000	1974-1978
5800-5836	37 GM	SD40-2	3000	1974
5838-5848	9 GM	SD40-2	3000	1977-1978
5849-5914	65 GM	SD40-2	3000	1978-1979
5915-5949	34 GM	SD40-2	3000	1979
5950-6024	72 GM	SD40-2	3000	1980
6025-6054	27 GM	SD40-2	3000	1982-1983
6055-6080	24 GM	SD40-2	3000	1977-1985
6400-6410	9 GM	SD40	3000	1970
6601-6607	4 GM	SD40-2	3000	1980
8106-8167	18 GM	SW1200RS	1200	1958-1960
8200-8270	44 GM	GP9	1750	1981-1990
9000-9024 B	24 GM	SD40-2F	3000	1988-1989
9100-9160	61 GM	SD90/43MAC	4300	1998

C P Cont

9300-9303		4 GM	SD90MAC	6000	1999
9500-9582		83 GE	AC4400CW	4400	1995
9583-9681		89 GE	AC4400CW	4400	1997
9682-9683		12 GE	AC4400CW	4400	1998
		1,021	EXCLUDES SLUGS		

RENTALS DURING THE YEAR

184-191	EMDX	4 GM	GP40-1*	3000	
200-203	EMDX	4 GM	GP40-2	3000	
504-518	HATX	7 GM	GP40-2	3000	1977
750-751	HATX	2 GM	SD40-2	3000	
800-806	HATX	6 GM	GP40-3	3000	1972
2003-2008	LLPX	3 GM	GP38-3	2000	
4201-4302	HLCX	4 GM	GP40-2**	3000	
4403-4410	HLCX	5 GM	GP40-3	3000	
6061-6092	HLCX	12 GM	SD40-3	3000	
6202-6401	HLCX	21 GM	SD40-2	3000	1973-1978
6500,6504	HLCX	2 GM	SD40-3	3000	1973
7349-7378	GSCX	15 GM	SD40-2	3000	1975
		85	* 188 IS GP40-2		
			** 4302 IS GP40-3		

NOTES

A   1404,1429 ARE MP15AC

B   EXCEPT 9010

CANADIAN RY MUSEUM-CRHA   St Constant-Delson QC

-C&SL	A	1	MITS	STEAM REP	2-2-2	1971
2-EBEC		1	MLW	STEAM	0-4-0T	1925
3-SAPC		1	MLW	STEAM	0-4-0T	1916
4-NHB		1	MLW	STEAM	0-6-0T	1914
5-MR		1	ALCO	STEAM	4-6-0	1895
Y5-MTC		1	MTC	ELECTRIC	SHOP	1923
7-COUR		1	MSR	ELECTRIC	B-B	1900
9-CAM		1	PORT	GAS-ELECT	12-TON	1928
20-R&S		1	MLW	RS2	1500	1949
25-O&C		1	BALD	STEAM	2-4-0	1900
30-CNR		1	GE	70-TON	600	1950
49-CNR		1	MLW	STEAM	4-6-4T	1914
54-LBSC		1	BALD	STEAM	0-6-0T	1875
77-CNR		1	CLC	BOXCAB	300	1929
144-CPR		1	CPR	STEAM	4-4-0	1886
492-CPR		1	CPR	STEAM	4-6-0	1915
713-CNR		1	GTR	STEAM	2-6-0	1900
805-CNR	B	1	GM	G8	875	1956
C841-SNCF		1	SACH	STEAM	0-6-0	1883
999-CPR		1	MLW	STEAM	4-6-0	1912
1002-NHB		1	MLW	S3	660	1951
1400-ONR		1	MLW	RS10	1600	1956
2231-CPR		1	CPR	STEAM	4-6-2	1914
2341-CPR		1	MLW	STEAM	4-6-2	1926
2601-CNR		1	MLW	STEAM	2-8-0	1907
2850-CPR		1	MLW	STEAM	4-6-4	1938
2928-CPR		1	MLW	STEAM	4-4-4	1938
3239-CNR		1	CLC	STEAM	2-8-2	1916
3388-CPR		1	ALCO	STEAM	2-8-0	1902
3684-CNR		1	MLW	RS11M	1800	1957
4100-CNR		1	CLC	STEAM	2-10-2	1924
4237-CPR		1	MLW	C424	2400	1966
4563-CPR		1	MLW	M630	3000	1969
4744-CPR		1	MLW	M640AC	4000	1971
5001-MTC		1	MTC	ELECTRIC	B-B	1917
5550-CNR		1	MLW	STEAM	4-6-2	1914
5702-CNR		1	MLW	STEAM	4-6-4	1930
5935-CPR		1	MLW	STEAM	2-10-4	1948
6153-CNR		1	MLW	STEAM	4-8-4	1929
6271-CPR		1	CPR	STEAM	0-6-0	1913
6711-CNR		1	GE	ELECTRIC	1100	1914
6765		1	MLW	FPA4	1800	1958
7000-CPR		1	H&W	BOXCAB	500	1937
7077-CPR		1	MLW	S2	1000	1948
8905-CPR		1	FM	H24-66	2400	1955
9171-CN		1	GM	F3AU	1500	1948
9400-CNR		1	MLW	FA1	1500	1950
12012-HQ		1	PLYM	GAS-MECH	200	1927
60010--BR		1	DW	STEAM	4-6-2	1937

```
                    49  A  OPERATING REPLICA  B  3'-6"GAUGE
```

C&NC RR Connorsville IN
| 345 | 1 GM | GP11 | 1800 | |

CANEY FORK & WESTERN RR CFWR McMinnville TN
531	1 GM	GP9	1750	1954
979,2345	2 GM	GP7	1500	1951-1952
	3			

CANON CITY & ROYAL GORGE RR Canon City CO
1	1 GM	NW2	1000	
402-403	2 GM	F7A	1500	1949
	3			

CANTON RR CTN Baltimore MD
1201	1 GM	SW1200	1200	1954
1501	1 GM	SW1500	1500	1967
1751	1 GM	GP16	1750	1980
	3			

CAPE BRETON & CENTRAL NOVA SCOTIA RY CBNS Port Hawkesbury NS
62.5967	2 GM	GP9	1750	1956-1955
2160,2176	2 GM	GP7	1500	1979
4022	1 GM	GP40	3000	1969
4700	1 GM	GP18	1800	1982
5000-5009	6 GM	GP50	2500	1980
	12 EXCLUDES 8-M630 AND 2-RS18 MODELS STORED			

CAPE COD CENTRAL RR Hyannis MA
| 2000-2001 | 2 MLW | M420 | 2000 | |

CAPE FEAR RYS CFR Fort Bragg NC
| USA-4604-4605 | 2 GM | GP10 | 1850 | 1991 |

CARLTON TRAIL RY Prince Albert SK
681,683,3532,				
3540,3549	5 MLW	M420	2000	
1004,1020	2 GM	GP10	1750	
	7			

CAROLINA COASTAL RY CLNA Midlothian VA
127	1 B-GM	SW10	1000	1959
148	1 GM	SW800	800	
	2			

CAROLINA PIEDMONT RR CPDR Laurens SC
70	1 GM	GP8	1500	1974
8379,8387	2 GM	GP10	1850	1974
	3			

CAROLINA RAIL SERVICE CRIJ Morehead City NC
| 203,1201-1202 | 3 GM | SW1200 | 1200 | 1966 |

CAROLINA SOUTHERN RR CALA Chadbourn NC/Conway SC
48,88,9158,9163	4 GM	F7A	1500*	1953-1950
87	1 GM	SW1200	1200	
100,943,950-951				
958	5 GM	GP18	1800	1961
520,4257	2 GM	E8A	2250	1952
2613	1 GM	GP30	2250	1963
6622	1 GM	F9BU	1750	1956
	14 * 9163 IS 1750HP			

CARTHAGE KNIGHTSTOWN & SHIRLEY RR Knightstown IN

1215	1	GE	45-TON	300	1951
28468	1	GE	44-TON	300	1946
	2				

CARTIER RY CART Port Cartier QC

34	1	ALCO	630	3000	1966
41-49	9	MLW	M636	3600	1970
62-68	7	MLW	RS18	1800	1959-1960
71-76	5	MLW	M636	3600	1972-1973
77-79	3	ALCO	C636	3600	1968
81-87	7	MLW	M636	3600	1975-1970
	32				

CASCADE & COLUMBIA RIVER RR CSCD Omak WA

1002	1	GM	GP10	1750	
6636-6637	2	GM	GP40	3000	1971-1966
	3				

C&S RR CSKR Jim Thorpe PA

7545,7563,7580	3	GM	GP10	1850	1977

CASS SCENIC RR WV DIVN OF TOURISM & PARKS CSRR Cass WV

2-6	5	LIMA	STEAM	3-TRUCK	1905-1945
6	1	HEIS	STEAM	3-TRUCK	1929
11	1	LIMA	STEAM	3-TRUCK	1923
20	1	GE	45-TON	300	1941
	8				

CATSKILL MOUNTAIN RR CMRR Shokan NY

1	1	DAV	30-TON	250	1942
2,2361	2	ALCO	RS1	1000	1950
29	1	PORT	50-TON	400	1942
	4				

CAYUGA RY Owego NY

1850	1	MLW	RS18	1800	1989

CEDAR POINT & LAKE ERIE RR (3'Gauge) Sandusky OH

1-MAUD L	1	DAV	STEAM	2-4-4RT	1927
2-JENNIE K	1	PORT	STEAM	2-4-0	1940
3-ALBERT	1	DAV	STEAM	2-6-0	1911
5-GEORGE R	1	PORT	STEAM	2-4-0	1942
22-MYRON H	1	VULC	STEAM	2-4-0	1922
44-JUDY K	1	VULC	STEAM	2-4-0	1920
	6				

CEDAR RAPIDS & IOWA CITY RY CIC Cedar Rapids IA

91	1	GM	SW8	800	1953
94	1	GM	SW900	900	1959
95	1	GM	SW9	1200	1951
97,99	2	GM	SW1200	1200	1966
100-105	6	GM	GP9	1750	1959
106-109	4	NRE	SW14	1400	1995
110-112,114	4	NRE	GP35	2500	1996-1997
	19				

CENTRAL CALIFORNIA TRACTION CCT Stocktkon CA

44,60	2	GM	GP7	1500	1978,1953
1790,1795	2	GM	GP18	1800	1965-1963
	4				

CENTRAL INDIANA & WESTERN RR CEIW Lapel IN

88	1	GM	SW7M	1200	1950

CENTRAL KANSAS RY CKRY Wichita KS

701,713,2016					
2083-2085,2087					
2199,2230,2232-					
2233,2238-2239					
2242-2243,2507					
2509	16	GM	GP7	1500	1973-1981
1006,1025,1040					
2510	4	GM	GP10	1850	
2501-2504	4	GM	GP35	2500	
2505-2506	2	GM	GP20	2000	
2508	1	GM	GP30	2250	
901,3332,3801					
4285,4436,4544					
4557,4912,4916	9	GM	GP9	1750	1981
	36	INCLUDES KANSAS SOUTHWESTERN			

CENTRAL MANITOBA RY Brandon MB

4000-4003	4	GM	GP9	1750	1984

CENTRAL MICHIGAN RY CMGN Bay City MI

8801-8802,8804	3	GM	GP38AC*	2000	1988
8902-8905	4	GE	U23B	2250	1973
9209-9210	2	GM	GP8	1800	1950
9712	1	GM	GP40-2W	3000	1977
	10	* REBUILT FROM GP40			

CENTRAL MONTANA RAIL CM Denton MT

1809-1810,1814					
1817,124,1838	6	GM	GP9	1750*	1954-1956
		* 1817 IS 2000			

CENTRAL NEW ENGLAND RR Newington CT

30, 670	2	ALCO	RS1	1000	1948-1955
0825	1	GE	25-TON	150	1949
905	1	GM	GP10	1750	1960
1922	1	GM	GP9	1750	1957
	5				

CENTRAL NEW YORK CHAPTER-NRHS MARTISCO STN MUSEUM

Syracuse NY

53	1	ALCO	STEAM	0-4-0T	1922
97A-WM	1	GM	FP7A	1500	1950
637-DL&W	1	GM	FP7A	1500	1950
807-808-DL&W	2	GM	E8A	2250	1951-1952
4933-PRR	1	PRR	ELECTRIC*	4850	1943
	6	*GG1 MODEL			

CENTRAL OF TENNESSEE RY CTRN Nashville TN

2001	1 GM	GP7	1500	1995
2005	1 GM	SW900	900	1991
2320	1 GM	SW1500	1500	
	3			

CENTRAL OREGON & PACIFIC RR - CORP

3805,3809-				
3811 LLPX	4 GM	GP38-3	2000	
3815-3817,3822-				
3832	14 GM	GP38	2000	1967-1970
3818-3819	2 GM	GP38-2	2000	1973
4000-4001,4021				
4023-4024	5 GM	GP40	3000	1966-1970
4020	1 GM	GP40-1	3000	1966
4165-4166	2 GM	SLUGS	0	1987
	26	EXCLUDES SLUGS		

CENTRAL PUGET SOUND REGIONAL RAIL-SOUND TRANSIT Seattle WA

901-903	3 GM	F59PHI	3000	1999
904-906	3 GM	F59PHI	3000	2000
907-911	5 GM	F59PHI	3000	2001
	11			

CENTRAL RR CO OF INDIANAPOLIS CERA Kokomo IN

2251-2255	5 GM	GP30	2250	1963-1964
		EXPECTING GP38-2 MODEL		

CENTRAL WESTERN RY CWRL Stettler/Boyle AB

1118	1 GM	SW1200RS	1200	1958
1753,7438	2 GM	GP9	1750	1954-1957
	3			

CHARLOTTE SOUTHERN RR

3	1 GE	44-TON	380	1956

CHATTAHOOCHEE INDUSTRIAL RR CIRR Cedar Springs GA

1,1810,1811	3 GM	GP10	1850	1978-1979
89-90	2 ALCO	SLUGS	0	1973
716,719,1500				
1505	4 GM	SW1500	1500	1969-1975
1830	1 GM	GP7	1500	1951
	8	EXCLUDES SLUGS		

CHATTOOGA & CHICKAMAUGA RY CCKY Lafayette GA

102	1 GM	GP7	1500	1979
103	1 GM	CF7	1500	1980
	2			

CHEHALIS-CENTRALIA RR Chehalis WA

9	1 VULC	45-TON	300	1941
15	1 BALD	STEAM	2-8-2	1916
	2			

CHEMIN DE FER BAIE DES CHALEURS QC

3536	1 BBD	HR412	2400	1987
3542,3545,3554	3 BBD	M420	2000	1986
	4			

CHEMIN DE FER CHARLEVOIX QC

1303,1323,1330	3 GM	SW1200RSM	1400		1991

CHEMIN DE FER MATANE ET DU GOLFE Mont Joli QC

104	1 GM	SW1200RS	1200	1958

CHEROKEE RAIL

1050	1 GM	NW2	1000	1949

CHESAPEAKE & ALBEMARLE RR CA Elizabeth City NC

2158	1 GM	GP7	1500	1979
2190	1 GM	GP16	1750	1979
	2			

CHESAPEAKE RR Ridgely MD

85,95	2 WHIT	80-TON	500	1944-1945

CHESTNUT RIDGE RY CHR Palmerton PA

11	1 GM	GP7	1500	1951
20	1 ALCO	S2	1000	1945
	2			

CHICAGO RAIL LINK CRL Chicago IL

14-15	2 GM	GP18	1800	
18-19	2 GM	SW1500	1500	
43	1 GM	SW8	800	1951
58-59	2 GM	GP9	1750	1958-1959
613-614,617	3 GM	GP7	1500	
1042	1 GM	GP10	1750	
	11			

CHICAGO SHORT LINE RY CSL Chicago IL

28-29	2 GM	SW1001	1000	1974
30-31	2 GM	SW1500	1500	1968-1971
	4			

CHICAGO SOUTHSHORE & SOUTH BEND RR CSS Michigan City IN

2000-2009	10 GM	GP38-2	2000	1981

CHICAGO TRANSIT AUTHORITY CTA Chicago IL

S-500	1 NIIG	44-TON	450	1980
S-501-S-503	3 NIIG	49-TON	680	1986
	4 NIIGATA			

CHILLICOTHE-BRUNSWICK RAIL Trenton MO

4485	1 GM	GP7	1500	1980

CIMARRON VALLEY RR Satanta KS

3020-3025	6 GM	GP30	2250	

CITY OF EDMONTON TRANSPORTATION EDMO Edmonton AB

2010	1 GE	50-TON	400	1998

CITY OF MADISON PORT AUTHORITY RY Madison WI

1229	1 DAV	44-TON	360	
2013	1 GM	SW8	800	
3634	1 GM	GP10	1800	
	3			

CITY OF PRINEVILLE RY COP Prineville OR

1	1 LIMA	STEAM	3-TRUCK	1923
985,989	2 GM	GP20	2000	1954
1837	1 GM	GP9	1750	1956
	4			

CITY OF ST LOUIS-WATER DIVISION RR MBST St Louis MO
3	1	PLYM	30-TON		1923

CITY PUBLIC SERVICE BOARD OF SAN ANTONIO SATX San Antonio TX
1999	1	SR	SRI600-CUM	600	1977

CLAREMONT CONCORD RR CCRR Claremont NH
1	1	GE	100-TON	500	
2	1	GE	25-TON	150	
30,118-119	3	GE	44-TON	380	1942-1947
	5				

CLARENDON & PITTSFORD RR CLP Rutland VT
203	1	GM	GP38	2000	1966
204	1	GM	GP38-2	2000	1973
802	1	GM	GP16*	1600	1979
	3	* REMOTE CONTROL			

CLINTON TERMINAL RR CTR Clinton NC
703B	1	GM	TR5B	1200	
2480,2627	2	GM	CF7	1500	1972
	3				

CMC RR Dayton TX
101-102	2	BL	MP1500D	1500	1997
103-104	2	BL	MP2000D	2000	1998
	4				

COAHUILA & DURANGO
3900	1	GE	U23B	2250	

COAST RAIL SERVICES CA
1234	1	GM	SW10	1000	
1965	1	GM	GP9	1750	
	2				

COE RAIL CRLE Walled Lake MI
52	1	ALCO	S1	660	1945
725	1	GM	F7A	1500	1957
1512	1	GM	SW1200	1200	1960
	3	EXPECTING 2 F7A MODELS			

COLORADO & WYOMING RY CW Pueblo CO
102-104	3	GM	GP7	1500	1951
201,203,205					
208-211	7	GM	SW8	800	1951
	10				

COLORADO RR MUSEUM CRRM (3'Gauge) Golden CO
1-AOC *	1	ALCO	STEAM	0-4-0T	1920
1-M&PP *	1	BALD	STEAM	0-4-2T	1893
3-USG	1	PLYM	8-TON	60	1948
20-RGS	1	SCH	STEAM	4-6-0	1899
50-DRGW	1	DAV	30-TON	200	1937
191-DL&G	1	BALD	STEAM	2-8-0	1880
318-DRGW	1	BALD	STEAM	2-8-0	1896
346-DRGW	1	BALD	STEAM	2-8-0	1881
491-DRGW	1	BALD	STEAM	2-8-2	1902
683-DRGW *	1	BALD	STEAM	2-8-0	1890

CRRM Cont

4455-UP *	1	LIMA	STEAM	0-6-0	1920
5629-CB&Q *	1	CB&Q	STEAM	4-8-4	1940
5762-DRGW *	1	GM	F9B	1750	1955
5771-DRGW *	1	GM	F9A	1750	1955
	14	* STANDARD GAUGE			

COLUMBIA & COWLITZ RY CLC Longview WA

700-701	2	GM	GP20	2000	1976-1977
702	1	GM	GP7	1500	
	3				

COLUMBIA BASIN RR Yakima WA

82,84	2	GM	F9A	1750	
100,102	2	GM	F7A	1500	1952
166,171	2	GM	SD9	1750	
201,203,211-212	4	GM	SW1200RS	1200	1965-1966
287,2184	2	GM	GP38	2000	1967
	12				

COLUMBIA TERMINAL RR (CITY OF COLUMBIA) Columbia MO

1	1	GM	SW1200	1200	1987

COLUMBUS & GREENVILLE RY CAGY Columbus MS

608,615,618,621	4	GM	GP7	1500	1952
701-702	2	GM	GP9	1750	1955
801-808	8	GM	CF7	1500	1977-1980
1000-1003	4	GM	GP7	1500	1979
2777,2785	2	GM	GP38	2000	1966
	20				

COMMONWEALTH RY CWRY Suffolk VA

517	1	GM	CF7	1500	1972

CONEMAUGH & BLACK LICK RR CBL Johnstown PA

100-102,122,125	5	GM	NW2	1200	1949-1945
104,110-112					
114,116	6	GM	SW7	1200	1949-1950
	11				

CONNECTICUT CENTRAL RR CCCL Middletown CT

36	1	ALCO	S4	1000	1953
53	1	GM	GP9E	1800	1979
1201	1	ALGM	RS3M	1200	1984
	3				

CONNECTICUT -DEPT OF TRANSPORTATION CTDT New Haven CT

605	1	ALCO	RS3M	1200	1962
2002,2006,2019					
2023	4	CL	FL9A	1750	1985
2011,2014,2016					
2024,2026,2027	6	BL	FL9A	1750	1993-1994
6690-6691	2	GM	F7AM	1750	1982
6694-6699	6	ALST	GP40PH-2	3000	1995-1996
	19				

CONNECTICUT ELECTRIC RY CER East Windsor CT

-PM	1 GE	ELECTRIC*	160	1894
1-HEL	1 GE	25-TON	150	1949
3-MK	1 CLIM STEAM		2-TRUCK	1910
5-HEL	1 ALCO STEAM		0-4-0T	1920
18-NYR	1 BLW	ELECTRIC	400	1918
6714-CN	1 GE	ELECTRIC	1200	1917
7926-HL&P	1 GE	44-TON	380	1944
	7	* GE'S OLDEST 2-TRUCK LOCOMOTIVE		

CONNECTICUT SOUTHERN RR CSOR

2008-2013	6 GE	B23-7	2250	1979

CONRAIL - CONSOLIDATED RAIL CR (SEE CSX TRANSPORTATION AND NORFOLK SOUTHERN SYSTEMS) SEE LAST ROSTER THIS BOOK

CONWAY SCENIC RR CONW North Conway NH

15-MC	1 GE	44-TON	380	1945
501-MCRR	1 ALCO STEAM		2-8-0	1910
573-MC	1 GM	GP7	1500	1950
1055-PT	1 ALCO S4		1000	1950
4266,4268-B&M	2 GM	F7A	1500	1949
6505,6516-CNR	2 GM	FP9A	1750	1954-1957
7470-CNR	1 GTR STEAM		0-6-0	1921
	9			

COOPERSVILLE & MARNE RY Coopersville MI

1	1 GE	50-TON	300	1957
2349	1 ALCO RS1		1000	1949
7014	1 GM	SW9	1200	1953
	3			

COPPER BASIN RY CBRY Hayden AZ

201-208	8 GM	GP9	1750	1955-1976
401-402	2 GM	GP39	2300	1970
403,501-502	3 GM	GP39-2	2300	1980-1993
503-505	3 GM	GP39CLC	2300	1995
	16			

R.J. CORMAN - ALLENTOWN LINES RJCN Allentown PA

1713	1 GM	GP16	1600	

R.J. CORMAN - BARDSTOWN LINE RJCR Bardstown KY

1940-1941	2 GM	FP7A	1500	1950
9002,9005,9009	3 GM	GP9	1750	1957
	5			

R.J. CORMAN - CLEVELAND LINE RJCL Dover OH

4119,4121	2 GM	GP20	2000	
9003	1 GM	GP9	1750	1958-1957
	3			

R.J. CORMAN - GREENVILLE LINE Greenville OH

1737,1806	2 GM	GP16	1600	

R.J. CORMAN - MEMPHIS LINE RJCM Guthrie KY

1601-1605,1607-					
1608	7	GM	GP16	1600	1980
1807	1	GM	GP18	1600	
9001,9004,9006					
9008	4	GM	GP9	1750	1955-1957
	12				

R.J. CORMAN - PENNSYLVANIA LINE RJCP Clearfield PA

1712	1	GM	GP16	1600
1827-1829.1831-				
1832.1858	6	GM	GP16	1600
7681,7697.7908-				
7910,7918	6	GM	GP38	2000
	13			

R.J. CORMAN - WESTERN OHIO LINE RJCW ST Marys PH

1606,1739,1836	3	GM	GP16	1600	1980
9007,9010	2	GM	GP9	1750	1955-1957
	5				

CORYDON 1883 SCENIC RR Corydon IN

101	1	GE	44-TON	300	1952

CORPUS CHRISTI TERMINAL RR

475,547	2	GM	CF7	1500
9576,9591	2	GM	SW1500	1500
	4			

COUNCIL BLUFFS RY Council Bluffs IA

714	1	GM	GP7	1500	1990

CRAB ORCHARD & EGYPTIAN RR COER Marion IL

6	1	GM	SW1	600	1953
1136,1161	2	GM	SW1200	1200	1966-1965
	3				

CRIPPLE CREEK & VICTOR RR (2'Gauge) Cripple Creek CO

1	1	ORA	STEAM	0-4-4-0	1902
2	1	HENS	STEAM	0-4-0	1936
3	1	PORT	STEAM	0-4-0T	1927
4	1	BAGN	STEAM	0-4-4-0T	1947
5	1	GE	16-TON	120	1951
	5				

1-30	CSX	29 GE	AC4400CW	4400 A	1994*	THIS BOOK
31-115	CSX	85 GE	AC4400CW	4400	1995	
116-173	CSX	58 GE	AC4400CW	4400	1996	
201-280	CSX	80 GE	AC4400CW	4400	1996	
281-301	CSX	21 GE	AC4400CW	4400	1997	
302-390	CSX	89 GE	AC4400CW	4400	1998	
391-421	CSX	31 GE	AC4400CW	4400	1999	
417	CSX	1 GM	FP7B	1500	1952	
418	CSX	1 GM	FB7A	1500	1952	
583-599	CSX	17 GE	AC6000CW	6000	2000	
600-602	CSX	3 GE	AC6000CW	6000	1996	
603-604	CSX	2 GE	AC6000CW	6000	1998	
605-697	CSX	93 GE	AC6000CW	6000	1999	
698-699	CSX	2 GE	AC6000CW	6000	2000	
700-724	CSX	25 GM	SD70MAC	4000	1997	
726-739	CSX	12 GM	SD70MAC	4000	1998	
740-759	CSX	20 GM	SD70MAC	4000	2000	
775-780	CON	3 GM	SD70MAC	4000	1998	
800-812	CON	13 GM	SD80MAC	5000	1996	
1004-1018	CON	15 GM	SLUG	0	1957-1958	
1021-1068	CSX	33 GM	SLUG	0	1984-1988	
1069-1099	CON	31 GM	SW1500	1500	1966-1973	
1100-1109	CSX	10 GM	SW1500	1500	1970	
1110-1119	CSX	10 GM	SW1500	1500	1971	
1120-1128	CON	9 GM	SW1001	1000	1973	
1129	CON	1 GM	SW1500	1500	1971	
1130-1139	CSX	10 GM	MP15AC	1500	1978	
1140-1149	CSX	10 GM	MP15	1500	1975	
1150-1169	CSX	20 GM	MP15AC	1500	1977	
1170-1194	CSX	25 GM	MP15AC	1500	1978	
1200-1214	CSX	15 GM	MP15T	1500	1984	
1215-1241	CSX	27 GM	MP15T	1500	1985	
1500-1524	CSX	25 GM	GP15T	1500	1982	
1525-1566	CON	42 GM	GP15	1500	1979	
1943	CON	1 GM	GP38	2000	1967	
1944-1948	CON	5 GM	GP38	2000	1970	
1949-1970	CON	22 GM	GP38	2000	1969	
1971-1998	CON	28 GM	GP38	2000	1971	
2011-2174	CSX	25 GM	GP38	2000	1967-1971	
2200-2350	CSX	149 GM	SLUG	0	1988-1998	
2400-2403	CSX	3 GM	SD20-2	2000 B	1979-1980	
2411-2419	CSX	9 GM	SD40-2	3000	1974	
2422-2423	CSX	2 GM	SD40-2	3000	1972	
2424-2436	CSX	13 GM	SD40-2	3000	1974	
2450-2454	CSX	5 GM	SD38-2	2000	1975	
2455-2467	CON	13 GM	SD38	2000	1970	
2500-2555	CSX	55 GM	GP38-2	2000 C	1973	
2556-2579	CSX	24 GM	GP38-2	2000	1972	

CSX Cont

2609-2650	CSX	41	GM	GP38-2	2000 D	1973
2651-2655	CSX	5	GM	GP38-2	2000	1978
2656-2701	CSX	46	GM	GP38-2	2000	1979
2702-2716	CSX	15	GM	GP38-2	2000	1980
2717-2759	CON	43	GM	GP38-2	2000	1973
2760-2769	CON	10	GM	GP38-2	2000 E	1977*
2770-2803	CON	34	GM	GP38-2	2000	1978
2804-2814	CON	11	GM	GP38-2	2000	1979
3100-3141	CSX	18	GE	B23-7	2250	1978
3144-3166	CON	23	GE	B23-7	2250	1978
3167-3179	CON	13	GE	B23-7	2250	1979
3180-3184	CON	5	GE	B23-7	2250	1977
3185-3188	CON	4	GE	B23-7R	2250	1972
3189	CON	1	GE	B23-7	2250	1979
3305	CSX	1	GE	U23B	2250	1975
4280-4299	CSX	16	GM	GP39	2300 F	1969
4300-4319	CSX	20	GM	GP39-2	2300 G	1974*
4400-4401	CON	2	GM	GP40-2	3000	1973
4402-4414	CON	13	GM	GP40-2	3000	1977
4415-4428	CON	14	GM	GP40-2	3000	1978
4429-4445	CON	17	GM	GP40-2	3000	1979
4446-4452	CON	7	GM	GP40-2	3000	1980
4600-4621	CSX	16	GM	SD40	3000 H	1966-1971
5500-5516	CSX	17	GE	B30-7	3000	1980
5517-5526	CSX	9	GE	B30-7	3000 I	1978
5527-5546	CSX	20	GE	B30-7	3000	1979
5547-5560	CSX	14	GE	B30-7	3000	1980
5561-5580	CSX	20	GE	B30-7	3000	1981
5581	CON	1	GE	B30-7	3000	1985
5783-5805	CON	23	GE	B36-7	3750	1983
5806-5925	CSX	118	GE	B36-7	3750 J	1985
5930-5949	CSX	20	GE	DASH8-40B	4000	1989
5950-5961	CON	11	GE	DASH8-40B	4000 K	1988
6000-6083	CSX	79	GM	GP40-2	3000 L	1972*
6084-6145	CSX	61	GM	GP40-2	3000 M	1975
6147-6160	CSX	14	GM	GP40-2	3000	1977
6201-6220	CSX	18	GM	GP40-2	3000 N	1978
6221-6249	CSX	29	GM	GP40-2	3000	1979
6276-6341	CSX	10	GM	GP40-2	3000 O	1980*
6346-6399	CSX	32	GM	GP40-2	3000 P	1972*
6400-6435	CSX	36	GM	GP40-2	3000	1978
6436-6461	CSX	26	GM	GP40-2	3000 Q	1981*
6462-6499	CSX	38	GM	GP40-2	3000	1980
6506-6854	CSX	41	GM	GP40	3000	1966-1971
6900-6923	CSX	24	GM	GP40-2	3000	1980
6924-6947	CSX	21	GM	GP40-2	3000 R	1979*
7000-7051	CSX	39	GE	C30-7	3000	1979
7052-7069	CSX	16	GE	C30-7	3000	1980
7072-7094	CSX	20	GE	C30-7	3000 S	1981
7095-7115	CON	21	GE	C30-7A	3100	1984

CSX Cont

7116-7126	CON	11	GE	C36-7	3750	1985
7300-7319	CON	20	GE	DASH8-40CW	4000	1990
7320-7340	CON	21	GE	DASH8-40CW	4000	1991
7341-7373	CON	33	GE	DASH8-40CW	4000	1993
7374-7396	CON	23	GE	DASH8-40CW	4000	1994
7476-7479	CON	4	GE	DASH8-32C	3200	1984
7480-7488	CON	9	GE	DASH8-39C	3900	1986
7489-7498	CON	10	GE	DASH8-40C	4000	1989
7500-7593	CSX	93	GE	DASH8-40C	4000 T	1989
7594-7646	CSX	53	GE	DASH8-40C	4000	1990
7650-7758	CSX	109	GE	DASH8-40CW	4000	1991
7759-7845	CSX	86	GE	DASH8-40CW	4000 U	1992
7846-7919	CSX	72	GE	DASH8-40CW	4000	1993
8000-8086	CSX	87	GM	SD40-2	3000	1979
8087-8130	CSX	44	GM	SD40-2	3000	1980
8131-8162	CSX	31	GM	SD40-2	3000 V	1981
8165-8211	CSX	27	GM	SD40-2	3000	1974
8212-8261	CSX	50	GM	SD40-2	3000 W	1977
8302-8488	CSX	124	GM	SD40-2	3000	1966-1971
8499	CON	1	GM	SD50	3500	1983
8500-8524	CSX	24	GM	SD50	3500 X	1983
8525-8602	GM	78	GM	SD50	3500	1984
8603-8643	CSX	41	GM	SD50	3500	1985
8644-8659	CON	16	GM	SD50	3500	1983
8660-8676	CON	17	GM	SD50	3500	1984
8677-8686	CON	10	GM	SD50	3600	1985
8687-8699	CON	13	GM	SD50	3600	1986
8700-8709	CSX	10	GM	SD60	3800	1989
8710-8711	CON	2	GM	SD60	3800	1985
8712-8721	CON	10	GM	SD60	3800	1989
8722-8723	CON	2	GM	SD60I	3800	1994
8724-8755	CON	32	GM	SD60I	3800	1995
8756-8786	CON	31	GM	SD60M	3800	1993
8800-8832	CSX	33	GM	SD40-2	3000	1977
8833-8846	CON	14	GM	SD40-2	3000	1978
8847-8869	CON	23	GM	SD40-2	3000	1979
8870-8885	CON	16	GM	SD40-2	3000	1966-1971
8886	CON	1	GM	SD45-2	3600	1972
8887-8888	CON	2	GM	SD40-2	3000	1977
8952-8954	CON	2	GM	SD45-2	3600 Y	1974
8972-8976	CON	5	GM	SD45-2	3600	1972
8973-8976	CSX	4	GM	SD45-2	3600	1972
9000-9002	CSX	3	GE	DASH9-44CW	4380	1993
9003-9052	CSX	50	GE	DASH9-44CW	4380	1994
9500-9508	CSX	9	GE	U18B	1800	1974,1973
9551-9555	CSX	5	GE	U23B	2250	1973-1975

CSX Cont

9556	CSX	1	GM	B23-7	2250	1978
9650-9664	CSX	14	GM	GP38	2000	1967-1971
9665-9699	CSX	5	GM	GP38	2000 Z	1967*
9700-9731	CSX	24	GM	GP40	3000	1971-1966
9992-9993	CSX	2	GM	F40PH	3000	1977-1979
		3,485	EXCLUDES SLUGS			

RENTALS DURING THE YEAR

104,109						
112	HATX	3	GM	GP38	2000	1967-1970
184,188-						
189,191	EMDX	4	GM	GP40	3000	1973-1967
200-203	EMDX	4	GM	GP40-2	3000	1966
3000-3010	GECX	11	GE	C30-7	3000	
7000-7024	EMDX	23	GM	SD70M	4000	1995
		45				

NOTES

A   EXCEPT   23 * 2 BUILT 1995 ORIGINAL NUMBERS 9100-9113
B   EXCEPT   2401 C EXCEPT 2528   D EXCEPT 2611
E   * 2769 BUILT 1973   F EXCEPT 4281,4284,4292,4296
G   * 4316 BUILT 1976   H EXCEPT 4603,4605,4608,4619-4620
I   EXCEPT   5522 J EXCEPT 5844,5890   K EXCEPT 5956
L   EXCEPT   6021,6036,6047,6069,6077   * 6000 BUILT 1971
M   EXCEPT   6102   N EXCEPT 6202,6208   O ACTUAL 6276,6279-6280
             6295-6297,6300-6301,6318-6341 * 6341 BUILT 1981
P   EXCEPT   6366-6387 *6388,6391 BUILT 1974
Q   *6457,6461 BUILT 1978
R   EXCEPT   6944-6946 *6947 BUILT 1980 S EXCEPT 7080
T   EXCEPT   7520 U EXCEPT 7770 V EXCEPT 8154
W   * 8245 BUILT 1981 X EXCEPT 8512
Y   ACTUAL   8952,8954,8972 *8954 BUILT 1972
Z   * 9665 BUILT 1970

DELTA VALLEY & SOUTHERN RY DVS Wilson AR

50	1 GE	50-TON	300	1954

DENVER ROCK ISLAND RR Denver CO

417,996	2 GM	NW2	1000	1947-1948
986	1 GM	SW1	600	
	3			

DEPEW LANCASTER & WESTERN RR DLWR Batavia/Depew NY

1800,1804,3603	3 ALCO	RS11	1800	1956

DEQUEEN & EASTERN RR DQE DeQueen AR

D7	1 GM	GP40-2	3000	
D27-D28	2 GM	GP38-2	2000	1980
	3			

DESERET-WESTERN RY Rangely CO

BME1-BME2	2 GE	ELECTRIC*	6000	1984
BME3-BME4	2 GE	ELECTRIC*	6000	1983
	4	* MODEL E60C		

DEVCO RY DVR Sydney NS

216-219,222,225-				
226,228	8 GM	GP38-2	2000	1979-1983
		PLANNING SALE OF LOCOMOTIVES SHORTLY		

DISNEYLAND RR (3'Gauge) Anaheim CA

1-2	2 WDI	STEAM	4-4-0	1954
3	1 BALD	STEAM	2-4-4T	1894
4	1 BALD	STEAM	2-4-0	1925
	4			

DISNEYWORLD RR (3'Gauge) Orlando FL

1,3	2 BALD	STEAM	4-6-0	1925
2	1 BALD	STEAM	2-6-0	1928
4	1 BALD	STEAM	4-4-0	1916
	4			

DODGE CITY FORD & BUCKLIN RR FBDC Dodge City KS

14	1 BALD	STEAM	2-8-0	1913
301	1 GE	44-TON	300	c1940
6001	1 ALCO	S11	660	1942
	3			

DOLLYWOOD EXPRESS (3'Gauge) Pigeon Forge TN

70,192-WP&Y	2 BALD	STEAM	2-8-2	1938-1943

DULUTH & NORTHEASTERN RR DNE Cloquet MN

31-33	3 GM	SW1	600	1940-1941
35	1 GM	SW1000	1967	
	4			

DULUTH MISSABE & IRON RANGE RY DMIR Proctor MN

11	1 GM	NW2	1000	1997
200-208	9 GM	SD38AC	2000	1971
209-210,212-213				
215,9002	6 GM	SD38-2	2000	1975-1976
214,216-217,221-				
223	6 GM	SD38	2000	1967-1971
301,303,305-308				
310-312,316-317				
321	11 GM	SD9M	1750	1979-1991
400-419	20 VMV	SD40-3	3000	1995-1997
	53			

DULUTH WINNIPEG & PACIFIC RY-DWP Duluth MN

5902-5911	10	GM	SD40	3000	1985

DUNN-ERWIN RY DER Dunn NC

5072	1	GM	NW2	1000	1949
5081	1	GM	SW9	1200	1952
	2				

DURANGO & SILVERTON RR DS (3'Gauge) Durango CO

42	1	BALD STEAM	2-8-0	1887	
473,476,478	3	ALCO STEAM	2-8-2	1923	
480-482,486	4	BALD STEAM	2-8-2	1925	
493,498-499	3	BALD STEAM	2-8-2	1902	
	11				

DURHAM TRANSPORT DRHY Edison NJ

66	1	GM	NW2M	1200	1948

E&N RY Victoria BC

344	1	GM	GP38	2000
1001	1	GM	GP10	1850
2796,2813,3809	3	GM	GP38	2000
	5			

EAST BROAD TOP RR EBTR (3'Gauge) Orbisonia PA

1,4-6	4	GE	60-TON	300	1964-1967
12,14-18	6	BALD STEAM	2-8-2	1911-1918	
M1	1	EBT	GAS-EL	250	1927
M4	1	PLYM 14-TON	150	1940	
M6	1	PLYM 16-TON	150	1941	
	13				

EAST CAMDEN & HIGHLAND RR EACH East Camden AR

60-61,63	3	GM	SW1200	1200	1956-1981

EAST COOPER & BERKELEY RR ECBR Charity Church SC

SC01,6155,6513					
6554	4	GM	GP9	1750	1954-1959

EAST ERIE COMMERCIAL RR EEC Erie PA

21-22	2	GE	85-TON	600	1980

EASTERN ALABAMA RY EARY Sylacauga AL

1510-1511,1551	3	GM	GP7	1500	1951-1953
1756-1757	2	GM	GP9	1750	1956
	5				

EASTERN IDAHO RR EIRR Twin Falls ID

782	1	GM	GP35L	2500	1980
2242,3001,3003- 3004,3006	5	GM	GP30	2250	1962
3133,3167,6513	3	GM	SD45	3600	1967-1970
3503-3505,3508 3510,3512,3518 3524	8	GM	GP35L	2500	
4203,4260	2	GM	GP30M	2250	1981
7004	1	GM	GP7	1500	
	20				

EASTERN ILLINOIS RR EIRC Charleston IL

4541	1 GM	GP9	1750	1979
7565	1 GM	GP10	1850	1977
	2			

EASTERN SHORE RR ESHR Cape Charles VA

1600	1 GM	GP8	1600	1953
2000-2001,8066				
8096	4 GM	GP10	1800	1976-1969
2085,2090	2 ALCO MRS1		1600	1952-1953
	7			

EAST JERSEY RR & TERMINAL EJR Bayonne NJ

18	1 GE	65-TON	400	1949
250	1 GM	SW900	900	1955
321	1 GM	SW800	800	1952
	3			

EAST PENN RY EPRY Pennsburg PA

25	1 GM	GP7	1500	1956
57	1 ALCO RS1		1000	1948
	2			

EAST PORTLAND DIVN OREGON PACIFIC Milwaukie OR

100	1 GM	SW1	600	1952
801	1 GM	SW8	800	1952
2501	1 GE	25-TON	150	1942
4501	1 GE	45-TON	300	1943
5100	1 GE	70-TON	660	1948
	5	INCLUDES SAMTRAK		

EAST TENNESSEE RY ETRY Johnson City TN

214	1 GM	SW1200	1200	1964
215	1 GM	SW7	1200	1951
	2			

EAST TEXAS CENTRAL RR ETC Antoine AR

1041	1 GM	GP10	1850	1978
1602,1610	2 GM	GP16	1850	1978
7530	1 GM	GP7	1500	
	4			

EFFINGHAM RR Vandalia IL

2716	1 GM	SW1200	1200	1963

ELDORADO & WESSON RY EDW El Dorado AR

25-26	2 GM	SW9	1200	1990

ELGIN JOLIET & EASTERN RY EJE Gary IN

300-307,310-324	23 GM	SW1200	1200	1960-1966
444-445	2 GM	SW1001	1000	1971
453	1 GM	NW2	1000	1947
459	1 GM	SW1000	1000	1971
612,614	2 GM	SD9	1750	1959
615-616	2 GM	SD18	1800	1960
650,654	2 GM	SD38	2000	1970
656-669	13 GM	SD38-2	2000	1974-1975
703	1 GM	GP38-2	2000	1972

EJE Cont

802,804	2	GM	SD9M	1750	1959
809,811,813,820	4	GM	SD18M	1800	1960
814-815,818	3	GM	SD9M	1750	1979
851-852	2	GM	SD18	1800	1962
	58				

ELK RIVER RR ELKR Summersville WV

1-3	3	GM	GP10	1850	1974
4-5	2	GM	GP9	1750	1959
	5				

ELLIS & EASTERN EE Sioux Falls SD

7	1	GM	SW1200	1200	1957
17	1	GM	SW900	900	1955
	2				

ESCANABA & LAKE SUPERIOR RR ELS Wells MI

101	1	BALD	DS4-660	660	1947
201-202	2	BALD	DS4-1000	1000	1948
207,300	2	BALD	RS12	1200	1952
400,402	2	GM	GP38	2000	1969
1200-1201	2	GM	SW8	800	1953
1220-1224	5	GM	SD9	1750	1955
	14				

ESSEX TERMINAL RY ETL Windsor ON

102,108	2	GM	GP9	1750	1963-1960
105	1	GM	SW9	1200	1956
107	1	GM	SW1500	1500	1971
	4				

EUREKA SPRINGS & NORTH ARKANSAS RY EKNA Eureka Springs AR

1	1	BALD	STEAM	2-6-0	1906
201	1	ALCO	STEAM	2-6-0	1906
226	1	BALD	STEAM	2-8-2	1927
4742	1	GM	SW1	600	1942
	4				

EVERETT RR EV Spoul PA

4	1	GE	80-TON	500	
5428	1	GM	GP8	1600	1989
6051	1	GM	GP9	1750	1957
8933	1	GM	SW9	1200	1951
	4	INCLUDES HOLLIDAYSBURG & ROARING SPRINGS			

FALLS ROAD RR Lockport NY

1801	1	MLW	RS18	1800	1959
1802	1	ALCO	RS11	1800	1959
	2				

FARMRAIL FMRC Clinton OK

169	1	GM	SW9	1200	1952
280,297,316-317	4	GM	GP9	1750	1954
8251	1	GM	GP10	1850	1971
	6				

FERROCARRIL MEXICANO FXE (FERROMEX)

EA001-EA039	23	GE	ELECTRIC*	6000	1982-1983
001-009	9	GE	C30-7	3000	1981-1986
105,114 HATX	2	GM	GP38	2000	1967
428-432	3	GE	C36-7	3600	1979
434-454	12	GE	C30-7	3000	1981
457-463	7	GE	C30-7	3000	1986
501	1	ALCO	RSD12	1800	1962
524-534	3	MLW	M420TR	2000	1975
540,542	2	GE	U23B	2250	1976
561-574	9	MLW	M424	2400	1981
707,724	2	MLW	M630	3000	1991-1992
903-911	7	GM	GP38-2	2000	1980
1004	1	GM	GP40-2	3000	1971
1008-1020	7	GM	GP40-2	3000	1975
1023-1036	9	GM	GP40-2	3000	1981
1232-1269 UP	15	GM	SW1000M	1200	1998
2104-2109	3	GM	GP40-2	3000	1972-1973
2110-2112	3	GM	GP40-2	3000	1976
2309-2310	2	GM	GP40-2	3000	1976
2311-2314	3	GM	GP40-2	3000	1981-1982
3608 HLCX	1	GM	GP38	2000	1969
4500-4549	50	GE	AC4400CW	4400	1999
5809-5845	5	GM	G12	1310	1956-1963
6700-6765	9	GE	C30-7	3000	1979
6749-6792	16	GE	C30-7	3000	1980
6757,6758	2	GE	C30-7	3000	1991
7219	1	ALCO	RS11	1800	1963
8208-8256	27	GM	GP38-2	2000	1964-1971
8402-8409	4	GM	GP40-2	3000	1967
8700-8755	40	GM	SD40-2	3000	1972-1973
8756-8766	10	GM	SD40-2	3000	1975
8768-8798	25	GM	SD40-2	3000	1980
8800-8818	18	GM	SW1504	1500	1973
9003	1	GE	U18B	1800	1974
9172	1	GE	B23-7	2250	1981
9221-9299	16	GM	GP38-2	2000	1975-1976
10028	1	GE	B23-7	2250	1981
11001-11057	20	GE	C30-7	3000	1982
11069-11126	20	GE	C30-7	3000	1984
11130	1	GE	C30-7	3000	1986
11158	1	GE	C30-7	3000	1988
13043-13074	28	GM	SD40-2	3000	1988
13075-13076	2	GM	SD40-2	3000	1989
13077-13083	7	GM	SD40-2	3000	1991
13084-13103	20	GM	SD40-2	3000	1992
14000-14001	2	GE	C30-SUPER7	3000	1989
14002-14031	25	GE	C30-SUPER7	3000	1990
14025-14050	22	GE	C30-SUPER7	3000	1991
14075-14088	6	GE	C30-SUPER7	3000	1992
14077-14091	11	GE	C30-SUPER7	3000	1993
15013-15033	21	GE	C30-SUPER7	3000	1994

537   *E60C MODEL

FERROCARRIL SURESTE-NDEM

Numbers		Qty	Builder	Model	HP	Dates
419-441		6	GE	U30C	3000	1979-1981
659,663		2	MLW	M636	3600	1973
702-718	A	4	MLW	M630	3000	1991-1993
3219		1	MLW	C424	2400	1978
5800-5889	B	24	GM	G12	1310	1956-1964
6701-6784		24	GE	C30-7	3000	1979-1980
7102		1	GM	GP9	1750	1959
8807-8838	D	3	BL	SW1504	1500	1994
9000-9043	E	6	GE	U18B	1800	1974
9106,9124	F	4	GE	U23B	2250	1975
9140-9151	G	3	GE	B23-7	2250	1980
9211-9417	H	25	GM	GP38-2	2000	1975-1979
9521,9530	NREX	2	GE	C30-7	3000	
9822-9825		4	BL	MP15AC	1500	1994
10011-10051	I	6	GE	B23-7	2250	1981-1982
11008-11150		2	GE	C30-7	3000	1982,1988
		117				

NOTES

A ACTUAL 702,709-710,718
B ACTUAL 5800,5803,5805,5810,5812,5814,5837,5844,5846
           5848,5852,5856,5864,5868,5870,5872,5874,5876
           5878-5881,5886,5888,5889
C ACTUAL 7405,7451,7454,7466
D ACTUAL 8807,8819,8838
E ACTUAL 9000,9005,9007,9024,9040,9043
F ACTUAL 9106,9110,9119,9124
G ACTUAL 9140,9148,9151
H ACTUAL 9211,9214,9216,9220,9224,9228,9254,9263,9267
           9271,9272,9276,9290-9291,9297,9400-9403,9405
           9407,9409-9410,9412,9414,9417
I ACTUAL 10011,10018,10030,10039,10044,10051

FILLMORE & WESTERN RY FWRY Fillmore CA

1	1	PORT	STEAM	0-4-0T	1891
51	1	BALD	STEAM	2-8-0	1906
100-101	2	GM	F7A	1500	1949
4009	1	ALCO	RS32	2000	1961
	5				

FILLMORE WESTERN RY Fremont NE

3033,3045	2	GM	GP20	2000	1985

FINGER LAKES RY FGLK Geneva NY

1701-1703,1751	4	GM	GP9	1750	1954-1956
1801	1	GM	GP10	1850	1973
1979,1989.2004	3	GE	B23-7	2250	1979
	8				

FLATS INDUSTRIAL RR Portland ME

12,1201	2	GM	SW9	1200	1986

FLORIDA CENTRAL RR FCEN Plymouth FL

47,49-50,53,56					
63-64	7	GM	CF7	1500	1973-1976
55,57	2	GM	GP7	1500	1979
207	1	GM	GP35	2000	1963
2565	1	GM	CF7	1500	
	11	NOW INCLUDES FLORIDA MIDLAND/FLORIDA NORTHERN			

FLORIDA EAST COAST RY FEC St Augustine FL

401,403-410	9	GM	GP40	3000	1991-1995
411-422,424-443	32	GM	GP40-2	3000	1991-1999
444-453	10	QR	GP40-3	3000	1995-1999
501-511	11	GM	GP38-2	2000	1992-1997
651-652,654-656					
658-661,663,666					
670,772-776	20	GM	GP9R	1750	1972-1973
	82	QR IS QUANTUM RAIL			

FLORIDA GULF COAST RR MUSEUM FGC Parrish FL

12-BEDT	1	PORT	STEAM	0-6-0T	1918
61-UBD	1	GM	NW5	1000	1947
100-USN-65-00345	1	GE	44-TON	300	1954
1633-NYC,8604-PRR	2	ALCO	RS3	1600	1951
1822,1835-USA	2	GM	GP7	1500	1951
	7				

FLORIDA WEST COAST RR FWCR Trenton FL

1337,1353	2	GM	GP18	1800	1960-1961

FORDYCE & PRINCETON RR FP Fordyce AR

1503-1504	2	GM	SW1500	1500	1970-1982
1805	1	GM	GP28	1800	1964
	3				

FORT MADISON FARMINGTON & WESTERN RR Donnellson IA

1	1	VULC	8-TON	100	1929
2	1	PLYM	35-TON	185	1928
4	1	BALD	STEAM	0-4-0	1913
348	1	DAV	30-TON	200	1941
	4				

FORT SMITH RR FSR Fort Smith AR

900-901	2	GM	GP9	1750	
1602-1603,1610	3	GM	GP16	1600	1980
	5				

FORT WORTH & WESTERN RR FWW Fort Worth TX

101-106,1500	7	GM	GP7	1500	1980
2248	1	COOK	STEAM	4-6-0	1896
4299,5004,5007					
5020	4	GM	GP7	1500	1953
	12				

FOUR STATES RY West Chester PA

3	1	ALCO	S2	1000	1949
9	1	GE	65-TON	500	1941
99	1	GM	GP9	1750	1955
1803	1	MLW	RS18	1800	1980
	4				

FRANKLIN INSTITUTE SCIENCE MUSEUM Philadelphia PA

ROCKET-RRR	1	BRAT	STEAM	2-2	1838
3-RRR	1	L&CC	STEAM	4-4-0	1842
60000-BALD	1	BALD	STEAM	4-10-2	1926
	3				

FREMONT & ELKHORN VALLEY RR Fremont NE

2	1	WHIT	50-TON	300	
481	1	DAV	44-TON	300	1953
1219	1	GM	SW1200	1200	1952
	3				

GALVESTON ISLAND RR MUSEUM Galveston TX

1-WBTS	1	BALD	STEAM	2-6-2	1920
112-CTC	1	LIMA	STEAM	2-TRUCK	1923
314-SP	1	ALCO	STEAM	4-6-0	1892
410-UP	1	FM	H20-44	2000	1954
555-CTC	1	ALCO	STEAM	2-8-0	1922
1303-SP	1	GM	NW2	1000	1949
1673-USAF	1	GE	80-TON	470	1952
	7				

GALVESTON RR GVSR Galveston TX

233	1	GM	SW1200	1200	1979
301-305	5	GM	SW1001	1000	1979
	6				

GARDEN CITY WESTERN RY GCW Garden City KS

201,801-804	5	GM	GP8	1600	1953

GATEWAY WESTERN RY GWWR Fairview Heights IL

1201-1204	4	GM	SW1200	1200	1964
1500-1507	8	GM	SW1500	1500	1968-1973
1510	1	GM	MP15AC	1500	1978
2000-2001,2036-					
2037,2040 *	5	GM	GP38	2000	1969
2101,4095-4099	6	VMV	GP38-3	2000	1997-1999

GWWR Cont

3008,3019-3020	3	GM	GP40	3000	1970-1971
4799	1	GM	GP40-3	2000	1999
	28	*	INCLUDES GATEWAY EASTERN GP38		
			2000-2001		

RENTALS

869,872 NREX	2	GM	SD40	3000	1966
1515,1518 HLCX	2	GM	SW1500	1500	1982
	4				

GAULEY RIVER RR Muddlety WV

1819,1821-1822	3	GM	GP16	1650	

GENESEE & WYOMING RR Rochester NY

	2	GM	MP15	1500	1981

GEORGETOWN LOOP RR GLRR (3'Gauge) Georgetown CO

8,12,14	3	LIMA	STEAM	3-TRUCK	1916-1927
15	1	GE	47-TON	380	1943
40,44	2	BALD	STEAM	2-8-0	1920
130,140	2	GE	52-TON	390	1956
	8				

GEORGETOWN RR GRR Georgetown TX

S1	1	ALCO	SLUG	0	1980
1007	1	BALD	DS44-10	1200	1956
9010-9012	3	GM	MP15	1500	1972-1980
9015	1	GM	GP9	1750	1954
9050-9060	9	GM	GP20	2000	1955-1953
	14	EXCLUDES SLUG			

GEORGIA & FLORIDA RAILNET Albany & Valdosta GA

500,502,517	3	GM	GP40-2	3000	1966
3605,3618	2	GM	GP38-3	2000	
8050-8396	13	GM	GP10	1850	
	18				

GEORGIA CENTRAL RY GC Vidalia GA

1004	1	GE	U30B	3000	1973
3907-3968 *	18	GE	U23B	2250	1973-1977
4629,6046	2	GM	GP9	1750	1959
4929	1	GM	GP7	1500	
7011	1	GM	SW9	1200	1952
	23	*	3707,3709-3712,3917,3919,3928,3933		
			3938,3946-3947,3950,3957,3959,3965		
			3968		

GEORGIA NORTHEASTERN RR GNRR Marietta GA

77	1	GM	SW1	600	
81	1	GM	NW2	1000	
316,4125	2	GM	GP20	2000	1960
2097	1	GM	GP7	1500	1952
5408	1	GM	GP8	1600	1976
6576	1	GM	GP9	1750	1957-1958
7529,7572	2	GM	GP10	1750	
8704-8705	2	GM	GP18	1800	1960
	11				

GEORGIA SOUTHWESTERN RR GSWR Americus GA

1900-1901	2 GM	SD9	1750	1957
3813,3837,3858				
4163	4 GM	GP38	2000	1965-1970
4005,4026-4029	5 GM	GP40	3000	1966-1968
4167	1 GM	SLUG	0	
	11	EXCLUDES SLUG	INCLUDES GEORGIA & ALABAMA	

GEORGIA WOODLANDS RR GWRC Washington GA

615	1 GM	GP7	1500	1953
6584	1 GM	GP9	1750	1958
	2			

GETTYSBURG RY Gettysburg PA

105	1 GM	GP9	1750	
106	1 GM	GP7	1500	
107	1 GM	GP10	1650	
	3			

GLOSTER SOUTHERN RR GLSR Gloster MS

1501-1502	2 GM	CF7	1500	1974-1972

GODERICH-EXETER RY GEXR Goderich ON

177,901	2 GM	GP9	1750	1963-1994
700,2127	2 GM	GP7	1500	1953-1978
3834-3835,3843				
3856	4 GM	GP38*	2000	1969-1984
4019,4022,4046	3 GM	GP40*	3000	1966-1968
4161	1	SLUG	0	1992
	11	EXCLUDES SLUG *4022 IS GP40-2 MODEL		
		3834 IS GP35M MODEL		

GOLD COAST RR MUSEUM GCRM Miami FL

C-RF&P	1 ALCO	SLUG	0	
1-NASA	1 ALCO	S2	1000	1942
7-PHOS	1 ALCO	STEAM	0-4-2T	1920
106-SRRY	1 ALCO	RS1	1000	1951
113-FEC	1 ALCO	STEAM	4-6-2	1913
153-FEC	1 ALCO	STEAM	4-6-2	1922
253-FEC	1 BALD	STEAM	2-4-2	
167-SCL	1 GM	SW9	1200	1951
1555-LIRR	1 ALCO	RS3	1600	1955
	8	EXCLUDES SLUG		

GOLDEN GATE RR MUSEUM GGRM Redwood City CA

2-USAF	1 GE	80-TON	500	1955
3-USN	1 GE	65-TON	500	1943
4-SFB	1 VULC	STEAM	0-6-0	1911
25-SFB, 49-SFB	2 ALCO	S2	1000	1944
1847-USA	1 FM	H12-44	1200	1953
2472-SP	1 BALD	STEAM	4-6-2	1921
3194	1 GM	GP9	1750	1954
4450	1 GM	SD9	1750	1955
6378-6380 (45-46)	2 GM	F7A	1500	1952
	11			

GOLDEN ISLES TERMINAL RR Brunswick GA

148	1 GM	SW900	900	
2000	1 GM	GP38	2000	
8235	1 GM	GP7	1500	1950·
	3			

GOLDEN SPIKE NATIONAL HISTORIC SITE Promontory Summit UT

51	1 GE	25-TON	150	1950
60-CPRR	1 OCON	STEAM REP	4-4-0	1979
119-UPRR	1 OCON	STEAM REP	4-4-0	1979
	3			

GOLDEN TRIANGLE RR GTRA Columbus MS

G1	1 GM	MP15AC	1500	1980
810,819	2 GM	GP38-2	2000	1981
	3			

GO TRANSIT - GREATER TORONTO SVCES BD GOTR Toronto ON

520-535	16 ALST	F59PH-1	3000	1998-1999
536-564 *	29 GM	F59PH-2	3000	1990-1994
	45	* 536-537 REFURBISHING BY CLN IN 2001		

GRAFTON & UPTON RR GU Worcester MA

9	1 GE	44-TON	300	1946
1001	1 ALCO	S4	1000	1952
	2			

GRAINBELT GNBC Clinton OK

3648,6083	2 GM	GP9	1750	1955-1956
4079	1 GM	GP20	1850	1962
8053,8180,8250				
8252-8255,8267				
8272	9 GM	GP10	1850	1971
	12			

GRAND CANYON RY GCRY Williams AZ

18,20,29	3 ALCO	STEAM	2-8-0	1910-1906
2134	1 GM	GP7	1500	1953
4960	1 BALD	STEAM	2-8-2	1923
6762,6768,6773				
6776,6793	5 MLW	FPA4	1800	1959
6860,6871	2 MLW	FPB4	1800	1959
	12			

GRAND FORKS RY GFR Grand Forks BC

| 6703 | 1 GM | SW8 | 800 | 1950 |

GRAND RAPIDS EASTERN RR GR Greenville MI

| 3836 | 1 GM | GP38 | 2000 | 1969 |

GRAND TRUNK WESTERN RR GTW (SEE CANADIAN NATIONAL ALSO ILLINOIS CENTRAL) + RENTALS

4600-4635	36 GM	GP9RB	1750	1989-1993
4900-4934 MP/UP	34 GM	GP38-2	2000	1972-1973
5800-5801,5807	3 GM	GP38AC	2000	1971
5900-5928 *	15 GM	SD40	3000	1969-1970
5930-5937 MP/UP	8 GM	SD40-2	3000	1975
6200-6203 DT&I	3 GM	GP38DC	2000	1966

GTW Cont

6401	DT&I	1 GM	GP40	3000	1968
6406-6413	DT&I	8 GM	GP40-2	3000	1972
6414-6421	DT&I	8 GM	GP40-2	3000	1973
6422-6425	DT&I	4 GM	GP40-2	3000	1979
		120	* EXCLUDES 10-SD40 MODEL # 5902-5911		
			LISTED AS DULUTH WINNIPEG & PACIFIC RY		

RENTALS DURING THE YEAR

869-892	NRE	8 GM	SD40	3000	

GREATER WINNIPEG WATER DISTRICT RY GWWD Winnipeg MB

200,202	2 MLW	RS23	1000	1960
201	1 MLW	S13	1000	1959
	3			

GREAT MIAMI & SCIOTO RY GMRY Cincinnati OH

1	1 GM	NW2	1000	1948
20	1 GM	GP9	1750	1959
30	1 GM	GP30	2250	1962
35	1 GM	GP35	2500	1964
70	1 GM	GP10	1800	1952
71	1 GM	GP7	1500	1951
	6			

GREAT PLAINS TRANSPORTATION MUSEUM Wichita KS

3-KG&E	1 GE	ELECTRIC	30-TON	1910
80	1 PLYM	35-TON	230	1943
93-ATSF	1 GM	FP45	3600	1967
421-BN	1 GM	NW2	1000	1949
889-MOC	1 WHIT	30-TON	230	1934
3768-ATSF	1 BALD	STEAM	4-8-4	1938
	6			

GREAT RIVER RR GTR - ROSEDALE-BOLIVAR CPC Rosedale MS

1	1 ALCO	S1	660	1941
2	1 ALCO	S2	1000	1943
	2			

GREAT SMOKY MOUNTAINS RY Dillsboro NC

210,223	2 GM	GP35	2500	1964-1963
711	1 GM	GP7	1500	1954
777	1 GM	GP9	1750	1956
1702	1 BALD	STEAM	2-8-0	1942
	5			

GREAT WALTON RR GRWR Monroe GA

3044	1 GM	GP35	2500	1968
4537,6400	2 GM	GP9R	1800	1968
6243,6580	2 GM	GP9	1750	1958
	5			

GREAT WESTERN RY OF COLORADO GWR Loveland CO

211,296	2 GM	GP9	1750	1976-1990
705	1 GM	GP7	1500	1954
914	1 GM	SD9	1750	1959
5625	1 GM	GP20M	2000	
	5			

GREEN MOUNTAIN RR GMRC Bellows Falls VT

302	1	GM	GP40	3000	1971
405	1	ALCO	RS1	1000	1951
803	1	GM	GP9	1750	1956
804	1	GM	GP9R	1750	1978
4265	1	GM	F7A	1500	
	5				

GUILFORD RAIL SYSTEM ST BOSTON & MAINE MAINE CENTRAL
SPRINGFIELD TERMINAL

BM	252	1	GM	GP38	2000
	322-342	17	GM	GP40	3000
	470	1	GM	GP9R	1750
	690,692	2	GM	SD39	2300
MEC	288	1	GE	U23B	2250
	300-321	22	GM	GP40	3000
	343-355	13	GM	GP40	3000
	370-381	12	GM	GP40	3000
	402-407	4	GE	U18B	1800
ST	10,12,13,15				
	18,25,32	7	GM	GP7	1500
	45,51-52,54				
	62,71-72,77	8	GM	GP9	1750
	200-216	17	GM	GP35	2500
	615-643	5	GM	SD26	2625
	681,686	3	GM	SD45	3600
		113			

GULF COLORADO & SAN SABA RY GCSR Brady TX

200,203-204	3	GM	GP9	1750	1957
4303,4308	2	GM	GP7	1500	1953
9626	1	GM	GP38	2000	
	6				

HAMPTON & BRANCHVILLE RR HB Hampton SC

120	1	GM	SW1000	1000	1967
667,686,859,906					
5943,6025,6249	7	GM	GP9	1750	1957-1959
	8				

HARBOR BELT CA

101-102	2	GM	GP7	1500

HARDIN SOUTHERN RR HSRR Hardin KY

4	1	BALD	STEAM	2-6-2	1914
863	1	GM	SW1	600	1940
	2				

HARTWELL RR HRT Hartwell GA

136	1	GM	GP35	2500	1965
3016,3021	2	GM	GP30	2250	1962-1963
4556	1	GM	GP9R	1800	1957
6525,6555	2	GM	GP9	1750	1957-1958
	6				

H & S RR HS Dothan AL

119,1007,1012	3 GM	SW1	600	1949

HAWAIIAN RY SOC (3'Gauge) Ewa Beach HI

1-EPC	1 BALD	STEAM	0-4-2T	1890
6-WA	1 BALD	STEAM	0-6-2T	1919
6-OR&L	1 BALD	STEAM	0-4-2T	1889
12-OR&L	1 ALCO	STEAM	0-6-0	1912
174-USN	1 WHIT	65-TON	400	1945
302,423-USN	2 WHIT	45-TON	300	1944
7750-USA	1 GE	25-TON	150	1942
	8			

HEART OF DIXIE RR MUSEUM Calera AL

1-HODX	1 GE	25-TON	150	
3-ARM	1 ALCO	STEAM	0-4-0T	1910
37-JWRR	1 BALD	S8	800	1953
38-WI	1 BALD	STEAM	2-8-0	1924
40-AP	1 DAV	STEAM	0-4-0F	1953
103-BS	1 ALCO	HH900	900	1937
570-NYC	1 GM	SC	600	1936
904-MUS	1 GM	SW1	600	1942
1850-C&S	1 FM	H12-44	1200	1953
2019,2022-USA	2 GM	SW8	800	1953
2430-VM	1 EUCL	25-TON	200	1935
4046	1 LIMA	STEAM	0-6-0	1944
	13	INCLUDES CALERA & SHELBY RR		

HEBER VALLEY RR Heber City UT

75,618	2 BALD	STEAM	2-8-0	1907
1011	1 GM	NW2	1000	1941
1218	1 DAV	44-TON	360	1953
1813	1 GM	MRS1	1600	1952
	5			

HENRY FORD MUSEUM & GREENFIELD VILLAGE RR MUSEUM
Dearborn MI

-L&M-ROCKET	1 RS	STEAM REP	0-2-2	1829
-M&H-DEWITT CLINT	1 NYC	STEAM REP	0-4-0	1831
-SA&G	1 ROG	STEAM	4-4-0	1858
-C OF D	1 PLYM	14-TON	GAS	1927
1-FORD	1 FORD	STEAM	4-4-0	1929
1-USN	1 GE	50-TON	380	1942
3-C&HM	1 MAS	STEAM	0-6-4T	1873
7-D&LN	1 BALD	STEAM	4-4-0	1897
7-WCR*	1 DAV	STEAM	0-4-0T	1922
8-D&M	1 BALD	STEAM	0-6-0	1914
45-MCRR	1 ALCO	STEAM	4-4-2	1902
90-IR	1 A-GE	BOXCAB	300	1926
154-B&LE	1 BALD	STEAM	2-8-0	1909
1601-C&O	1 LIMA	STEAM	2-6-6-6	1941
	14	* 3'GAUGE		

HERITAGE PARK HISTORICAL VILLAGE HP Calgary AB

-	2	PORT	COMP AIR	0-4-0FT	1909
3	1	VUL	STEAM	0-4-0T	1902
4-CP	1	CPR	STEAM	0-6-0	1905
2023-USA	1	ALCO	STEAM	0-6-0	1942
2024-USA	1	LIMA	STEAM	0-6-0	1944
5931-CPR	1	MLW	STEAM	2-10-4	1949
7019-CPR	1	MLW	S2	1000	1944
	8				

HISTORIC RR SHOPS - COASTAL HERITAGE SOCIETY Savannah GA

- *	1	PORT	STEAM	0-4-0	1921
1-CofG	1	BALD	STEAM	2-8-0	1907
8-CRRBC	1	BALD	STEAM	0-6-0T	1886
15-SLC **	1	BALD	STEAM	2-4-2	1914
30-CB&TC	1	ALCO	STEAM	0-4-0T	1913
2715-S&A	1	GM	GP35	2500	1964
3250-AS	1	PORT	STEAM	0-4-0T	1905
	7	* NARROW GAUGE ** OWNED BY MIKE BUCKNER			

HOCKING VALLEY SCENIC RY HVSR Nelsonville OH

3-0P	1	BALD	STEAM	0-6-0	1925
33-LS&I	1	BALD	STEAM	2-8-0	1916
4005-USAF	1	BLH	60-TON	500	1954
5833-C&O	1	GM	GP7	1500	1952
7315-USA	1	GE	45-TON	300	1943
	5				

HOLLIS & EASTERN RR HE Duke OK

39	1	GM	SW1	600	1952
70	1	GM	GP20	2000	1961
	2				

HOOSIER SOUTHERN RR HOS Tell City IN

464	1	GM	GP8	1600	1968
465	1	GM	GP9	1750	1957
466-467	2	GM	GP7	1500	1952
	4				

HOOSIER VALLEY RR MUSEUM North Judson IN

6	1	PORT	STEAM	0-4-2T	1913
11-HVRM	1	GE	95-TON	600	1952
27-USA	1	WHIT	44-TON	380	1941
310-ERIE	1	ALCO	S1	660	1947
2789-C&O	1	ALCO	STEAM	2-8-4	1947
	5				

HOUSATONIC RR HRRC Canaan CT

300	1	GE	45-TON	300	1942
3600-3604	5	GM	GP35	2500	1964-1965
7324	1	GM	GP9	1750	1977
9935	1	ALCO	RS3M	1200	1979
	8				

HOUSTON & GULF COAST RR Houston TX

1706,1708 ECRX					
4472	3	GM	GP9	1750	

HUDSON BAY RY The Pas MB

643,685	2	MLW	M420	2000	
3530-3559*	16	MLW	M420	2000	
	18	* 3530,3533,3538-3539,3542-3545,3547-3548
		3550-3551,3555,3557-3559

HULL CHELSEA WAKEFIELD STEAM TRAIN Hull QC

244	1	SWED	5670D	1750	1962
909	1	SWED	STEAM	2-8-0	1907
	2				

HUNTSVILLE & LAKE OF BAYS PRESERVATION SOC (3'-6" Gauge)

Huntsville ON

1-2	2	MLW	STEAM	0-4-0T	1928
3	1	GE	25-TON	150	1948
9-ET*	1	MLW	STEAM	0-6-0	1922
10*	1	GE	70-TON	600	1946
	5	* STANDARD GAUGE SOME LOCOMOTIVES ON LOAN

HUNTSVILLE & MADISON COUNTY RR HMCR Huntsville AL

527	1	GM	NW2	1000	1946
8923	1	GM	SW9	1200	1951
	2				

HURON & EASTERN RY HESR Saginaw MI

201-204	4	GM	GP38-2	2000	1977
301	1	GM	GP38	2000	1969
	5				

HURON CENTRAL RY Sudbury ON

201,204,208-209	4	GM	GP9	1750	
458-462	5	GM	SD45-2	3600	1997-1998
	9				

HUTCHINSON & NORTHERN RY HN Hutchinson KS

6-7	2	GM	SW900	900	1957-1955

I & M RAIL LINK IMRL Davenport IA

12-16	5	GM	SW7/9	1200	1950-1954
101-103,105-106	5	GM	GP9	1750	1950-1958
200-218,220-233	29	GM	SD40	3000	1966-1970
352-389	22	GM	SD45	3600	1967-1970
393	1	GM	F45	3600	1971
600-612	10	GM	SD9	1750	1952-1954
2025-2039 NREX	8	GM	SD40-3	3000	
6077-6525 HLCX	4	GM	SD40-3	3000	
8905-8940	24	GM	SD45	3600	1966-1971
	108	(SEE ALSO MONTANA RAIL LINK)

IDAHO NORTHERN & PACIFIC RR INPR Emmett ID

1707	1	GM	GP16	1600	1980
2074,2094	2	GM	GP7	1500	1977
4500-4506	7	GM	GP40	3000	1966-1969
4506-4510	4	GM	GP35	2500	1967-1965
	14				

ILLINOIS & MIDLAND RY IMR Springfield IL

30-31	2	GM	RS1325	1325	1960
40-43	4	GM	SW1500	1500	1970
50,52-54	4	GM	SD9	1750	1955
60-61	2	GM	SD18	1800	1960-1961
80-84	5	GM	SD20	2000	1980
	17				

ILLINOIS CENTRAL RR IC (SEE CANADIAN NATIONAL)

100-101	2	GMBN	E9A	2400	1973
1000-1019	20	GM	SD70	4000	1995
1020-1039	20	GM	SD70	4000	1998
1300-1301	2	GMIC	SW13	1200	1971
1400-1511	45	GMIC	SW14	1200	1978-1982
1765,1788 CCP	2	GM	GP10	1750	1970
2000 ELC	1	GM	SD40-3	3000	
2025-2041	17	GMIC	SD20	2000	1982
3100-3139	35	VMV	GP40R	3000	1987-1991
3140	1	GM	GP40-2	3000	1965
4011-4035 CN	20	ALST	GP9RM	1800	1981-1982
5812-5831 GT	20	GM	GP38-2	2000	1978
5832-5836 GT	5	GM	GP38-2	2000	1980
5844-5849 GT	6	GM	GP38-2	2000	1977
5850-5861 GT	12	GM	GP38-2	2000	1978
6000-6071	35	VMV	SD40-2R	3000	1994-1995
6030,6032	2	GM	SD40-2	3000	1975
6034	1	GMIC	SD40-2	3000	1982
6072	1	NREX	SD40-2	3000	1978
6100-6160	52	GM	SD40-2	3000	1976
6200-6204	5	VMV	SD40-3	3000	1997-1998
6221-6228 GT	8	GM	GP38-2	2000	1975
6250-6251	2	VMV	SD40-3	3000	1999
8057-8465	14	GMIC	GP10	1850	1971-1977
8400-8417 CCP	9	GM	GP10	1750	1970-1971
8701-8753	39	GMIC	GP11	1850	1979-1981
9438 CCP	1	GM	GP28	1800	1964
9560-9639	53	GM	GP38-2	2000	1972-1974
	420	CCP IS CHICAGO CENTRAL & PACIFIC RR			

ILLINOIS RAILNET Ottawa IL

3	1	GM	F7A	1500	
5	1	GM	GP7	1500	
6-7	2	GE	B23-7	2250	
	4				

ILLINOIS RY MUSEUM ILM Union IL

BN1-BN	1	GM	F9A-2	2000	1968
BN2-BN	1	GM	F9B-2	2000	1990
BN3-BN	1	GM	E9A-2	2000	1990
2-JM	1	WHIT	12-TON	-	1951
L3-TMER	1	TMER	ELECTRIC	50-TON	1920
L4-WEPCO	1	TMER	ELECTRIC	50-TON	1920
4-UE	1	PORT	STEAM	0-4-0F	1946

ILM Cont

4-CE	1 A-GE	ELECTRIC	60-TON	1911
5-STRP	1 LIMA	STEAM	3-TRUCK	1929
5-CE	1 BALD	STEAM	0-6-0	1922
7-PSC	1 BALD	STEAM	0-6-0T	1926
7-ACW	1 VULC	STEAM	0-4-0T	1917
L7-WEPCO	1 TMER	ELECTRIC	37-TON	1931
L10-TMER	1 TMER	ELECTRIC	55-TON	1944
14-CSRL	1 BALD	ELECTRIC	50-TON	1929
14-D&R	1 GM	SC600	600	1937
16-T&D	1 BALD	STEAM	4-4-0	1914
18A&B-UP	1 GE	GAS-TURBINE	8500	1960
21-MN&S	1 BALD	DT6-6-2000	2000	1948
26-GN&A	1 BALD	STEAM	2-6-0	1926
30-ITR	1 MCG	ELECTRIC	35-TON	1915
33C-MILW	1 GM	E8A	2250	1956
35-LS&I	1 BALD	STEAM	2-8-0	1916
37A-MILW	1 GM	E9A	2400	1961
66-DC	1 ALCO	S1	660	1945
92-AT&SF	1 GM	FP45	3600	1968
96B-MILW	1 GM	F7B	1500	1951
99-L&A	1 BALD	STEAM	2-8-0	1919
101-TRR	1 BALD	STEAM	2-6-2	1924
103-WT	1 BALD	V0660	660	1945
104C-MILW	1 GM	FP7A	1500	1952
E110-ARM	1 LIMA	DIESEL	1200	1951
118C-MILW	1 GM	F7A	1500	1951
121-DRINW	1 GM	SW7	1200	1950
200-MT	1 ALCO	RS3	1600	1951
207-L&NE	1 BALD	STEAM	0-6-0	1936
265-MILW	1 ALCO	STEAM	4-8-4	1944
305,308-METRA	2 GM	F7A	1500	1949
314-L&N	1 ALCO	FA2	1500	1960
400-TP&W	1 ALCO	RS11	1800	1958
428-UP	1 BALD	STEAM	2-8-0	1901
508-CTC *	1 B-W	ELECTRIC	MINING	1908
606-C&G	1 BALD	AS416	1600	1950
637-CB&Q	1 ROG	STEAM	4-6-0	1892
671-UP	1 GM	E9B	2400	1955
760-MILW	1 FM	H10-44	1000	1944
803-CSSB	1 GE	ELECTRIC	2-D-D-2	1949
938-CRI&P	1 ALCO	STEAM	4-6-2	1910
975-SP	1 BALD	STEAM	2-10-2	1918
1366-UP	1 FM	H20-44	2000	1947
1518-C&NW	1 GM	GP7	1500	1948
1565-IT	1 ITS	ELECTRIC	60-TON	1910
1603-MILW	1 ALCO	HH600	600	1939
1605-IT	1 GM	GP7	1500	1953
1630-SLSF	1 BALD	STEAM	2-10-0	1918
1792-PULL	1 DAV	10-TON	GAS	1928

ILM Cont

1951-GTW	1	ALCO	RS1	1000	1957
2050-N&W	1	ALCO	STEAM	2-8-8-2	1923
2407-GB&W	1	ALCO	RSD15	2400	1959
2707-C&O	1	ALCO	STEAM	2-8-4	1943
2903-AT&SF	1	BALD	STEAM	4-8-4	1943
3001-DL&W	1	A-GE	DIESEL	300	1926
3007-CB&Q	1	BALD	STEAM	4-6-4	1930
3719-IC	1	BRKS	STEAM	2-6-0	1900
4715-PC	1	A-GE	ELECTRIC	2-D-2	1906
4939-AMTK	1	P-GE	ELECTRIC	2-C-C-2	1942
4963-CB&Q	1	BALD	STEAM	2-8-2	1923
5056-MILW	1	GE	U25B	2500	1965
5383-BN	1	GE	U30C	3000	1974
6244-BN	1	GM	SD24	2400	1959
6323-GTW	1	ALCO	STEAM	4-8-4	1942
6930-UP	1	GM	DDA40X	6600	1970
8380-GTW	1	BALD	STEAM	0-8-0	1929
8537-USA	1	GE	44-TON	300	1944
9911A-CB&Q	1	GM	E5A	2000	1940
	76	* 2'GAUGE			

ILLINOIS WESTERN RR Vandalia IL

7570	1	GM	GP10	1850	1976

INDIANA & OHIO RAIL SYSTEM INOR + RENTALS Cincinnati OH

53	1	GM	GP7	1500	1953
61	1	GM	GP9	1750	1956
71	1	GM	GP18	1800	1960
81-87,2252	8	GM	GP30	2000	1962-1983
251-252	2	GM	GP35	2500*	1964
3803-3807,3864	4	GM	GP38-3	2000	1969
3838 HLCX	1	GM	GP38DC	2000	
4030	1	GM	GP40	3000	1969
4031-4036,4050	7	GM	GP40-1	3000	1968-1971
5001,5003,5005-5006	4	GM	GP50	3500	1980
	30	* SOME RATED 2000-2250HP			

RENTALS

423 HATX	1	GM	GP40	3000	
2001-2007 LLPS	5	GM	GP38DC	2000	1969
3076,3140 NREX	2	GM	GP40	3000	1967-1968
6403-6427	7	GM	SD40	3000	
	15				

INDIANA HARBOR BELT IHB Gibson IN

BU50-BU55	6	GM	NW2/SW7	1200	1987-1989
PB1-PB5	5	GM	SLUGS	0	1981
477-479	3	GM	SLUGS	0	1962-1975
1505	1	GM	MP15	1500	1970
2256,2272 NREX	2	GM	SW1200	1200	1953-1954
2920-2925 NREX	6	GM	SD20	2000	1980
3801-3802	2	GM	GP38-2	2000	1995

IHB Cont

3901-3902	2 GM	SD39	2300	1970
4001-4002	2 GM	SD40	3000	1970
8719-8834	34 GM	NW2	1000	1948-1981
8835-8877	9 GM	SW7	1200	1949-1986
9002-9008	7 GM	SW9	1200	1953-1985
9200-9222	23 GM	SW1500	1500	1966-1970
	94	EXCLUDES SLUGS		

INDIANA NORTHEASTERN RR IN South Milford IN

47*,1601,1603	3 GM	GP7	1500	1952
1766,1770	2 GM	GP9	1750	1957
	5	* LEASED FROM PRRR		

INDIANA RAIL ROAD INRD Indianapolis IN

549-550,554-555				
558,560	6 GM	SD10	1850	1974
600	1 GM	SD15H	1500	1968
1701,1704,1718				
1728,1736,1753	1757,1791,1809			
1813	10 GM	GP16	1600	1980-1979
2543	1 GM	CF7	1500	1973
7305,7308-7310				
7314,7317	6 GM	SD18	1800	1963-1962
	24			

INDIANA RY MUSEUM FLWB French Lick IN

B-WTP	1 GE	ELECTRIC	150	1920
2-TFC	1 PLYM	25-TON	150	1929
3-EL&C	1 GE	80-TON	500	1947
5-CM	1 PLYM	30-TON	150	1936
11	1 BALD	STEAM	0-4-0T	1936
97	1 BALD	STEAM	2-6-0	1925
101,119-AW&W	2 ALCO	S4	1000	1953-1957
104-AW&W	1 ALCO	RS1	1000	1947
208	1 BALD	STEAM	2-6-0	1912
	10			

INDIANA SOUTHERN RR ISRR Petersburg IN

1-2 PSI-WG	2 GM	GP38	2000	
3814	1 GM	GP38AC	2000	
3977,3983,3988	3 GE	B23-7	2250	1979
4037,4043	7 GM	GP40-1	3000	1970-1971
4162,5215	2 GM	SLUGS	0	1992
4218	1 GM	GP30M	2250	
	14			

INDIANA TRANSPORTATION MUSEUM ITM Noblesville IN

44-BRR	1 GE	44-TON	300	1950
50-CIL	1 GM	SW1	600	1942
83A-MONON	1 GM	F7A	1500	1949
96C-MILW	1 GM	FP7A	1500	1951
99-NWSC	1 BALD	VO1000	1000	
587-NKP	1 BALD	STEAM	2-8-2	1918
	6			

INTERNATIONAL RAIL ROAD SYSTEMS Columbia Gardens BC

4519	1 GM	GP9	1750	1957

IOWA INTERSTATE RR IAIS Iowa City IA

100-103 NREX	4 GM	SD20	2000	R1979-1980
250	1 GM	SW1200	1200	1966
303	1 GM	GP9	1500	1956
325	1 GM	GP7	1500	1953
400	1 GM	GP7M	1750	R1976
401-403	3 GM	GP10	1850	R1968-1972
405,407-408	3 GM	GP8	1850	R1974-1975
413,431	2 GM	GP10	1850	R1969
466,468,481	3 GM	GP8	1850	R1968-1969
483-484	2 GM	GP10	1850	R1969
495	1 GM	GP16	1750	R1982
600-604	5 GM	GP38	2000	1966-1969
625-628	4 GM	GP38AC	2000	1971
800-802	3 MLW	M420R	2000	1974-1975
	34			

IOWA NORTHERN RY IANR Greene IA

2000-2004 NREX	5 GM	GP20	2000	1974
3607,3609	2 GM	GP38	2000	1969-1971
	7			

IOWA TRACTION RR IATR Mason City IA

50-51,54	3 BW	ELECTRIC	600	1919-1921
60	1 BW	ELECTRIC	1000	1917
	4			

ISS RAIL ISSR New Castle PA

605	1 ALCO RS11		1800	1957
3003	1 ALCO S2		1000	1946
	2			

JEFFERSON WARRIOR RR JEFW Birmingham AL

51-54	4 GM	SW1500	1500	1972
55-56	2 GM	SW9M	1200	1972
	6			

JK LINE TIPP Monterey IN

7311	1 GM	SD18	1800	1963

JOHNSON COUNTY AIRPORT COMM RY New Century KS

1992	1 GM	SW900R	900	1992

JUNIATA TERMINAL Philadelphia PA

7250-7251	2 GM	GP10	1850	1989
7650	1 ALCO SLUG		0	1957
9251	1 GM	NW2	1000	1947
9277	1 GM	SW1500	1500	1973
	4 EXCLUDES SLUG			

JUNIATA VALLEY RR JVRR Lewistown PA

1865	1 GM	SW9	1200	1953

KANKAKEE BEAVERVILLE & SOUTHERN RR KBSR Beaverville IL

312,321,324	3 ALCO RS11		1800	1956-1960
308	1 ALCO RS11M		2000	1956
315	1 ALCO C420		2000	1966
	5			

KANSAS CITY SOUTHERN RY KCS

1-2,4		3	GM	F9A-3	1750	1997
3		1	GM	F9B	1750	1997
103-104	TMR	2	GM	SW1001	1000	1974-1980
600-634		35	VMV	SD40-3	3000	1995
637-656		20	GM	SD40-3	3000	1972
657-666		10	GM	SD40-3	3000	1974
667-669		3	GM	SD40-3	3000	1976
670-676		7	VMV	SD40-3	3000	1996
677-686		10	GM	SD40-3	3000	1978
687-692		6	GM	SD40-3	3000	1980
695-699		5	ALST	SD40-3	3000	1996
700-703		4	GM	SD40X	3500	1979
704-713*		9	GM	SD50	3500 A	1981
714-723		10	GM	SD60	3800	1989
724-735		12	GM	SD60	3800	1990
736-759		24	GM	SD60	3800	1991
871-889	TMR	19	BL	GP40-3	3000	1997-1998
1001-1086	MSRC	29	GM	GP10	1850	1968-1974
1161-1179		19	GM	GP40-3	3000	1998
1803-1804	MSRC	2	GM	GP18	1850	1963,1960
2000-2074		75	GE	AC4400CW	4400	2000
2075-2099		25	GE	AC4400CW	4400	2001
4000-4009		10	GM	GP38-2	2000	1974
4010-4011		2	GM	GP38-2	2000	1978
4012-4023		12	GM	GP38-2	2000	1973
4024-4028		5	GM	GP38-2	2000	1990
4029-4031		3	GM	GP38-2	2000	1978
4032-4033		2	GM	GP38-2	2000	1975
4078-4257		8	GM	SLUG	0	1968-1973
4300		1	GM	SW1001	1000	1981
4301		1	GM	SW900	900	1988
4319		1	GM	SW1500	1500	1980
4320-4323		4	GM	SW1500	1500	1966
4324-4337		13	GM	SW1500	1500 B	1968
4338-4351		14	GM	SW1500	1500	1971
4352-4361		10	GM	SW1500	1500	1972
4362		1	GM	SW1500	1500	1971
4363-4367		5	GM	MP15	1500	1975
4500-4509		10	BL	SD45-3	3600	1996
4700-4722		22	GM	GP40-3	3000 C	1974
4736-4739		4	GM	GP40-3	3000	1978
4740-4748		9	VMV	GP40-3	3000	1995
4805-4824		20	GM	GP40-3	3000	1994
6600-6627 *		28	ALST	SD40-3	3000	1998
6628-6639 *		12	ALST	SD40-3	3000	1999

519   * SHARED WITH CANADIAN NATIONAL

A 712 IS 2000   B EXCEPT 4332   C EXCEPT 4703

KENTUCKY CENTRAL RY KCRY Paris KY

9	1 BALD	VO1000	1000	1945
11	1 BALD	STEAM	2-6-2	1925
2016	1 GM	SW800	800	1951
	3			

KENTUCKY RY MUSEUM KRM New Haven KY

11-LC	1 VULC	STEAM	0-4-0T	1913
32-MON	1 GM	BL2	1500	1948
76-77-USN	2 GE	45-TON	380	1940-1942
152-L&N	1 ROG	STEAM	4-6-2	1905
285-L&N	1 L&N	STEAM	0-8-0	1920
770-L&N	1 GM	E6A	2000	1939
1846-USA	1 FM	H12-44	1200	1953
2112	1 ALCO	MRS1	1600	
2546-ATSF	1 GM	CF7	1500	1973
2918-WAB *	1 GM	GP35	2500	1963
4010,4044	2 WHIT	60-TON	500	1955
2716-C&O	1 ALCO	STEAM	2-8-4	1943
7374-USA	1 ALCO	S1	660	1941
	14	* LOANED FROM MUSEUM OF TRANSPORT		

KEOKUK JUNCTION RY KJRY Keokuk IA

105	1 GM	NW2	1000	1949
400-401	2 GM			
406	1 GM	F7A	1500	
600	1 GM	CF7	1500	1974
702	1 GM	GP7	1500	
806-807	2 GM	GP8	1600 *	
909-911	3 GM	GP9	1750	
1609	1 GM	GP16	1850	
	12	* 807 RATED 1850HP		

KETTLE MORAINE RY KMRY North Lake WI

1-W&OV	1 BALD	STEAM	4-6-0	1906
3M-USAF	1 DAV	30-TON	300	1943
3-CMRR	1 HEIS	STEAM	2-TRUCK	1917
6-CIPS	1 VULC	STEAM	0-4-0T	1920
9-MMCR,16-LTC	2 BALD	STEAM	2-6-2	1901,1919
107	1 GE	65-TON	400	1944
	7			

KIAMICHI RR KRR Hugo OK

702-707	3 GM	GP7	1500	1953-1951
901-907	5 GM	GP9	1750	1952-1959
1001-1006	6 GM	GP10	1750	1951-1955
3501-3502	2 GM	GP35	2500	1969
3801-3805	4 GM	GP35M	2000	1964
3811-3815	5 GM	GP38	2000	1964-1969
	25			

KISKI JUNCTION RR New Castle PA

7135	1 ALCO	S1	660	1943

KNOX & KANE RR KKRR Marienville PA

1		1 PORT	50-TON	300	1945
38		1 BALD	STEAM	2-8-0	1927
39		1 GM	GP9	1750	1957
44		1 ALCO	S4	1000	1957
58		1 SINO	STEAM	2-8-2	1989
70		1 ALCO	RS36	1800	1962
		6			

KNOXVILLE & HOLSTON RIVER RR Knoxville TN

109,361,3617	3 GM	GP38	2000	
134	1 GM	NW2	1000	1946
52,2313,2318,9573	4 GM	SW1500	1500	1977
2391	1 GM	GP9R	1750	1956
8056,8068	2 GM	GP10	1850	1974-1976
	11			

KWT RY KWT Paris TN

300	1 GM	GP7	1500	1953
301-302	2 GM	GP9	1750	1959-1960
303	1 GM	GP18	1800	1960
	4			

KYLE RR KYLE Phillipsburg KS

1101-1102	2 GM	SW8	800	1952
1125	1 GM	SW1000	1000	1966
1827-1829	3 GM	GP28	1800	1964
2036	1 GM	GP20E	2000	1974
2200,2210	2 GM	GP30	2250	1963
2500,2504-2506	4 BL	GP35	2500	1979-1980
5321-5332	4 GE	U30C	3000	1972
5794-5796,5799	4 GE	U30B	3000	1974-1975
5808-5928	8 GE	U30C	3000	1973
6230-6233	4 GM	SD39	2300	1968-1970
	33			

LAHAINA KAANAPALI & PACIFIC RR LKP (3'Gauge) Lahaina HI

1,3	2 PORT	STEAM	2-4-0	1943
5	1 BALD	STEAM	0-6-2	1908
45	1 PLYM	30-TON	330	1959
85	1 ALCO	STEAM	4-6-0	1910
	5			

LAKE COUNTY RR Lakeview OR

700,1617	2 GM	GP7	1500	

LAKELAND & WATERWAYS RY Edmonton AB

1400-1401	2 GM	FP9A	1800	
1701,1754,1758-				
1759,4001	5 GM	GP9	1750 *	1998
2099	1 GM	GP38	2000	
2210,5010-5011				
5013	4 GM	GP7	1500	1953
	12	* 4001 IS GP9-2TR RATED 1800HP		

LAKE SHORE RY MUSEUM North East PA

6-CEI	1	HEIS	STEAM	0-6-0F	1937
25-ECIW	1	WHIT	23-TON	125	1941
802-CSS&SB	1	GE	ELECTRIC *	5120	1949
1700-WAG	1	GE	132-TON	1000	1940
2500-NYC	1	GE	U25B	2500	1964
	5	* MODEL 2-D-D-2			

LAKE STATE RY LSRC Tawas City MI

181,281,381,1280	4	A-GE	C425M *	2000	1981
469	1	ALCO	RS2	1500	1977-1956
646	1	ALCO	S1	660	1946
698	1	BBD	HR412	2000	1981
798	1	BBD	M420	2000	1977
974-975	2	BL	TE56-4A	1800	1974-1975
976	1	BL	C420	2000	1976
1195	1	ALCO	RS11	1800	1977
	12	* 181 IS C425MAC MODEL			

LAKE SUPERIOR & ISHPEMING RR LSI Negaunee MI

3000-3053	16	GE	U30C	3000	1974-1975
3071-3074	4	GE	C30-7	3000	1977
	20				

LAKE SUPERIOR MUSEUM OF TRANSPORTATION LSMT/LSMR Duluth MN

1-FC	1	MACK	15-TON	200	1931
1-NP	1	SM-F	STEAM	0-4-0T	1870
1-GN	1	PATT	STEAM	4-4-0	1861
7-MS	1	PORT	STEAM	0-4-0T	1915
14-D&NM	1	BALD	STEAM	2-8-2	1913
28-D&NE	1	ALCO	STEAM	2-8-0	1906
46-FP LS&M	1	GE	45-TON	380	1945
71B-MILW	1	GM	F7B	1500	1950
192-GN	1	GM	NW5	1000	1946
193-DMIR	1	GM	SD18	1800	1960
227-DMIR	1	BALD	STEAM	2-8-8-4	1941
307-HM	1	GE	ELECTRIC	600	1928
400-GN	1	GM	SD45	3600	1966
900-OIM	1	ALCO	HH1000	1000	1940
2435-NP	1	ALCO	STEAM	2-6-2	1907
2500A-SOO	1	GM	FP7A	1500	1949
7243-EM	1	BALD	S12	1200	1955
10200-MILW	1	GE	ELECTRIC	1500	1915
	18	INCLUDES LAKE SUPERIOR & MISSISSIPPI RR			

LAKE TERMINAL RR LT Lorain OH

1021,1023	2	GM	SW1001	1000	1968-1975
1022	1	GM	SW1000	1000	1970
	3				

LAKE WHATCOM RY LWRY Acme WA

30-NPT	1	ALCO	S1	660	1940
1070-NP	1	ALCO	STEAM	0-6-0	1907
	2				

LANCASTER & CHESTER RY LC Lancaster SC

90-91	2	GM	SW900	900	1982
92	1	GM	SW900M	1000	1984
93-94,97-98	4	GM	SW1200	1200	1997-1998
95-96	2	GM	SW1500	1500	1966-1968
	9				

LANDISVILLE RR AMHR Landisville PA

8651	1	GM	SW900M	900	1956

LAONA & NORTHERN RR CAMP FIVE MUSEUM CF Laona WI

4	1	VULC	STEAM	2-6-2	1916

LAPEER INTER RR

5	1	GE	65-TON	500	1950
6	1	PLYM	MST		1984
	2				

LAUREL HIGHLANDS RR Scottsdale PA

1	1	WHIT	80-TON	600	1941
7	1	PORT	STEAM	2-4-0	1934
	2				

LAURINBURG & SOUTHERN RR LRS Laurinburg NC

138	1	GM	SW9	1200	1951
2318,9528	2	GM	SW1500	1500	1966
	3				

LEADVILLE-COLORADO & SOUTHERN RR Leadville CO

641	1	ALCO	STEAM	2-8-0	1906
1714,1918	2	GM	GP9	1750	1955-1957
	3				

LEWIS & CLARK RY LINC Battle Ground WA

81-82	2	GM	SW8	800	1953-1954

LEWISBURG & BUFFALO CREEK RR Lewisburg/Strasburg PA

1500	1	GM	SW8	800	1953
9425	1	GM	SW1	600	1950
	2				

LEXINGTON & OHIO RR Versailles TN

7738	1	GM	GP8	1600	
9528	1	GM	SW1500	1500	
	2				

LITTLE KANAWHA RIVER RAIL LKRR Parkersburg WV

714	1	GM	SW1200	1200	1955

LITTLE RIVER RR LRR White Pigeon MI

110	1	BALD	STEAM	4-6-2	1911
220	1	PLYM	20-TON	GAS	1929
	2				

LITTLE ROCK & WESTERN RY LRWN Perry AR

101-102	2	ALCO	C420	2000	1982
103	1	GM	GP9	1750	1986
7736	1	VMV	GP38	q1600	1975
	4				

LITTLE ROCK PORT RR LRPA Little Rock AR

902	1	GM	SW900	900	1952

LIVONIA AVON & LAKEVILLE RR LAL Lakeville NY

4-5	2	ALCO	S1	660	1950
20	1	ALCO	RS1	1000	1949
72	1	ALCO	S2	1000	1941
420	1	ALCO	C420	2000	1964
425	1	ALCO	C425	2500	1965
450-452,454	4	ALCO	C424M	2000	1980
	10				

LONGHORN RR Austin TX

2003-2005	3	GM	GP9	1750	
2006-2007	2	GM	GP35	2500	
9275	1	GM	SW1500	1500	1973
	6				

LONG ISLAND RR LI Jamaica NY

100-107	5	GM	SW1001	1000	1977
150-172	20	GM	MP15AC	1500	1977
250-277	24	GM	GP38-2	2000	1976-1977
300-302	3	ABB	FL9AC	2000	1993
397-399	3	GE	25-TON	150	1958
400-422 *	23	GM	DE30AC	3000	1997-1999
500-522 *	23	GM	DE30AC-DM**	3000	1999
	101				

```
                * COMPLETELY NEW STREAMLINED STAINLESS-
                  STEEL MONOCOQUE DESIGN
               ** DM OPERATES DUAL MODE
```

LONGVIEW PORTLAND & NORTHERN RY LPN Gardiner OR

111	1	ALCO	S2	1000	1949
130	1	GM	SW1500	1500	1969
	2	LOCOMOTIVES FOR SALE			

LOS ANGELES JUNCTION RY LAJ Los Angeles CA

2563,2568,2571				
2619	4	GM	CF7	1500

LOUISIANA & DELTA RR LDRR New Iberia LA

1200	1	GM	SW1200	1200	1964
1500-1514	15	GM	CF7	1500	1972-1973
1850-1853	4	GM	GP10	1850	1975-1974
	20				

LOUISIANA & NORTH WEST RR LNW Homer IA

50,52-53	3	GM	GP7	1500	1950-1953
51	1	GM	GP9	1750	1955
54	1	GM	GP35	2500	1965
	5				

LOUISVILLE & INDIANA RR LIRC Jeffersonville IN

201	1	GM	GP10	1850	1979
220-221,223	3	GM	GP38-2	2000	1982
1607-1610	4	GM	GP16	1600	1951-1954
9321-9373	2	GM	SW1200	1200	1962
	10				

LOUISVILLE NEW ALBANY & CORYDON RR Corydon IN

101	1	GE	44-TON	300	1962
1951	1	GE	45-TON	300	1951
86,1000-1001	3	ALCO	CS9-CAT	975	1980
850	1	ALCO	C420	2000	R1979
900	1	ALCO	RS36	1800	1963
	7				

LOWVILLE & BEAVER RIVER RR Lowville NY

1947,1950-1951	3	GE	44-TON	380*	1947-1951
			* 1951 RATED AT 400HP		

LTV STEEL MINING RR Hoyt Lakes MN

4201-4204	4	NRE	GP38-3	2000	1997
4206-4209	4	GM	GP20	2000	
4210-4211,4214	3	GM	F9A	1750	
4215-4216	2	GM	GP38	2000	
4222-4225	4	GM	F9B	1750	
7201-7216	15	ALCO	RS11	1800	
7212-7222	3	ALCO	C420	2000	
7230	1	ALCO	C424	2400	
7245-7246	2	BALD	S12	1200	
	38				

RENTALS

-	LRCX	3	GE	C30-7	3000

LUXAPALILA VALLEY RR LXVR Columbus MS

2880,2885	2	GM	GP38	2000	1965-1966

LUZERNE & SUSQUEHANNA RY Wilkes Barre PA

30	1	GM	SW1	600	1953
50	1	GM	SW7	1200	1959
	2				

LYCOMING VALLEY RR LVRR Williamsport PA

231,238-239	3	GM	SW9	1200	1953

M & B RR Meridian MS (FORMERLY MERIDIAN & BIGBEE RR)

107,109,7735					
8371	4	VMV	GP10	1850	1995

MACKENZIE NORTHERN RY Edmonton AB

1700,1702,1750					
1755-1757	6	GM	GP9	1750	1998
1802	1	GM	GP18	1800	1960
2000-2001,2003					
2009　　HELM	4	GM	GP38	2000	1969
2120-2122	3	GM	GP38-2	2000	
4000-4002,4004	4	GM	GP9-2R	1800	1998
4301-4303	3	GM	GP7	1500	1951
9304,9306,9309	3	GM	GP40	3000	1966
	24				

MADISON RR CMPA Madison IN

3634	1	GM	GP10	1800	1971
2013	1	GM	SW800	800	1955
	2				

MAD RIVER & NKP RR MRRM Bellevue OH

-AFCO	1	PLYM	18-TON	150	1944
1-B&M	1	ALCO	S5	800	1954
2-NJI&I *	1	GM	NW2	1000	1948
7-C&EI	1	PORT	STEAM	0-6-0F	1943
329-NKP	1	ALCO	RSD12	1800	1957
671-WAB	1	GM	F7A	1500	1951
740-MILW	1	FM	H12-44	1200	1952
900-NKP	1	GM	GP30	2250	1962
1190-BR&P	1	ALCO	STEAM	0-6-0	1904
9096-B&O	1	ALCO	S4	1000	1956
	10	* NOT OWNED BY MR&NKP			

MAGMA ARIZONA RR MAA Superior AZ

9	1	ALCO	RS3	1600	1951

MAHONING VALLEY RY MVRY Campbell OH

466-467	2	GM	SW1	600	1949

MAINE COAST RR MC Rockland ME

367	1	ALCO	RS1	1800	1958
958	1	ALCO	S1	660	1949
2002,2204	2	MLW	M420R	2000	1974-1975
	4				

MAINE NARROW GAUGE RR & MUSEUM (2'Gauge) Portland ME/
South Carver MA

1,3	WHM	2	GE	23-TON	150	1949
3-4	MRR	2	VULC	STEAM	0-4-4T	1912-1918
6,10-11	USM	3	PLYM	8-10-TON	200	
7-8	B&H	2	BALD	STEAM	2-4-4T	1913-1924
12-13	EDA	2	BRKV	2-TON	220	
14,16	EDA	2	PLYM	6-TON		
		13	FORMERLY EDAVILLE RR			

MANUFACTURERS JUNCTION RY MJ Cicero IL

22,33	2	GM	SW1	600	1946-1947

MANUFACTURERS RY MRS St Louis MO

251-252	2	GM	MP15	1500	1975
253	1	GM	SW1200	1200	1976
254	1	GM	MP15AC	1500	1983
255-257	3	GM	SW1500	1500	1967-1970
	7				

MARC-MARYLAND RAIL COMMUTER-DEPT OF TRANSPORTATION MDDT
Baltimore MD

51-69	19	BL	GP40WH-2	3000	1993-1994
70-75	6	BL	GP39H-2	2300	1998
91-92	2	GM	E9A	2500	1999
100-102	3	ALCO	RS3M	1200	1978-1979
4900-4903 A	4	A-GM	ELECTRIC	7000	1986
4904-4909 B	6	B-AL	ELECTRIC	8000	1999-2000
7100	1	BL	AUX POWER	0	1999
	40	EXCLUDES AUX POWER UNIT			

A AEM7 MODEL   B AEM10 MODEL BUILDER IS BOMBARDIER-ALSTOM

MARTA-METROPOLITAN ATLANTA RAPID TRANSIT
Atlanta GA

815	1	REP	50-TON	740	1988
1001	1	GE	50-TON	335	1983
	2				

MARYLAND & DELAWARE RR MDDE Federalsburg MD

801-802	2	GM	SW900	900	1996
1201-1203	3	ALCO	RS3M	1200	1978
2628,2630,2632	3	GM	CF7	1500	1972
	8				

MARYLAND & PENNSYLVANIA RR MPA York PA

82,84	2	GM	SW9	1200	1951-1952
1500,1502,1504	3	GM	CF7	1500	1978
	5				

MARYLAND MIDLAND RY MMID Union Bridge MD

200-202	3	GM	GP9	1750	1957
300-302	3	GM	GP38DC	2000	1967
	6				

MASSACHUSETTS BAY TRANSPORTATION AUTH MBTA Boston MA

902-904,1921	4	GM	GP9	1750	1957
1000-1017	18	ALST	F40PH	3000	1989-1990
1025-1036	12	BL	F40PHM-2C	3000	1991-1993
1050-1075 *	25	GM	F40PH2C	3000	1987-1988
1115-1139	25	ALST	GP40LH-2	3000	1996-1997
	84	* EXCEPT 1073			

MASSACHUSETTS CENTRAL RR MCER Palmer MA

960,1728	2	GM	GP9R	1750	1954
2100	1	GM	NW5	1000	1948
4243	1	ALCO	C424	2400	1964
4264	1	ALCO	C425	2500	1965
	5				

MASSENA TERMINAL RR MSTR Massena NY

14-15	2	GM	MP15	1500	1974-1980

MAUMEE & WESTERN RR Defiance OH

12,16	2	GM	GP10	1750
221	1	GM	SW1200	1200
325	1	ALCO	C425	2500
344	1	GM	GP7	1500
373,2257,2393	3	GM	GP35	2500
	8			

McCLOUD RY MCR McCloud CA

18	1	BALD	STEAM	2-8-2	1914
25	1	ALCO	STEAM	2-6-2	1925
30	1	BLH	S12	1200	1953
36-38	3	GM	SD38	2000	1969
	6				

METRA-CHICAGO COMMUTER RAIL SERVICE BOARD-RTA CCRS

1-2		2 GM	SW1	600	1939-1954
3		1 GM	SW1200	1200	1954
4-9		6 GM	SW1500	1500	1968-1972
100-127		28 GM	F40PH-2	3200	1977
128-184		57 GM	F40PH-2	3200	1979-1989
185-214		30 GM	F40PHM-2	3200	1991-1992
600-614		15 GM	F40C	3200	1974
		139			

METRO NORTH RR-STATE OF NEW YORK MNCR New York NY

101-106		6 GM	GP35R	2000	1993-1994
201-205	A	5 GE	DSH9-P32ACDM	3200	1995
206-218	A	13 GE	DSH9-P32ACDM	3200	1997-1998
401-403		3 GE	ELECTRIC	1000	1952
410-413	A	4 IC	F10A-DM	1750	1979
543		1 GM	GP8	1500	1979
605		1 ALCO	RS3M	1000	1979
750		1 GM	GP9	1750	1955
2002-2033 AB		21 GM	FL9DC-DM	1800	1957-1960
2040-2046 A		7 ABB	FL9AC-DM	1800	1991-1993
		62	A OPERATES IN DUAL MODE		
			B 10 OWNED BY CONNECTICUT-DOT 2006-2027		

MG RAIL MGRI Jeffersonville IN

1221	1 GM	SW9	1200	1955
1841,1847	2 GM	GP16	1750	1950
	3			

MICHIGAN SHORE RR MS Greenville MI

73	1 GM	SW1200	1200	1964

MICHIGAN SOUTHERN RR MSO White Pigeon MI

16	1 GM	SW8	800	1952
66,78	2 ALCO	S1	660	1951
101	1 ALCO	T6	900	
466	1 ALCO	RS2	1600	1946
	5			

MID-CONTINENT RY MUSEUM MCRY North Freedom WI

-WP&L	1 PLYM	30-TON	260	1952
1-WC&C	1 MLW	STEAM	4-6-0	1913
2-ST	1 BALD	STEAM	2-8-2	1912
2-WFHP	1 WHIT	50-TON	400	1946
2-LCL	1 LIMA	STEAM	2-6-0	1906
2-IWSG	1 PLYM	HL18	125	1928
4-PULL	1 GE	45-TON	300	1943
7-AAR	1 ALCO	S1	660	1944
9-D&R	1 BP&W	STEAM	2-6-0	1884
9-GL	1 LIMA	STEAM	2-TRUCK	1909
22-LS&I	1 ALCO	STEAM	2-8-0	1910

MCRY Cont

49-KGBW	1	ALCO	STEAM	2-8-0	1929
401-AT&N	1	BALD	STEAM	2-10-0	1928
440-UP	1	BWC	STEAM	2-8-0	1900
701-C&IW	1	ALCO	STEAM	0-4-0	1914
988-MILW	1	ALCO	RSC2	1500	1947
1385-C&NW	1	ALCO	STEAM	4-6-0	1907
2645-SOO	1	BRKS	STEAM	4-6-0	1900
	18				

MIDDLETOWN & HUMMELSTOWN RR MIDH Hummelstown PA

1-2	2	GE	65-TON	400 *	1941-1955
66	1	GE	ELECTRIC	65-TON	1948
91	1	CLC	STEAM	2-6-0	1910
151	1	ALCO	S6	900	1956
1016	1	ALCO	T6	1000	1969
	6	* 2 RATED 440HP			

MIDDLETOWN & NEW JERSEY RY MNJ Middletown NY

1-2	2	GE	44-TON	400	1946
11	1	ALCO	STEAM	2-6-0	1920
	3				

MIDLAND RY MRHA Baldwin City KS

1	1	GE	25-TON	150	1938
9	1	WHIT	25-TON	150	1926
10	1	ALCO	STEAM	2-8-2T	1930
28	1	GE	45-TON	300	1944
142	1	ALCO	RS3M	1500	1959
460	1	GE	44-TON	380	1942
524	1	GM	NW2	1000	1946
652	1	GM	E8A	2250	1952
2123	1	DAV	STEAM	0-4-0T	1928
8255	1	ALCO	RS3	1600	1951
	10				

MIDLAND TERMINAL MDLR Midland PA

431-432	2	GM	NW2	1000	1951
1200,1215	2	GM	SW9	1200	1953
	4				

MID-MICHIGAN RR MMRR Greenville MI

24	1	GM	GP9	1750	1976
3839	1	GM	GP38	2000	1967
	2				

MIDWEST CENTRAL RR MDCR (3'Gauge) Mt Pleasant IA

1	1	BALD	STEAM	2-8-0	1897
2	1	BALD	STEAM	2-6-0	1906
6	1	BALD	STEAM	2-6-0	1891
9	1	LIMA	STEAM	3-TRUCK	1923
9,14	2	PLYM	25-TON	250	1956-1965
16	1	HENS	STEAM	0-4-0	1951
101	1	VULC	15-TON	GAS	1935
	8				

LOCOMOTIVE PHOTOGRAPH MODEL IDENTIFICATION

NEW BUILDERS

EMD-GM

UNION PACIFIC	8522	SD90MAC	6000HP
CANADIAN NATIONAL	5787	SD75I	4300HP
ONTARIO NORTHLAND	2101	SD75I	4300HP
ILLINOIS CENTRAL	1020	SD70	4000HP
AMTRAK	453	F59PHI	3200HP
LONG ISLAND RR	400	DE30AC	3000HP
CONRAIL	6758	SD50	3500HP
ALASKA	2801	GP49	2800HP
SSW COTTON BELT	7249	GP40-2	3000HP
BURLINGTON NORTHERN	2707	GP39-2	2300HP
GRAND TRUNK	5836	GP38-2	2000HP
NORTHERN PACIFIC	202	GP9	1750HP
SOUTHERN PACIFIC	2702	MP15AC	1500HP
GALVESTON WHARVES	305	SW1001	1000HP

GE

CSX	604	AC6000CW	6000
UNION PACIFIC	7333	AC44/6000CW	4400
CANADIAN PACIFIC	9648	AC4400CW	4400
CSX	349	AC4400CW	4400
UNION PACIFIC	7105	AC4400CW	4400
BNSF	4881	DASH9-4400CW	4400
NORFOLK SOUTHERN	9387	DASH9-4000CW	4000+HP
METRO NORTH	209	DASH9-P32ACDM	3200HP

BOMBARDIER ALSTOM CONSORTIUM

AMTRAK AMERICAN FLYER	2006	ACELA	6000HP

MIDWEST RAIL MWRX Parkville MO

91	1	GM	SW1	600	1940
201,205,3338	3	GM	GP9	1750	1955-1959
317	1	ALCO	S3	660	1953
630	1	GM	E6A	2000	1941
1308,4153	2	GM	GP7	1500	1952
4390	1	GM	SD9	1750	1955
	9				

MILFORD-BENNINGTON RR Milford NH

901	1	GM	SW900	900	1983
1423	1	GM	SW9	1200	1953
	2				

MINNESOTA CENTRAL RR MCTA Morton MN

100	1	GM	NW2	1000	1956
701	1	GM	GP7	1500	
800,805	2	GM	GP8C	1800	1982
906-908	3	GM	GP9	1750	
1616	1	GM	GP16	1600	1979
	8				

MINNESOTA COMMERCIAL RY MNNR St Paul MN

TB-1	1	BL	SLUG	0	1974
50	1	GE	C30-7	3000	1973
62-63	2	ALCO	C424M	2400	1980
73	1	MLW	M630	3000	1969
80	1	MLW	RS23	1000	1958
100	1	GM	NW2	1000	1949
110,200	2	GM	SW1200	1200	1954-1955
302,306	2	GM	SW1500	1500	1968-1970
307	1	ALCO	RS20M	2000	1975
313-314	2	ALCO	C424	2400	1963-1965
316,318	2	ALCO	RS27	2400	1960-1962
484	1	GM	CF7	1500	1974
1604,1608	2	GM	RS3	1600	1950
4711	1	MLW	M636-CAT	3100	1971
	19	EXCLUDES SLUG			

MINNESOTA DAKOTA & WESTERN RY MDW International Falls MN

16-20	5	ALCO	S2	1000	1947-1949

MINNESOTA NORTHERN RR MNN

104	1	GM	GP7	1500	
1208	1	GM	SW1200	1200	
1463,1471	2	GM	GP9	1750	
2796,2813					
3806,3810	4	GM	GP38	2000	
	8				

MINNESOTA TRANSPORTATION MUSEUM St Paul MN

5-NSP	1	GE	45-TON	300	1951
559	1	GM	GP7	1500	1976
B71-ARM	1	WEST	BOXCAB	380	1929
100-DP	1	GE	BOXCAB	175	1913

MTM Cont

Number		Qty	Builder	Model	Type	Year
101,103		2	GM	NW2	1000	1946
105-LSTT	O&SCV	1	GM	SW1200	1200	1958
328-NP	O&SCV	1	ALCO	STEAM	4-6-0	1907
2156-NP		1	BALD	STEAM	4-6-2	1909
		9	INCLUDES OSCEOLA & ST CROIX VALLEY			

MINNESOTA ZEPHYR STILLWATER DEPOT Stillwater MN

Number	Qty	Builder	Model	HP	Year
787	1	GM	FP9A	1750	
788	1	GM	F7A	1500	1951
	2				

MISSISSIPPIAN RY MISS Fulton MS

Number	Qty	Builder	Model	HP	Year
261	1	GM	SW9	1200	1952

MISSISSIPPI & SKUNA VALLEY RR MSV Bruce MS

Number	Qty	Builder	Model	HP	Year
D-4	1	GM	SW9	1200	1952
D-5	1	GM	CF7M	1600	1978
	2				

MISSISSIPPI & TENNESSEE RAILNET New Albany MS

Number		Qty	Builder	Model	HP	Year
5002	NREX	1	GM	GP20	2000	
9001,9004,9005		3	GM	GP9	1750	
		4				

MISSISSIPPI CENTRAL RR MSCI Holly Springs MS

Number	Qty	Builder	Model	HP	Year
1604-1606	3	GM	GP16	1600	1980

MISSISSIPPI DELTA RR MSDR Clarksdale MS

Number	Qty	Builder	Model	HP	Year
202	1	GM	GP7	1500	1953
6226	1	GM	GP9	1750	1957
	2				

MISSISSIPPI EXPORT RR MSE Moss Point MS

Number	Qty	Builder	Model	HP	Year
60	1	GM	GP9	1750	1957
64	1	GM	SW1500	1500	1973
65-66	2	GM	GP38-2	2000	1975-1979
95	1	GM	GP40	3000	1966
	5				

MISSOURI & NORTHERN ARKANSAS RR MNA Carthage MO

Number	Qty	Builder	Model	HP	Year
483	1	GM	GP20	2000	1984
751	1	GM	SW1200	1200	1964
1011,1021,1023	3	GM	SD20	2000	1981
2210	1	GM	GP16	1850	1979
3840-3842	3	GM	GP38AC*	2000	1969
4003-4011,4044	9	GM	GP40	3000	1968
4012-4015,4045	5	GM	GP40-1	3000	1970
4163-4164,2167	3	GM	SLUGS	0	1979-1993
	23	EXCLUDES SLUGS * 3840 IS GP38DC			

MODESTO & EMPIRE TRACTION MET Modesto CA

Number	Qty	Builder	Model	HP	Year
600-609	10	GE	70-TON	600	1947-1955

MOHAWK ADIRONDACK & NORTHERN RR MWHA Carthage/Utica NY

Number	Qty	Builder	Model	HP	Year
642,645 *	2	ALCO	C420	2000	1964-1973
804-806,2453	4	ALCO	C425	2500	1964
2448-2449	2	ALCO	C424	2400	
	8	* 645 BUILT BY MLW			

MOLALLA DIVN-OREGON PACIFIC-OPRR MWRL

187	1	GM	NW5	800	1946
602,801-803	4	GM	SW8	800	1951-1953
1810	1	GM	GP7U	1800	1976
	6				

MONONGAHELA CONNECTING RR MCRR Pittsburg PA

1000-1001	2	GM	SW1001	1000	1973

MONTANA RAIL LINK MRL Missoula MT

17-18	2	GM	SW12	1200	1952-1965
51-52	2	GM	SW1500	1500	1978
106-135	21	GM	GP9	1750	1952-1958
151	1	GM	GP19-1	1900	1991
250	1	GM	SD40-2	3000	1972
251-289	15	GM	SD40-2XR	3000	1989-1994
290	1	GM	SDP40-2XR	3000	1990
301-304,306-331	31	GM	SD45-2	3600	1973-1980
332	1	GM	SDP45-2	3600	1976
350-389	18	GM	SD45	3600	1967-1968
390-392	3	GM	F45	3600	1971
401-406	6	GM	GP35	2500	1964
607-608,610	3	GM	SD9	1750	1952-1953
651-652	2	GM	SD19-1	1900	1991
701-705	5	GM	SD35	2500	1966-1971
	112	(SEE I&M RAIL LINK)			

MONTANA WESTERN RY MWRR Butte MT

201-203	3	GM	GP9	1750	1957
2010-2011	2	GM	GP38-2	2000	1973
	5				

MONTICELLO RY MUSEUM MRYM Monticello IL

1-MONT	1	ALCO	STEAM	0-4-0	1930
44-HORM	1	DAV	44-TON	300	1940
191-RS	1	ALCO	STEAM	0-6-0	1916
301-LI	1	ALCO	RS3	1600	1955
401-SR	1	BALD	STEAM	2-8-0	1907
1189-WAB	1	GM	F7A	1500	1953
6789-CNR	1	MLW	FPA4	1800	1959
6862-CNR	1	MLW	FPB4	1800	1959
9838-SR	1	ALCO	SLUG	0	1977
	8	EXCLUDES SLUG			

MORRISTOWN & ERIE RY ME Morristown NJ

16-17	2	ALCO	C430	3000	1967
18-19	2	ALCO	C424	2400	1964
20	1	GM	SW1500	1500	1966
21-23	3	ALCO	M424	2400	1964
	8				

MOSCOW CAMDEN & SAN AUGUSTINE RR MCSA Camden TX

1	1	GM	SW1200	1200	1960
3	1	GM	SW8	800	1957
	2				

MOUNT HOOD RR MH Hood River OR

88-89	2	GM	GP9	1750	1959

MOUNT RAINIER SCENIC RR MRSR Elbe WA

3-RAY	1	LIMA	STEAM	2-TRUCK	1910
5-PGH	1	PORT	STEAM	2-8-2	1924
7-DRL	1	BALD	STEAM	2-4-4-2	1910
10-HL	1	CLIM	STEAM	3-TRUCK	1928
11-PL	1	LIMA	STEAM	3-TRUCK	1929
12-PL	1	HEIS	STEAM	3-TRUCK	1912
17-HL	1	ALCO	STEAM	2-8-2T	1929
30-NPT	1	ALCO	S1	660	1940
41-DOT	1	ALCO	RSD1	1000	1941
42-USA	1	ALCO	S1	660	1942
45-RAY	1	BALD	STEAM	2-6-2	1906
70-RAY	1	BALD	STEAM	2-8-2	1922
91-KPM	1	HEIS	STEAM	3-TRUCK	1930
7012A-NP	1	GM	F9A	1750	1956
	14				

MOUNT VERNON TERMINAL RY MVT Mount Vernon WA

1200	1	GM	SW9	1200	1953

MUSEO NACIONAL DE LOS FERROCARRILES MEXICANOS Puebla MEX

10-CZ	1	BALD	STEAM	2-8-0	1908
19-DH *	1	ALCO	PA1	2000	1947
40-NM	1	TAM	STEAM	2-8-0	1913
650-VCI	1	BALD	STEAM	2-6-0	1901
802-CZ	1	GM	GA8	800	1964
1001-FCM	1	A-GE	ELECTRIC	2520	1923
1150-NM	1	ALCO	STEAM	2-8-0	1921
3034-NM	1	ALCO	STEAM	4-8-4	1946
6328B-NM	1	GM	FP7AM	1750	1951
7020A-NM	1	GM	FP9A	1750	1956
	10	* 17-DH MEXICO CITY-FED ELECTRICAL MUSEUM			

MUSEUM OF ALASKA TRANSPORTATION Wasilla AK

1000	1	ALCO	RS1	1000	1945
1500	1	GM	F7A	1500	1948
1841-1842	2	BLH	S12	1200	1952
7324	1	GE	44-TON	300	1942
	5				

MUSEUM OF SCIENCE & INDUSTRY Chicago IL

JOHN STEVENS	1	STEV	STEAM REP	0-2-2	1825
ROCKET-L&M	1	R&S	STEAM REP	0-4-0	1829
YORK-B&O	1	YORK	STEAM REP	0-4-0	1831
MISSISSIPPI	1	MISS	STEAM ORIG	0-4-0	1834
999-NYC	1	NYC	STEAM	4-4-0	1893
9900-CB&Q	1	BUDD	PIONEER ZEPH	600	1934
	6				

-DANIEL NASON	1	B&P	STEAM	4-4-0	1858
-RDG B DIAMOND	1	BALD	STEAM	2-2-2T	1889
-MBM	1	PLYM	30-TON	200	1942
1-UE A	1	BALD	STEAM	0-4-0T	1926
1-GE	1	GE	ELECTRIC	30-TON	1892
1-B&O	1	A-GE	DIESEL	300	1925
1-CSTL	1	WHIT	DIESEL	15-TON	1924
1-J-P	1	PLYM	70-TON PROP	440	1936
2-UE	1	HEIS	STEAM	0-6-0F	1940
2-LC A	1	DAV	STEAM	0-4-0T	1907
2-CSTL	1	PLYM	30-TON	200	1930
E2-MILW	1	GE	ELECTRIC	3200	1919
3-CRI&P	1	GM	AEROTRAIN	1200	1955
7-GLC	1	PORT	STEAM	0-4-0F	1941
7-NCR	1	LIMA	STEAM	0-4-0F	1910
8-ASF	1	WHIT	65-TON	400	1948
9-LSE	1	RI	STEAM	0-4-4T	1893
12-A&S	1	ALCO	STEAM	0-8-0	1926
39-B&A	1	B&A	STEAM	4-4-0	1876
50-B&O	1	GM	DIESEL	1800	1935
64,66-CB&Q	2	GM	E8A	2250	1950
95-SS	1	BALD	STEAM	0-6-0	1906
103-GM	1	GM	FTA	1350	1939
113-NYC	1	A-GE	ELECTRIC	2-D-2	1906
146-TRRA	1	ALCO	STEAM	0-6-0	1916
170-NKP	1	ALCO	STEAM	4-6-4	1927
173-B&O	1	B&O	STEAM	4-6-0	1873
211-MFR	1	ALCO	S2	1000	1948
274-C&NW	1	BALD	STEAM	4-4-0	1873
311-MKT	1	BALD	STEAM	4-4-0	1890
318-TRRA	1	TRRA	STEAM	0-8-0	1928
408-SR&N	1	GM	NC	900	1937
502-DMIR	1	BALD	STEAM	2-10-2	1916
546-M&STL	1	ALCO	RS1	1000	1946
E-550-FDS	1	WEST	ELECTRIC	2000	1910
551-C&IM	1	LIMA	STEAM	2-8-2	1928
573-WAB	1	RI	STEAM	2-6-0	1899
635-STL	1	BALD	STEAM	4-6-0	1889
662-PNMA B	1	GE	ELECTRIC	60-TON	1914
724-GRR	1	BALD	STEAM	0-6-0	1896
764-ICRR	1	ALCO	STEAM	2-8-0	1904
952-DL&W	1	ALCO	STEAM	4-4-0	1905
1015-C&NW	1	ALCO	STEAM	4-4-2	1900
1149-USA-TC	1	DAV	GAS-TURBINE	1-B-1	1950
1522-SLSF	1	BALD	STEAM	4-8-2	1926
1575-IT	1	IT	ELECTRIC	B-B	1918
1595-IT	1	IT	ELECTRIC	B-B-B-B	1929

NMT Cont

1621-SLSF	1	BALD	STEAM	2-10-0	1918
1843-USA	1	FM	H12-44	1200	1955
2002-USA	1	GM	SW8	800	1952
2069-USA	1	ALCO	MRS1	1600	1953
2156-N&W	1	N&W	STEAM	2-8-8-2	1942
2727-C&O	1	ALCO	STEAM	2-8-4	1944
2918-N&W	1	GM	GP35	2250	1964
2933-NYC	1	ALCO	STEAM	4-8-2	1929
3607-EL	1	GM	SD45	3600	1967
4006-UP	1	ALCO	STEAM	4-8-8-4	1941
4460-SP	1	LIMA	STEAM	4-8-4	1943
4502-MP	1	ALCO	RS3	1500	1955
4700-PRR	1	PRR	ELECTRIC	3750	1931
4916-PRR C	1	PRR	ELECTRIC *	4620	1942
5011-AT&SF	1	BALD	STEAM	2-10-4	1944
5529-CNR	1	MLW	STEAM	4-6-2	1906
5677-CONR	1	GM	GP7	1500	1952
6944-UP	1	GM	DDA40X	6600	1971
7768-USA	1	GE	25-TON	150	1943
9008-CB&Q	1	GM	E-PASS	1000	1939
	68	A 2'-6"GAUGE B PANAMA CANAL RR			
		BROAD GAUGE C* GG1 MODEL			

NAPA VALLEY RR NVWT Napa CA

52	1	GE	65-TON	550	1943
62	1	ALCO	RS11	1800	1959
70-73	4	MLW	FPA4	1800	1958-1959
	6				

NARRAGANSETT BAY RR Newport RI

1943	1	GE	65-TON	500	1943

NASH COUNTY RR NCYR Spring Hope NC

345	1	GM	GP38	2000	
8047,8330,8420	3	GM	GP10	1850	1974
	4				

NASHVILLE & EASTERN RR NERR Lebanon TN

805	1	GE	B23-7	2250	
3901,3927,3954	3	GE	U23B	2250	1972-1974
5323,5328,5338-					
5345	8	GE	U30B	3000	1966-1972
5772	1	GE	U36B	3600	1971
8319	1	GM	GP10	1850	1977
9910-9912	2	GM	E9A	2400	1955
	16				

NATIONAL MUSEUM OF SCIENCE & TECHNOLOGY Ottawa ON

1-CZ	1	LIMA	STEAM	2-TRUCK	1925
40-GTR	1	PRTD	STEAM	4-4-0	1872
247-GTR	1	GTR	STEAM	0-6-0T	1894
926-CPR	1	CPR	STEAM	4-6-0	1912
1001-GM	1	GM	H1	500	1956
1201-CPR	1	CPR	STEAM	4-6-2	1944

NMST Cont

2858-CPR	1	MLW	STEAM	4-6-4	1938
3100-CPR	1	CPR	STEAM	4-8-4	1928
4065-CPR	1	CLC	C-LINER	1600	1951
6200-CNR	1	MLW	STEAM	4-8-4	1942
6400-CNR	1	MLW	STEAM	4-8-4	1936
6715-CNR	1	GE	ELECTRIC	1100	1914
	12				

NATIONAL RR MUSEUM NRRM Green Bay WI

2-CRIP	1	GM	AEROTRAIN	1200	1955
5-P&CL*	1	LIMA	STEAM	2-TRUCK	1917
10-GB&W	1	ALCO	S3	660	1952
24-LS&I	1	ALCO	STEAM	2-8-0	1910
29-PULL	1	ALCO	STEAM	0-4-0T	1929
38A-MILW	1	GM	F9A	2400	1962
101-USA	1	BALD	STEAM	2-8-0	1918
102-S&C	1	BALD	STEAM	2-8-2	1924
106-USA	1	WHIT	44-TON	310	1940
261-MILW	1	ALCO	STEAM	4-8-4	1944
315-GB&W	1	ALCO	C430	3000	1968
441-SPUD	1	GE	44-TON	400	1941
506-DM&IR	1	ALCO	STEAM	2-10-2	1918
538-M&STL	1	GM	NW1	900	1938
702-WPS	1	PLYM	20-TON	150	1950
715-WC	1	GM	GP30	2500	1963
767-MILW	1	FM	H10-44	1000	1949
1201-SP	1	ALCO	S6	900	1954
2718-S00	1	ALCO	STEAM	4-6-2	1923
2736-C&O	1	ALCO	STEAM	2-8-4	1944
4017-UP	1	ALCO	STEAM	4-8-8-4	1941
4890-PRR	1	PRR	ELECTRIC	GG1	1941
5017-ATSF	1	BALD	STEAM	2-10-4	1944
8651-USA	1	ALCO	RSD1	1000	1944
60008-L&NE	1	DONC	STEAM	4-6-2	1937
	25	* 3'GAUGE			

NAUGATUCK RR Waterbury CT

42	1	GE	45-TON	360	1942
529,557	2	ALCO	RS3	1600	1952-1953
1732	1	GM	GP9	1750	1952
2525	1	GE	U25B	2500	1968
	5				

NEBKOTA RY NRI Chadron NE

49	1	GM	GP7	1500	1952
1381-1382 ILSX	2	GM	GP9	1750	
	3				

NEBRASKA CENTRAL RR NCRC Columbus NE

2101,2106	2	GM	GP7	1500	1966
4200-4204	5	NRE	GP38MAC	2000	1993
5315,5332	2	GM	SD45	3600	1997
	9				

NEBRASKA KANSAS & COLORADO RAILNET Grant NE

1		1	GM	GP10	1850
2,4		2	GM	GP7	1500
5		1	GM	GP30M	2250
15,5003		2	GM	GP30	2250
23		1	GM	GP35	2500
		7			

NEBRASKA MIDLAND RR-STUHR MUSEUM (3'Gauge) Grand Island NE

69-WP&Y		1	BALD STEAM	2-8-0	1908

NEBRASKA NORTHEASTERN RY Osmond NE

1380	ILSX	1	GM	GP10	1850
9601		1	GM	GP9	1750
9603		1	GM	GP10	1850
9701-9703		3	GM	GP38	2000
		6			

NEVADA COUNTY NARROW GAUGE RR MUSEUM (3'Gauge) Nevada City CA

*		1	PORT 12-TON	GAS	
5-NCNG		1	BALD STEAM	2-6-0	1875
5-AL		1	LIMA STEAM	2-6-2	1910
9	*	1	HENS STEAM	0-4-0T	1939
10-AP		1	PLYM 5-TON	45	1935
		5	* 2'GAUGE		

NEVADA NORTHERN RY MUSEUM NNRM East Ely NV

40-NN		1	BALD STEAM	4-6-0	1910
80-81-KCC		2	GE ELECTRIC	750	1937-1941
81-NN		1	BALD STEAM	2-8-0	1917
93-KCC		1	ALCO STEAM	2-8-0	1909
105-KCC		1	ALCO RS2	1500	1948
109-KCC		1	ALCO RS3	1600	1952
310-KCC		1	GE 25-TON	150	1950
801-KCC		1	BALD VO1000	1000	1943
802-KCC		1	BLH S12	1200	1952
		10			

NEVADA STATE RR MUSEUM NSRM Carson City/Boulder City NV

1-C&TLF	*	1	BALD STEAM	2-6-0	1875
1-DS&CV	*	1	PORT STEAM	0-4-2T	1882
2-SV&E		1	BALD STEAM	2-6-2T	1908
4-YL		1	LIMA STEAM	3-TRUCK	1920
8-NSRM		1	COOK STEAM	4-4-0	1888
8-SP		1	BALD STEAM	4-6-0	1907
12-UIN	*	1	BALD STEAM	2-8-0	1896
18-V&T		1	CP STEAM	4-4-0	1873
22-V&T		1	BALD STEAM	4-4-0	1875
25-V&T		1	BALD STEAM	4-6-0	1905
27-V&T		1	BALD STEAM	4-6-0	1913
35-PL		1	BALD STEAM	2-8-2	1923
99-NSRM		1	DAV 5-TON	GAS	1922
110-RAY		1	BALD STEAM	2-6-6-2T	1928

NSRM Cont

264-UP	1	BALD	STEAM	2-8-0	1907	
844-UP	1	GM	GP30	2250	1962	
1000-UP	1	GM	NW2	1000	1939	
1005-TOC	1	PLYM	8-TON	63	1944	
1855-NSRM	1	FM	H12-44	1200	1953	
	19	* 3'GAUGE				

NEW BRUNSWICK EAST COAST RAIL Campbellton NB

1813-1868 CPR	23	MLW	RS18	1800	1980	1989
6900-6910 CNR	11	ALST	SD40-3	3000	1999	
	34					

NEW BRUNSWICK SOUTHERN RY NBSR Saint John NB

3700-3701	2	GM	GP9	1750	
3702-3703	2	GM	SW1200	1200	
3735,3744,3757					
3760,3764,3787-					
3788,3795	8	GM	GP9	1750	
9801-9803	3	CLN	GP38-3	2000	1998
	15				

NEWBURGH & SOUTH SHORE RR NSR Cleveland OH

1019,1021	2	GM	SW1001	1000	1971-1975

NEW ENGLAND CENTRAL RR NECR St Albans VT

1237	1	GM	SW1200	1200	
3844-3855,3857	13	GM	GP38 *	2000	
4047-4049	3	GM	GP40	3000	1969-1971
5032-5033,6281	3	GM	SD40	3000	1971
	20	* 3857 IS GP38AC MODEL			

NEW ENGLAND SOUTHERN RR NEGS Concord NH

503	1	GM	GP18	1800	1960
566	1	GM	GP10	1800	1984
	2				

NEW HAMPSHIRE & VERMONT RR NHVT Whitefield NH

669	1	GM	GP9	1750	1957

NEW HAMPSHIRE CENTRAL RR NHCR Meredith NH

360	1	GE	44-TON	360	1943

NEW HAMPSHIRE NORTHCOAST NHNC Ossipee NH

1755-1760	6	GM	GP9R	1750	1979-1980

NEW HOPE & IVYLAND RR NHRR New Hope PA

9-USA	1	ALCO	STEAM	0-6-0	1941
28	1	WHIT	50-TON	300	1951
40-L&C	1	BALD	STEAM	2-8-0	1925
614-C&O	1	LIMA	STEAM	4-8-4	1948
1533-CNR	1	MLW	STEAM	4-6-0	1911
2198-PRR	1	GM	GP30	2250	1963
3028-NDEM	1	ALCO	STEAM	4-8-4	1946
7064,7087	2	GE	C30-7	3000	1980-1981
9423-PRR	1	GM	SW1	600	1950
	10				

NEW ORLEANS & LOWER COAST GULF RR NOLR Belle Chasse LA

1229	1 GM	SW1200	1200	1979
2180	1 GM	GP16	1750	1979
	2			

NEW ORLEANS PUBLIC BELT RR NOPB New Orleans LA

105	1 GM	SW1000	1000	1971
151-153	3 GM	SW1500	1500	1971
1501	1 BL	MP1500D	1500	1996
2001-2002	2 BL	MP2000D	2000	1998
8708	1 GM	SW900	900	
	8			

NEW YORK & ATLANTIC RY Fresh Pond NY

101,105-106	3 GM	SW1001	1000	1977
151,155-156,159	4 GM	MP15	1500	1977
261,268,270-271	4 GM	GP38-2	2000	1976-1977
	11			

NEW YORK & GREENWOOD LAKE RY Suffern NY

436	1 GM	SW9	1200	1952
935	1 ALCO	RS3	1600	1952
	2			

NEW YORK & LAKE ERIE RR NYLE Gowanda NY

1013	1 ALCO	C425	2500	1965
1700 *	1 GE	132-TON	1000	1940
	2	* OWNED BY LSRHS		

NEW YORK & OGDENSBURG RR Ogdensburg NY

10	1 GE	70-TON	600	1956
12	1 GM	SW9	1200	1951
14	1 GM	SW8	800	1959
	3			

NEW YORK CROSS HARBOR RR TERMINAL NYCH Brooklyn NY

11	1 ALCO	S4	1000	1951
21,25	2 ALCO	S1	660	1947
59	1 GM	NW2	1000	1946
319-321	2 ALCO	C424	2400	1963
1337	1 GM	SW1200RS	1200	1963
	7			

NEW YORK SUSQUEHANNA & WESTERN RY Cooperstown NY

116	1 GM	NW2	1000	1948
120	1 GM	SW9	1200	1953
142	1 SINO	STEAM	2-8-2	1989
1800,1802,1804	3 GM	GP18	1800	1962
2012	1 GM	GP38	2000	1967
2400,2402	2 GM	E9A	2400	1973
3000,3006	2 ALCO	C430	3000	1967
3040	1 GM	GP40	3000	1968
3612,3614,3618				
3634	4 GM	SD45	3200*	1970-1971
3636	1 GM	F45	3200*	1971
4002,4004,4006				
4008	4 GE	DASH8-40B	4000	1988
4050,4052,4054	3 GM	SD70M	4000	1995
	24	* ORIGINALLY 3600HP		

NILES CANYON RY MUSEUM (PACIFIC LOCOMOTIVE ASSN PLA) Sunol CA

1-BB	1 WHIT	20-TON	100	1925
1-PL	1 HEIS	STEAM	3-TRUCK	1913
2-QRR	1 ALCO	STEAM	2-6-2T	1924
3-RDL	1 ALCO	STEAM	2-6-2T	
3-SVMS	1 PORT	STEAM	0-4-0T	1914
4-CVR	1 BALD	STEAM	2-6-6-2T	1924
5-SPR	1 HEIS	STEAM	3-TRUCK	1913
6-NCB	1 PLYM	30-TON	6-WHL	1929
7-FGS	1 LIMA	STEAM	3-TRUCK	1926
12-SR	1 LIMA	STEAM	3-TRUCK	1903
30-SR	1 BALD	STEAM	2-6-2	1922
65-298-USN	1 GE	80-TON	500	1945
65-600-USN	1 GE	65-TON	500	1942
101-OTR	1 BALD	DS44-10	1000	1948
103-SCI	1 PLYM	10-TON	120	1929
233-CPRR	1 CP	STEAM	2-6-2T	1882
462-ATSF	1 GE	44-TON	300	1943
713-WP	1 GM	GP7	1500	1953
918D-WP	1 GM	F7A	1500	1950
1269-SP	1 SLW	STEAM	0-6-0	1921
1856-USA	1 FM	H12-44	1200	1953
2467-SP	1 BALD	STEAM	4-6-2	1921
5623-SP	1 GM	GP9	1800	1955
	23			

NIMISHILLEN & TUSCARAWAS RY NTRY Canton OH

1203-1285	7 GM	SW1200	1200	1954-1992

NITTANY & BALD EAGLE RR NBER Bellefonte PA

1601-1603	3 GM	GP8	1600	1982
1804	1 GM	GP10	1850	1976
2427	1 GM	CF7	1500	1977
4174	1 GM	GP7	1500	1953
	6			

NJ TRANSIT RAIL OPERATIONS NJTR Newark NJ

500-503	4 GM	SW1500	1500	1972-1989
4100-4112	13 GM	GP40PH-2-0	3000	1991
4113-4129	17 GM	F40PH-2CAT	3000	1997-1998
4130-4144	15 BL	GP40FH-2	3000	1987-1989
4145-4150	5 BL	GP40PH-2A	3000	1993
4184-4189 A	6 BL	GP40PH-2M	3000	1988-1990
4190 A	1 BL	GP40PH-2M	3000	1992
4200-4219	20 CR	GP40PH-2B	3000	1993-1997
4300-4303	4 CR	GP40-2	3000	1995
4400-4414 B	15 ABB	ELECTRIC	7000	1990
4415-4419 B	5 ABB	ELECTRIC	7000	1995
4420-4431 B	12 ADT	ELECTRIC	7000	1996-1997
	117	A INCLUDES LEASED UNITS FROM MTA		
		B ALP44 MODEL BUILT BY ABB - ASEA-		
		BROWN BOVERI AND AD TRANZ/ASEA-BB-		
		DAIMLER BENZ		

NOBLES ROCK RR DAKOTA DIVN NRR Luverne MN

302		1	GM	GP7	1500	1950
1365		1	GM	GP9	1750	1954
		2				

NORFOLK SOUTHERN RY SYSTEM CONSOLIDATED ROSTER *
HERITAGE NS, CON(CONRAIL) NW(NORFOLK & WESTERN) SOU(SOUTHERN)
* AS A COURTESY WE HAVE LISTED CONRAIL'S 1998 ROSTER AT THE END
OF THIS BOOK

50-59	NW	10	GM	SD9M	1750		1989-1995
115-116	RTA	2	GM	F40PH	3000		1977
1001,1003	CON	2	CONR	SLUG	0		1957
1002,1004		2	GM	SW1	600		1947,1950
1102-1115	CON	14	CONR	SLUG	0		1978-1979
1355-1388	NW	29	GM	GP40	3000	A	1966-1967
1400-1457	CON	58	GM	GP15-1	1500		1979
1580-1624	NW	44	GM	SD40	3000	B	1966-1971
1625-1635	NW	10	GM	SD40-2	3000	C	1973
1636-1652		16	GM	SD40-2	3000	D	1974
1700-1705	CON	6	GM	SD45-2	3600		1972
2292-2347		20	GM	SW1500	1500		1968-1970
2348-2373	SOU	26	GM	MP15DC	1500		1977
2374-2393		19	GM	MP15DC	1500	E	1979
2394-2435		42	GM	MP15DC	1500		1982
2501-2531	NS	31	GM	SD70	4000		1993
2532-2556	NS	25	GM	SD70	4000		1994
2557-2580	CON	24	GM	SD70	4000		1998
2717-2775		35	GM	GP38	2000		1969
2778-2832		29	GM	GP38	2000		1970
2823-2878		54	GM	GP38AC	2000	F	1971
2879		1	GM	GP38	2000		1968
2880	CON	1	GM	GP38	2000		1967
2881-2884	CON	4	GM	GP38	2000		1970-1971
2885-2957	CON	73	GM	GP38	2000		1969-1971
3000-3002	CON	3	GM	GP40-2	3000		1973
3003-3022	CON	18	GM	GP40-2	3000		1977
3023-3039	CON	17	GM	GP40-2	3000		1978
3040-3062	CON	23	GM	GP40-2	3000		1979
3063-3070	CON	8	GM	GP40-2	3000		1980
3170-3187		16	GM	SD40	3000	G	1971
3188-3208		19	GM	SD40	3000	H	1972
3209-3240		31	GM	SD40-2	3000	I	1977
3241-3243		3	GM	SD40-2	3000		1974
3255-3302		46	GM	SD40-2	3000	J	1978
3303-3328		26	GM	SD40-2	3000		1979
3329-3385	CON	57	GM	SD40-2	3000		1977
3386-3404	CON	19	GM	SD40-2	3000		1978
3405-3447	CON	43	GM	SD40-2	3000		1979-1966
3500-3521		22	GE	B30-7A	3000		1982
3522-3566	SOU	45	GE	DASH8-32B	3200		1989

3600-3631	CON	32	GE	B36-7	3600		1983
3800-3820	CON	21	GM	SD38	2000		1970
3973,3978		2	GE	B23-7	2250		1978
3981-3987		6	GE	B23-7	2250	K	1979
3996-4023		7	GE	B23-7	2250	L	1981
4024-4056	CON	33	GE	B23-7	2250		1978
4057-4085	CON	16	GE	B23-7	2250		1979
4086-4091	CON	6	GE	B23-7	2250		1977
4093-4099	CON	7	GE	B23-7R	2250		1972
4100-4159	NW	56	GM	GP38AC	2000	M	1971
4600-4605		6	GM	GP49	2800		1980
4606-4608	SOU	3	GM	GP59	3000		1986
4609-4641	SOU	32	GM	GP59	3000	N	1989
4800-4817	CON	18	GE	DASH8-40B	4000		1988
5000-5058		56	GM	GP38-2	2000	O	1972
5059-5103		44	GM	GP38-2	2000	P	1973
5104-5162		56	GM	GP38-2	2000	Q	1974
5165-5171	SOU	7	GM	GP38-2	2000		1975
5172-5201		30	GM	GP38-2	2000		1976
5202-5231		30	GM	GP38-2	2000		1977
5232-5256		24	GM	GP38-2	2000	R	1979
5257-5329	CON	73	GM	GP38-2	2000		1973
5330-5340	CON	11	GM	GP38-2	2000		1977
5341-5380	CON	40	GM	GP38-2	2000		1978
5381-5393	CON	13	GM	GP38-2	2000		1979
6073-6138	NW	65	GM	SD40-2	3000		1975
6139-6188	NW	49	GM	SD40-2	3000	S	1978
6189-6206	NW	18	GM	SD40-2	3000		1980
6400-6422	CON	23	GM	SD50	3500		1983
6423-6445	CON	23	GM	SD50	3500		1984
6446-6460	CON	15	GM	SD50	3500		1985
6461-6477	CON	17	GM	SD50	3500		1986
6500-6505	NW	6	GM	SD50	3500		1980
6506-6525		20	GM	SD50	3500		1984
6550-6553	NS	4	GM	SD60	3800		1985
6554-6603	SOU	50	GM	SD60	3800		1985
6604-6650		47	GM	SD60	3800		1986
6651-6675	SOU	25	GM	SD60	3800		1988
6676-6696	SOU	21	GM	SD60	3800		1990
6697-6700	SOU	4	GM	SD60	3800		1991
6701-6716	CON	16	GM	SD60	3800	T	1989
6717-6718	CON	2	GM	SD60I	3800		1994
6719-6762	CON	44	GM	SD60I	3800	U	1995
6763-6806	CON	44	GM	SD60M	3800		1993
7000-7002	SOU	3	GM	GP40X	3500		1978
7003-7072		70	GM	GP50	3500		1980
7073-7092		20	GM	GP50	3500		1981
7100-7143	NS	43	GM	GP60	3800		1991
7144-7150	NS	7	GM	GP60	3800		1992

NS Cont

7200-7216	CON	17	GM	SD80MAC	5000		1996
8004-8031	NW	10	GE	C30-7	3000	W	1978
8041-8082	NW	13	GE	C30-7	3000	X	1979
8083-8111	CON	29	GE	C30-7A	3000		1984
8200-8212	CON	13	GE	DASH8-39C	3900		1986
8300-8313	CON	14	GE	DASH8-40C	4000		1989
8314-8342	CON	29	GE	DASH8-40CW	4000		1990
8343-8371	CON	29	GE	DASH8-40CW	4000		1991
8372-8418	CON	47	GE	DASH8-40CW	4000		1993
8419-8451	CON	33	GE	DASH8-40CW	4000		1994
8480-8493	CON	14	GE	C36-7	3600		1985
8500-8505	NW	6	GE	C36-7	3600		1981
8506-8530	NW	25	GE	C36-7	3600		1982
8531-8563	NW	26	GE	C36-7	3600	Y	1984
8543-8548	CON	6	GE	DASH8-32C	3200		1984
8564-8613	NW	48	GE	DASH8-39C	3900	Z	1985
8614-8663	SOU	46	GE	DASH8-39C	3900		1986
8664-8688	SOU	24	GE	DASH8-39C	3900	AA	1987
8689-8709	SOU	21	GE	DASH8-40C	4000		1990
8710-8713	SOU	4	GE	DASH8-40C	4000		1991
8714-8763	NS	49	GE	DASH8-40C	4000	AB	1992
8764-8888	NS	125	GE	DASH9-40C	4000		1995
8889-9008	NS	119	GE	DASH9-40CW	4000*	AC	1996
9009-9128	NS	120	GE	DASH9-40CW	4000*		1997
9129-9247	NS	119	GE	DASH9-40CW	4000*		1998
9248-9394	NS	147	GE	DASH9-40CW	4000*		1999
9395-9534	NS	**140	GE	DASH9-40CW	4000*		2000
9400-9422	CON	12	GM	SW1001	1000	AD	1973
9503-9507	CON	3	GM	SW1500	1500	AE	1971
9510-9553	CON	17	GM	SW1500	1500		1972
9560-9581	CON	12	GM	SW1500	1500		1973
9588-9620	CON	11	GM	SW1500	1500		1966-1972
9712-9713	NW	2	NW	SLUG	0		1983
9714-9741	NW	26	NW	SLUG	0		1984-1988
9834	SOU	1	SR	SLUG	0		1976
9835-9841		5	SR	SLUG	0		1976-1977
9842-9855	SOU	14	NWGE	SLUG	0		1982-1990
9902-9910	NW	4	NW	SLUG	0		1973-1975
9920-9923	NW	4	NW	SLUG	0		1982,1981
		3550					

EXCLUDES SLUGS * 4000HP RATED BUT CAN
BE UPRATED TO 4400HP ** SUBJECT TO
FINAL APPROVAL

NOTES

A EXCEPT 1356,1377,1381-1382,1384
B EXCEPT 1616   C EXCEPT 1628   D EXCEPT 1640
E EXCEPT 2376   F EXCEPT 2842,2852   G EXCEPT 3181,3186
H EXCEPT 3191,3198   I EXCEPT 3217   J EXCEPT 3257,3276
K EXCEPT 3982-3983,3986,4011,4014

NS Cont

NOTES

L	ACTUAL	3996,4010-4011,4014,4018,4021,4023		
M	EXCEPT	4103,4107,4110,4152	N	EXCEPT 4636
O	EXCEPT	5021-5023	P	EXCEPT 5068
Q	EXCEPT	5133,5149,5159	R EXCEPT 5251	S EXCEPT 6164
T	6716 BUILT 1985	U 6728 BUILT 1994	V 7145-7146 BUILT 1991	
W	ACTUAL	8004,8008-8011,8016,8022,8024,8030-8031		
X	ACTUAL	8041-8042,8051,8055,8065-8066,8068,8070,8072		
		8076,8078-8079		
Y	EXCEPT	8543-8549	Z EXCEPT 8587,8589	AA EXCEPT 8679
AB	EXCEPT	8746	AC EXCEPT 8917	
AD	ACTUAL	9400,9409,9412-9416,9418-9422		
AE	EXCEPT	9504-9505		

NORTH ALABAMA RR MUSEUM NARM Huntsville AL

11-UC	1 A-GE BOXCAB		300	1926
484-RM *	1 ALCO S2		1000	1949
1534-TBD-LI	1 ALCO S4		1000	1954
	3	* INCLUDES MERCURY & CHASE RR		

NORTHAMPTON SWITCHING Northampton PA

51,101	2 ALCO S6	900	
99	1 ALCO RS3M	1200	
	3	FORMERLY NDC RR	

NORTH CAROLINA & VIRGINIA RR NCVA Ahoskie NC

1326	1 GM	GP16	1850	1983
4120	1 GM	SLUG	0	1983
6244	1 GM	GP9	1750	1990
	2	EXCLUDES SLUG		

NORTH CAROLINA-DEPT OF TRANSPORTATION RAIL DIVN Raleigh NC

1755,1797	2 GM	F59PHI	3000	1998
1768,1792	2 ALST	GP40H-2	3000	1992
	4			

NORTH CAROLINA PORTS RY NCPR Wilmington NC

1801-1802	2 FM	H12-44	1200

NORTH CAROLINA RR MUSEUM NHVR New Hill NC

7	1 HEIS STEAM		3-TRUCK	1941
67	1 GE	45-TON	300	1942
70	1 WHIT 50-TON		360	1943
71	1 GE	80-TON	500	1945
75	1 WHIT 80-TON		500	1947
	5	INCLUDES NEW HOPE VALLEY RY		

NORTH CAROLINA TRANSPORTATION MUSEUM NCTH Spencer NC

3-CP&L	1 PORT STEAM		0-4-0F	1937
L3-NCPA	1 GE	45-TON	300	1943
7-WRB	1 PORT STEAM		0-6-0	1942
65-00556-NAVY	1 DAV	44-TON	380	1953
111-DPC	1 ALCO STEAM		0-4-0T	1922
501-NCDT *	1 GM	E3A	2000	1939

NCTH Cont

542-SR	1	BALD	STEAM	2-8-0	1903
544-SAL	1	ALCO	STEAM	2-10-0	1918
604-SR	1	BALD	STEAM	2-8-0	1926
620-N&W	1	GM	GP9	1750	1958
1031-ACL	1	BALD	STEAM	4-6-0	1913
1415-SAL	1	BALD	VO1000	1000	1944
1616-NS	1	BALD	AS616	1600	1955
1925-GCRR	1	LIMA	STEAM	3-TRUCK	1925
2601-SR	1	GM	GP30	2250	1963
5103-P&N	1	GE	ELECTRIC	67-TON	1913
5951-DPC	1	GE	25-TON	150	1953
6133-SR	1	GM	FP7A	1500	1950
6900-SR	1	GM	E8A	2250	1951
7497-USA	1	GE	45-TON	360	1943
	20	* ON LOAN			

NORTH COUNTY TRANSIT DISTRICT-COASTER TRAIN Oceanside CA

1501	1	GM	SW1500	1500	
2101-2105	5	BL	F40PHM-2C	3000	1994
	6				

NORTHERN CENTRAL RY New Freedom PA

800,6763	2	MLW	FPA4	1800
1689	1	ALCO	RSD5	1600
1513	1	ALCO	RSC3	1600
	4			

NORTHERN COUNTIES LOGGING MUSEUM Eureka CA

1-BHLC	1	M&C	STEAM	0-4-0	1892
1-ERMLC	1	M&C	STEAM	0-4-0	1884
2-BHLC	1	BALD	STEAM	2-4-2T	1898
7-A&MR	1	LIMA	STEAM	2-TRUCK	1918
15-HLC	1	BALD	STEAM	2-8-2	1916
29-PLC	1	BALD	STEAM	2-8-2	1910
33-HLC	1	LIMA	STEAM	3-TRUCK	1922
54-MPC	1	HEIS	DIESEL *	2-TRUCK	1927
	8	* CONVERTED FROM STEAM			

NORTHERN OHIO & WESTERN RY NOW Tisson OH

3372	1	GM	GP7M	1750	
4435	1	GM	GP7	1500	
4497	1	GM	GP9	1750	1957
	3				

NORTHERN PLAINS RR Fordville ND

701	1	GM	GP7	1500	
901	1	GM	GP9	1750	
3501,3503,6326-6327	4	GM	GP35M	2500	1963-1979
	6				

NORTHERN VERMONT RR Newport VT

510-513	4	GM	GP35R	2000

NORTHSHORE MINING RY Babbitt MN

650-652,1211	3	LRC	SD40-3	3000	1999
1050	1	GM	GP9	1750	1956
1212	1	GM	SW1200	1200	1962
1214	1	GM	SW1000	1000	
1226-1227,1230-1232	5	GM	SD18R	2000	1991
1233-1236	4	GM	SD28	2000	1991
	15				

NORTH SHORE RR NSHR Northumberland PA

364-366	3	GM	SW8	800	1950-1952
446	1	GM	SW9	1200	1952-1953
	4				

NORTHWESTERN OKLAHOMA RR NOKL Woodward OK

3	1	GE	65-TON	400	1942

NORTHWESTERN PACIFIC RR NWP Eureka CA

70	1	GM	GP7	1500	1952
171	1	VMV	SW1500	1500	1999
2872,3190,3779 3786,3804,3857	6	GM	GP9E	1750	1956
6412-6413	2	GM	SD40	3000	1970
	10				

NYCTA-NEW YORK CITY TRANSIT AUTH NYCT/MTA Brooklyn NY

D50-D82	33	GE	50-TON	400	1966-1977
EL01-EL10	10	GE	ELECTRIC	400	1983
N1-N2	2	GE	50-TON	400	1975
OL883-OL902	20	GE	50-TON	400	1983
OL903-OL909	7	REP	50-TON	400	1991
VT101,VT105	2	VAK	45-TON	400	1997
VT201,VT205	2	SF	45-TON	400	2000
	76				

OAKLAND TERMINAL RY OTR Oakland CA

97	1	GM	GP7	1500	1980
5623 *	1	GM	GP9R1	1750	1955
	2	* PRIVATELY OWNED			

OGDENSBURG BRIDGE PORT AUTH Ogdensburg NY

10	1	GE	70-TON	600	1956
12	1	GM	SW9	1200	1951
14	1	GM	SW8	800	1959
	3				

OGEECHEE RY OGEE Sylvania GA

101-102	2	GM	SW8	800	1948-1951
1320,1325	2	GM	GP35	2500	1964
1551	1	GM	GP7	1500	1951
4215	1	GM	GP30M	2250	1986
	6				

OHIO CENTRAL RR OHCR Coshocton OH

3-SWP	1	ALCO	STEAM	0-4-0	1928
13-BC&G	1	ALCO	STEAM	2-8-0	1920
14,1695	2	ALCO	S4	1000	1950

OHCR Cont

71	1	GM	SW7	1200	
82	1	GE	80-TON	500	
96-CNR	1	ALCO	STEAM	2-6-0	1910
558-C&OR	1	GM	GP30	2250	
1000-1002,1005	4	GM	SLUGS	0	
1077	1	ALCO	RS3	1600	
1278,1293-CPR	2	MLW	STEAM	4-6-2	1948
1314,1329	2	GM	SW1200	1200	
1501	1	GM	GP7	1500	
1551-CNR	1	MLW	STEAM	4-6-0	1912
1663	1	ALCO	S3	660	
2175	1	GM	GP38-2	2000	
2187	1	GM	GP30	2250	
2257,2393-C&OR	2	GM	GP35	2500	
2401	1	GM	SD20-2	2000	
2490,2494-C&OR	2	GM	SW1500	1500	
3216-3217,3253- 3254,3262,3247 3553-3554,3567	6	GM	GP40	3000	1968
3588	4	BBD	HR412 *	2000	
4032	1	GM	GP9M	1800	
6325-GT	1	ALCO	STEAM	4-8-4	1942
6632,6636,6642	3	GM	SD18	1800	
7537,7547,7573- 7574,7585-7586 7591,7594	8	GM	GP10	1850	
	46	EXCLUDES SLUGS * 3567 IS MLW M420W MODEL 1976			

OHI-RAIL CORP OHIC Mechanicstown OH

101-102	2	ALCO	S2	1000	1945-1946

OIL CREEK & TITUSVILLE LINES OCTL Meadville PA

75,85	2	ALCO	S2	1000	1947-1950

OKANAGAN VALLEY RY Vernon BC

1038,1049,1064	3	GM	GP10	1750	1955-1956

OLD AUGUSTA RR OAK New Augusta MS

100	1	GM	NW2	1000	1952
200	1	GM	MP15	1500	1974
	2				

OLD COLONY & NEWPORT RY NCNR Newport RI

84,4764	2	GE	45-TON	300	1941-1945

OLYMPIC RR OLYR Bellevue WA

52	1	GM	SW1	600	1940

OMAHA LINCOLN & BEATRICE RY OLB Lincoln NE

47	1	GM	SW1200CAT	1500	1965
101	1	GE	44-TON	400	1950
102	1	GE	70-TON	700	1951
	3				

ONTARIO CENTRAL RR Victor NY

86	1	ALCO	RS36	1800	1962

ONTARIO L'ORIGNAL RY Hawkesbury ON

179-180	GEXR	2 GM	GP9	1750	1963

ONTARIO MIDLAND RR OMID Sodus NY

36	1 ALCO	RS11	1800	1956
408	1 ALCO	RS36	1800	1962
	2			

ONTARIO NORTHLAND RY ONT North Bay ON

1600-1605	6 GM	GP9	1750	1956-1957
1730-1737 *	7 GM	SD40-2	3000	1973-1974
1800-1809 *	8 GM	GP38-2	2000	1974-1984
2000-2002	3 GM	FP7A-CAT	2000	1994-1997
2100-2105	6 GM	SD75I	4300	1999
	30	* EXCEPT 1732,1803,1807		

ORANGE EMPIRE RY MUSEUM OERY Perris CA

1-ASARCO	1 B-W	ELECTRIC	18-TON	1912
1-GF *	1 BALD	STEAM	0-4-2T	1883
1-H&N	1 GE	ELECTRIC	260	1921
2-GF *	1 BALD	STEAM	2-6-0	1881
2-MN	1 DAV	STEAM	0-6-0T	1917
2-VC	1 BALD	STEAM	2-6-2	1922
8-USN	1 BLW	VO1000	1000	1945
12-SCE	1 PLYM	ML-6	200	1941
015-DOT	1 ALCO	RSD1	1000	1942
E-60-AP&C	1 GE	25-TON	200	1941
98-ATSF	1 GM	FP45	3600	1967
297-YVT	1 B-W	ELECTRIC	400	1923
E-513-AP&C	1 BALD	SH2300B	200	1956
560-ATSF	1 FM	H12-44	1200	1957
589-GF *	1 PLYM	HSG	92	1968
653-SN	1 GE	ELECTRIC	1000	1928
942-UP	1 GM	E8A	2250	1953
1006-SP	1 GM	SW1	600	1939
1474-SP	1 ALCO	S4	1000	1952
1550-SP	1 BLH	S12	1200	1953
1624-PE	1 PE	ELECTRIC	1000	1925
1956-OERM	1 ALCO	RSD1	1000	1941
2564-UP	1 ALCO	STEAM	2-8-2	1921
2594,2598-SP	2 ALCO	RSD12	1800	1961
3100-SP	1 GE	U25B	2500	1963
7441,8580-USAF	2 GE	45-TON	400	1942-1944
9550-LAMTA **	1 LARY	ELECTRIC	100	1904
	29	* 3'GAUGE ** 3'-6"GAUGE		

ORANGE PORT TERMINAL RY OPT Orange TX

	1 GE	65-TON	400	1943
125	1 GE	125-TON	1200	1979
3816	1 GM	GP9	1750	1958
	3			

OREGON ELECTRIC RY MUSEUM OERM Glenwood OR

-SBS	1 GE	25-TON		150	1942
254-KCC	1 GE	ELECTRIC	25-TON	c1920	
351-KCC	1 GE	ELECTRIC	35-TON	1903	
401-KCC	1 B-W	ELECTRIC	45-TON	c1930	
	4				

OTTAWA CENTRAL RY Ottawa ON

1815,1824,1828				
1838,1842,1865	6 MLW	RS18	1800	1981-1984
4202	1 MLW	C424	2400	1964
	7			

OTTAWA VALLEY RY North Bay ON

1703	1 GM	GP9	1750	
1800	1 GM	SD18	1800	1998
2002	1 GM	GP38	2000	1970
3509,3582,3586	3 BBD	HR412	2000	1981-1998
4200-4201,4203	3 GM	GP9	1750	1957-1959
5006	1 GM	GP35	2250	
	10	* 3509 IS MLW M420 MODEL		

OTTER TAIL VALLEY RR OTVR Fergus Falls MN

181,192,194	3 GM	GP18	1800	1963
1483-1484	2 GM	GP9	1750	
	5			

OUACHITA RR OUCH El Dorado AR

63	1 GM	SW9	1200	1952
64	1 GM	NW2	1000	1939
1151,1159	2 GM	GMD1	1200	1959
	4			

OWEGO & HARFORD RY Owego NY

40	1 GM	SW1	600	1953
1216	1 GM	NW2	1200	1956
1811,1816	2 MLW	RS18U	1800	1956-1980
9089	1 GM	SW9	1200	
	5			

PACIFIC HARBOR LINES Wilmington CA

32,35-38	5 GM	SW1200	1200	
40-43	4 GM	SD18	1800	
101	1 GM	GP7	1500	
	10	FORMERLY HARBOR BELT LINE		

PADUCAH & LOUISVILLE RY PAL Paducah KY

1798,8355	2 GM	GP10	1850	1974-1977
3600	1 VMV	GP35M	2000	1988
8200	1 GM	GP7	1500	1974
8237,8300-8303				
8356-8357	6 GM	GP10	1850	1972-1974
8307,8319-8321				
8325,8333,8347	7 GM	GP8	1600	1970-1975

PAL Cont

8305-8306,8308
8310-8311,8314
8317,8322-8324
8326-8327,8329-
8332,8334-8335
8337,8339-8346
8348-8349,8351-
8353,8361,8370

8464,8466	35 GM	GP10	1850	1970-1974
8350,8354	2 GM	GP9	1750	1978
8507	1 GM	GP39	2300	1970
8600-8604	5 GM	GP10	1850	1994
	60			

PALOUSE RIVER & COULEE CITY RR PCC Colfax/Coulee City WA

2268,2353,2357

3651,4229	5 GM	GP35	2500
3004,4109	2 GM	GP30	2250
4202,4229	2 GM	GP35M	2500
	9		

PANHANDLE NORTHERN RR PNR Borger TX

2067,2069,4284

4433-4434	5 GM	GP7	1500	R1974-1981
4310,4370,4425	3 GM	SD9	1750	1955-1960
	8			

PARR TERMINAL RR PRT Richmond CA

52	1 GM	SW1200	1200	1965
1195	1 GM	SW900	900	1954
1402	1 GM	NW2	1000	1949
2285	1 GM	SW1200	1200	1965
	4			

PATAPSCO & BACK RIVERS RR PBR Sparrows Point MD

2,15	2	SLUGS	0	1962-1985
5-6,215-218	6 GM	SW1500	1500	1967-1969
116,936	2 GM	SW7	1200	1951-1950
113,135,205-206				
904	5 GM	SW9	1200	1951-1956
128,132	2 GM	SW1200	1200	1957
140,147	2 BALD	VO-1000M	1200	1943-1947
	17	EXCLUDES SLUGS		

PEARL RIVER VALLEY RR PRV Picayune MS

1	1 GE	65-TON	470	1947

PECOS VALLEY SOUTHERN RY PVS Pecos TX

7-8	2 GE	70-TON	600	1949-1952
9	1 GM	SW900	900	1956
	3			

PEE DEE RIVER RY PDRR Bennettsville SC

1764,1797,1800

1842	4 GM	GP16	1600	
2486	1 GM	CF7	1500	1975
	5			

PEND OREILLE VALLEY RR POVA Newport WA

102	1 GM	GP9	1750	1957
159	1 GM	SD9	1750	1957
1745,8043,8310				
8325	4 VMV	GP10	1850	1974-1977
	6			

PENINSULA TERMINAL PT Portland OR

3,20,50	3 GE	70-TON	600	1949-1956
40	1 GE	45-TON	300	c1947
60,1295	2 GM	GP10	1850	
138,140	2 GM	SW1200	1200	
7548,7556	2 GM	GP10	1850	
	10			

PENN JERSEY RAIL LINES Morrisville PA

116,302	2 BALD	DS44-1000	1000	1949

PENN EASTERN RAIL LINES York PA

57	1 GM	GP10	1850	1982
75	1 GM	GP16	1750	1972
99,9008	2 GM	NW2	1000	1948,1946
261	1 GE	U28B	2800	1970
1506	1 GM	GP7	1500	1952
1756	1 GM	GP9	1750	1956
	7			

PEORIA & PEKIN UNION RY PPU Creve Coeur IL

601	1 GM	NW2U	1200	1947
602	1 GM	SW7	1200	1950
700	1 GM	SW14	1200	1974
701-702	2 GM	SW10M	1395	1984-1997
800-802	3 PLW	CATSC15A-3	1500	1994-1998
2000-2001	2 GM	GP35C	2000	1989
	10			

PHILADELPHIA BETHLEHEM & NEW ENGLAND RR PBNE Bethlehem PA

9-10	2 BLW	SLUGS	0	1971-1982
11-14	4 GM	SLUGS	0	1976-1982
22-27	6 GM	NW2	1200	1946-1949
31-33,44,90	5 GM	SW7	1200	1950-1951
35-38,93-94	6 GM	SW9	1200	1951-1956
39,42-43	3 GM	SW1200	1200	1956-1957
50-51	2 GM	SW900	900	1936-1937
203,207	2 GM	SW1200	1200	1957,1955
204	1 GM	SW9	1200	1956
XBSC33	1 GM	NW2	1200	1941
XBSC61	1 GM	SW1	600	1950
	27	EXCLUDES SLUGS		

PICKENS RY PICK Anderson SC

1802	1 FM	H12-44	1200	

PICKENS RY-HONEA PATH DIV PKHP Pickens SC

6	1 A-GM	S2M-CUM	1200	1946
7-8	2 A-GM	S2M-CUM	600	1950
	3			

PINE BELT SOUTHERN RR South Pittsburg TN

3059	1 GM	GP30	2250	
3986	1 GE	B23-7	2250	
	2			

PIONEER INDUSTRIAL RY Peoria IL

102	1 ALCO RS3M		1600	

PIONEER VALLEY RR PVRR Westfield MA

2558,2597,2647	3 GM	CF7	1500	1970-1973

PITTSBURGH ALLEGHENY & McKEES RR PAM McKees Rocks PA

17,20	2 GE	70-TON	600	1951

PITTSBURGH INDUSTRIAL RR Pittsburgh PA

2340,2342	2 GM	SW1500	1500	1970

PLYMOUTH & LINCOLN RR Lincoln NH

959,1186	2 ALCO S1		660	1949-1950

POINT COMFORT & NORTHERN RY PCN Lolita TX

12,14-15	3 GM	MP15	1500	1980
16	1 GM	GP38	2000	1969
3000	1 GM	GP40	3000	1969
3726,3731	2 GM	GP38	2000	1969
	7			

PORT BIENVILLE RR PBVR Bay Saint Louis MS

L-140	1 GM	SW9	1200	1954
L-1056	1 GM	GP18	1800	1968
L-1790	1 GM	GP16	1600	1982
	3			

PORT COLBORNE HARBOUR RY Port Colborne ON

308	1 ALCO S1		660	1940
6101	1 ALCO C425		2500	1966
	2			

PORT JERSEY RR Jersey City NJ

1197	1 GM	SW1200	1200	1962

PORT MANATEE RR Tampa FL

	1 GM	GP18	1600	
	1 GM	GP10	1850	
	2			

PORT OF CORPUS CHRISTI Corpus Christi TX

1	1 GE	25-TON	150	
2	1 GE	45-TON	380	
3	1 GE	65-TON	500	
4	1 GE	35-TON	275	
5	1 GM	NW2	1000	
	5			

PORT OF MONTREAL RY Montreal QC

7601-7602	2 GM	SW1001	1000	1976
8403-8406	4 GM	MP15	1500	1984
	6			

PORT OF MUSKOGEE Muskogee OK

3349,3361	2 GM	GP9	1750	

PORT OF PALM BEACH DISTRICT RR West Palm Beach FL

1311	1 GM	SW1200M	1300	1977

PORT OF TILLAMOOK BAY RR POTB Tillamook OR

101,3771	2	GM	GP9E	1750	1956-1953
201,4368,4405-					
4406,4414,4432	6	GM	SD9E	1800	1955-1956
	8				

PORTOLA RR MUSEUM-FEATHER RIVER RAIL SOCIETY PRM/FRRS

Portola CA

1-FR&W	1	PLYM	ML8	180	1943
2-3-KCC	2	ALCO	RS3	1600	1950
3-QRR	1	GE	44-TON	300	1940
3-4-O&NW	2	BLH	AS616	1600	1952
4-QRR	1	ALCO	S1	660	1941
20-USS	1	BLH	S12	1200	1951
51-NVR	1	BALD	DS44-660	660	1946
81-FR&W	1	GE	80-TON	500	1953
110-1-FBC	1	GEIR	BOXCAB	600	1929
146-SN	1	GE	44-TON	320	1946
244,544	2	ALCO	MRS1	1600	1953
501-WP	1	GM	SW1	600	1939
506,512-WP	2	ALCO	S1	660	1942-1941
608-WP	1	GM	NW2	1200	1940
707-708-WP	2	GM	GP7	1500	1952
725,731-WP	2	GM	GP9	1750	1955
737-UP	1	BALD	STEAM	4-4-0	1887
778-KCC	1	GE	ELECTRIC	900	1958
805A-WP	1	GM	FP7	1500	1950
849-UP	1	GM	GP30	2250	1962
908-KCC	1	ALCO	RS2	1500	1949
921D-WP	1	GM	F7A	1500	1950
925C-WP	1	GM	F9BU	1750	1951
1215-SP	1	BALD	STEAM	0-6-0	1913
1857-FR&W	1	FM	H12-44	1200	1953
2001-WP	1	GM	GP20	2000	1959
2873-SP	1	GM	GP9E	1750	1956
3051-WP	1	GE	U30B	3000	1967
4004-SP	1	ALCO	RS32	2000	1962
4404-SP	1	GM	SD9E	1750	1955
5057-MILW	1	GE	U25B	2500	1965
6946-UP	1	GM	DDA40X	6600	1971
	38				

PORT ROYAL RR PRYL Port Royal SC

1740,1849	2	GM	GP16	1600	1956-1952

PORT STANLEY TERMINAL RAIL PSTR Port Stanley ON

L1	1	GE	25-TON	300	1952
L2	1	CLC	50-TON	440	1950
L3	1	GE	44-TON	400	1947
L5	1	CLC	25-TON	220	1948
	4				

PORT TERMINAL RR ASSN PTRA Houston TX

9601-9632 *	32 BL	MP1500D	1500	1996

* 9625-9632 OWNED BY BNSF-BELT RR

PORT TERMINAL RR OF SOUTH CAROLINA PTR North Charleston SC

1002,5105	2 ALCO S4	1000	1954

PORT UTILITIES COMM OF SOUTH CAROLINA PUCC Charleston SC

1001,1003,2001-2002	4 GM	SW1001	1000	1975-1977

POTOMAC EAGLE Romney WV

116	1 GM	F7A	1500	1948

POWAY MIDLAND RR PMRR (3'-6"Gauge) Poway CA

3-CPCC	1 BALD STEAM	0-4-0	1907

PRESCOTT & NORTHWESTERN RR PNW Prescott AR

23-25	3 GE	70-TON	600*	1954-1956

* 25 IS 720HP

PRINCE GEORGE & FORESTRY MUSEUM Prince George BC

O-LP	1 GE	25-TON	150	1948
2-USA	1 ATL	65-TON	500	1943
101-USN	1 GE	65-TON	500	1943
307-CN	1 GE	70-TON	600	1950
455B	1 GM	F7BU	1750	1950
586-PGE	1 MLW	RS10S	1600	1956
1520-CNOR	1 CLC	STEAM	4-6-0	1906
9169-CN	1 GM	F7AU	1750	1951
8				

PROGRESSIVE RAIL Lakeville MN

67,74	2 GM	SW1500	1500	1966

PROVIDENCE & WORCESTER RR PW Worcester MA

120	1 A-GM RS3M	1200	1950
150	1 GE	25-TON	150	1945
1201-1202	2 GM	SW7	1200	1950
1801	1 GE	U18B	1800	1976
1802	1 GM	GP9E	1800	1977
2006-2009	4 GM	GP38-2	2000	1980-1982
2010-2011	2 GM	GP38	2000	1969
2201,2212-2216	6 GE	B23-7	2250	1978-1989
2202-2211	10 GE	U23B	2250	1977-1975
9401-9403	3 GM	GP40	3000	1971
31				

PUGET SOUND & PACIFIC RR Elmo WA

1001-1004	4 GM	GP10	1850	
3005	1 GM	GP30	2250	1959
3802	1 GM	GP38	2000	1969
6				

QUEBEC & GATINEAU RY Montreal QC

1500-1507	6 GM	SW1500	1500	
1801,1847	2 MLW	RS18	1800	
2004-2009	6 GM	GP38	2000	
2500-2502	3 GM	GP35	2500	
4212	1 MLW	C424	2400	
18				

QUEBEC NORTH SHORE & LABRADOR RY QNSL Sept Iles QC

259,261	2	GM	SD40-2	3000	1971-1975
301-322	22	ALST	SD40-2CLC	3000	1993-1995
401-403	3	GE	DASH8-40CM	4000	1994
404-414	11	GE	DASH9-44CW	4400	1998
9501-9503	3	ALST	GP38M	2000	1995
9511-9512	2	ALST	SLUGS	0	1995
	41	EXCLUDES SLUGS			

QUEBEC SOUTHERN RY Montreal QC

500-509	10	ICG	GP35R	2500	1997

QUEEN ANNE'S RR Lewes DE

3-USN	1	VULC	STEAM	0-6-0T	1943
19-PRR	1	ALCO	T6	1000	1959
	2				

QUINCY BAY TERMINAL QBT Quincy MA

19	1	ALCO	S4	1000	1950
20	1	GM	SW9	1200	1981
21	1	GE	U23B	2250	1975
22	1	GE	B23-7	2250	1979
	4				

QUINCY RR QRR Quincy CA

5	1	GM	SW1200	1200	1963

RAILCRUISE AMERICA-ST LOUIS CAR St Louis MO

101-102	2	BL	F9A	1750	1982
103-104	2	BL	F7B	1500	1999
	4				

RAILROAD MUSEUM OF NEW ENGLAND Waterbury CT

28-PV	1	GM	SW1	600	1939
42-SW	1	GE	45-TON	300	1942
103-S&C	1	BALD	STEAM	2-6-2	1925
300-NYNH	1	GE	ELECTRIC	3300	1956
0401-NYNH	1	ALCO	FA1	1500	1947
529-NYNH	1	ALCO	RS3	1600	1950
557-MEC	1	ALCO	RS3	1600	1953
1109-B&M	1	GM	SW1	600	1939
1246-CPR	1	MLW	STEAM	4-6-2	1946
1732-B&M	1	GM	GP9	1750	1957
2525-NYNH	1	GE	U25B	2500	1965
5562-PC	1	ALCO	RS3	1600	1951
	12	OPERATES NAUGATUCK RR			

RAILROAD MUSEUM OF PENNSYLVANIA RMP Strasburg PA

-PRR	1	PRR	STEAM REP	0-4-0	1825
-DOT	1	ALCO	RS1	1000	1942
1-LSC	1	BRKV		GAS	1951
1-C&A-JOHN BULL	1	PRR	STEAM REP	4-2-0	1831
1-LR	1	LIMA	STEAM	3-TRUCK	1905
4-CML	1	HEIS	STEAM	2-TRUCK	1918
4-WHML	1	CLIM	STEAM	2-TRUCK	1913
4-LR	1	LIMA	STEAM	3-TRUCK	1905

RMP Cont

13-BEDT		1	PORT	STEAM	0-6-0T	1919
20-V&T		1	BALD	STEAM	2-6-0	1875
81-M&P		1	GM	NW2	1000	1946
94-PRR		1	JUNI	STEAM	0-4-0	1917
111-BSC		1	HEIS	STEAM	0-4-0F	1941
460-PRR		1	JUNI	STEAM	4-4-2	1914
520-PRR		1	BALD	STEAM	2-8-2	1916
701-MONC		1	ALCO	C415	1500	1968
757-NKP		1	LIMA	STEAM	2-8-4	1944
1187-RDG		1	BALD	STEAM	0-4-0	1903
1187-PRR		1	ALT	STEAM	2-8-0	1888
1200-USN		1	BALD	S12	1200	1952
1223-PRR		1	JUNI	STEAM	4-4-0	1905
1251-RDG		1	READ	STEAM	0-6-0T	1918
1670-PRR		1	JUNI	STEAM	0-6-0	1916
2233-PRR		1	GM	GP30	2250	1963
2846-PRR		1	BALD	STEAM	2-8-0	1905
3750-PRR		1	JUNI	STEAM	4-6-2	1920
3936-3937-PRR	A	2	JUNI	ELECTRIC	2-B-B-2	1911
4094-PP&L		1	HEIS	STEAM	0-8-0F	1939
4465-PRR	B	1	GE	ELECTRIC	4400	1963
4800-PRR	C	1	B-GE	ELECTRIC	2-C-C-2	1934
4935-PRR	C	1	JUNI	ELECTRIC	2-C-C-2	1943
5690-PRR		1	ALT	ELECTRIC	B-1	1934
5741-PRR		1	JUNI	STEAM	4-6-0	1924
5901-PRR		1	GM	E7A	2000	1945
6755-PRR		1	ALT	STEAM	4-8-2	1930
7002-PRR		1	JUNI	STEAM	4-4-2	1902
7006-PRR		1	GM	GP9	1750	1955
7688-PRR		1	LIMA	STEAM	2-8-0	1915
		39	A	DD1 MODEL	B	E44A MODEL
			C	GG1 MODEL		

RAILROAD SWITCHING SERVICE OF MISSOURI RSM St Louis MO

2020	1	GM	SW8	800	

RAIL TOURS RTI Jim Thorpe PA

11-STRT	1	GM	SW900MSC	900	1937
1098-CPR	1	CLC	STEAM	4-6-0	1913
	2				

RAILWAY EXPOSITION RECO Covington KY

1-I&M	1	BRKV	15-TON	140	1949
2-JV	1	PLYM	18-TON	150	1937
332-P&BR	1	BALD	VO1000	1000	1939
1053-GTW	1	ALCO	S4	1000	1956
5888-PRR	1	GM	E8A	2250	1951
9408-PRR	1	GM	SW1	600	1947
	6				

RARUS RY RARW Anaconda MT

102-103	2	GM	GP7	1500	1952-1954
104-107	4	GM	GP9	1750	1957
301	1	GM	GP7	1500	1953
302	1	GM	GP9	1750	1957
	8				

READER RR RR Reader AR

2	1	BALD	STEAM	2-6-0	1907
4,7	2	BALD	STEAM	2-6-2	1914,1908
	3				

READING BLUE MOUNTAIN & NORTHERN RR RBMN Port Clinton PA

425	1	BALD	STEAM	4-6-2	1928
800-803	4	GM	SW8/M	800	1950-1952
1000	1	GM	NW2	1000	1948
1200-1201	2	GM	SW7	1200	1950-1951
1202	1	GM	SW1200	1200	1956
1503-1504	2	GM	CF7	1500	1977
1545-1548	4	GM	SW1500	1500	1969-1971
2000	1	GM	SD38	2000	1970
2102	1	RDG	STEAM	4-8-4	1945
2300-2301	2	GE	B23-7	2250	1979
2392-2399	5	GE	U23B	2250	1972-1978
3600-3601	2	GM	SD45-2	3600	1972
	26				

READING CO TECH & HIST SOC RCTH Reading PA

103-RDG	1	GM	NW2	1000	1947
485-RDG	1	ALCO	RS3	1600	1952
702-RDG	1	BLW	DS44-10	1000	1948
730-WSR	1	BLW	DS44-75	750	1950
900-RDG	1	GM	FP7A	1500	1950
3640-RDG	1	GM	GP35	2500	1964
5204-RDG	1	ALCO	C424	2400	1963
5308-RDG	1	ALCO	C630	3000	1967
5513-RDG	1	GM	GP30	2250	1962
6300-RDG	1	GE	U30C	3000	1967
	10				

REDMONT RY Red Bay AL

101	1	GM	CF7	1500	1975

RED RIVER VALLEY & WESTERN RR RRVM Breckenridge MN

301,304	2	GM	CF7	1500	1974-1977
302,309	2	SF	SLUGS	0	1974-1977
401-404,406-407	6	GM	GP10	1850	
601	1	GM	SD20	2000	
2051-2053	3	GM	GP20	2000	
	12	EXCLUDES SLUGS			

RIO VALLEY SWITCHING RR RVSC McAllen TX

1233	1	GM	SW1200	1200	
1705,1729,1749	3	GM	GP16	1600	
4159	1	GM	GP7M	1650	
	5				

RIVER TERMINAL RY RT Cleveland OH

98,100	2	GM	SW900	900	1956-1957
101-108	8	GM	SW1001	1000	1968-1978
	10				

RMW VENTURES Connorsville IN

4,7	2	VMV	GP11	1850	1981
6,12,16	3	VMV	GP10	1850	1981
203	1	GM	GP20	2000	1960
221,223	2	GM	SW1200	1200	1957-1965
325,327	2	ALCO	C425	2500	1965-1966
342-345	4	GM	GP7U	1500	1981
	14	FORMERLY INDIANA HI-RAIL			

ROARING CAMP & BIG TREES RR RCBT (3'Gauge) Felton CA

1-CPC	1	LIMA	STEAM	2-TRUCK	1912
2-WSL	1	HEIS	STEAM	2-TRUCK	1899
3-KP	1	BALD	STEAM	0-4-2T	1890
5-CP&W	1	CLIM	STEAM	2-TRUCK	1928
6-WMRL	1	LIMA	STEAM	2-TRUCK	1912
7-WSL	1	LIMA	STEAM	3-TRUCK	1911
	6				

ROBERVAL & SAGUENAY RY RS Jonquiere QC

50-52	3	GE	B23-SUPER 7	2250	1990-1991
60-63	4	ALST	GP38-3	2000	1996
64-65	2	ALST	GP38-3	2000	1997
66	1	ALST	GP38-3	2000	1998
	10				

ROCHESTER & GENESEE VALLEY RR MUSEUM ODRM Rochester NY

6-EK	1	GE	80-TON	500	1946
9-EK	1	ALCO	RS1	1000	1951
12-BNY	1	VULC	STEAM	0-4-0T	1918
79-NKP	1	ALCO	S4	1000	1953
211-LV	1	ALCO	RS3M	1200	1979
1843-USA	1	FM	H12-44	1200	1953
1941-RG&E	1	GE	45-TON	300	1941
	7				

ROCHESTER & SOUTHERN RR RSR Rochester NY

879,887,926	3	GM	GP9	1750

ROCKDALE SANDOW & SOUTHERN RR RSS Rockdale TX

13-15	3	GM	MP15	1500	1974

ROCKY MOUNTAIN RAILTOURS Vancouver BC

800-801,803-					
805 HATX	5	GM	GP40-2	3000	1979

RUTLAND LINE Wahpeton SD

401-404,406-407	6	GM	GP10	1750
601	1	GM	SD20	2000
2051-2053	3	GM	GP20CAT	2000
	10	EXPECTING 2 GENII GP15CAT		

SABINE RIVER & NORTHERN RR SRN Mulford TX

1505-1506	2	GM	GP7	1500	1953
1759,17510	2	GM	GP9	1750	1955-1954
	4				

SAGINAW VALLEY RY SGVY Vassar MI

998-999	2	GM	SW1200*	1200	1954-1955

* 999 IS SW9 MODEL

SALT LAKE CITY SOUTHERN RR SL Salt Lake City UT

272	1	GM	GP9	1750	1984
2151	1 — 2	GM	GP7	1500	1978

SALT LAKE GARFIELD & WESTERN RY SLGW Salt Lake City UT

DS5	1	GE	65-TON	420	1943
DS8	1 — 2	GM	SW1200	1200	1956

SANDERSVILLE RR SAN Sandersville GA

90-91 1100,1300,1400	2	GM	SLUGS	0	1980
1500	4	GM	SW1500	1500	1968-1970
1200	1 — 5	GM	SW1200	1200	1964

EXCLUDES SLUGS

SAN DIEGO & IMPERIAL VALLEY RR SDIV San Diego CA

5911	1	GM	GP9	1750	1955
2162,2168	2	GM	GP7	1750	1978-1979
3820,3861	2 — 5	GM	GP38	2000	1967-1969

SAN DIEGO NORTHERN RY

1501	1	GM	SW1500	1500

SAN DIEGO RR MUSEUM PSRM Campo CA

AGREX	1	WHIT	45-TON	300	1945
1-O&NW	1	BALD	AS616	1600	1953
10-ESL	1	ALCO	STEAM	0-6-0T	1923
11-CBL	1	ALCO	STEAM	2-8-2T	1929
46-CW	1	BALD	STEAM	2-6-6-2	1937
65-00608-USN	1	GE	44-TON	380	1942
104-SDAE	1	BALD	STEAM	2-8-0	1904
1366-UP	1	FM	H20-44	2000	1947
1809,1820-USA	2	GM	MRS1	1600	1952
2098-ATSF	1	ALCO	RS2	1500	1949
2104-USAF	1	ALCO	MRS1	1600	1953
2353-SP	1	BALD	STEAM	4-6-0	1912
3873-SP	1	GM	GP9R	1750	1977
6920-ARCO +-	2	BLH	SH2300	300	1954
7285-USMC	1	GE	80-TON	500	1943
7485-USA	1	GE	45-TON	300	1941
8157	1 — 19	PORT	25-TON	150	1948

INCLUDES SAN DIEGO & ARIZONA

SAND SPRINGS RY SS Sand Springs OK

100-102	3	GM	SW900	900	1956-1957

SAN JOAQUIN REGIONAL RAIL-ACE-ALTAMONT COMMUTER EXPRESS San Jose C

3101-3103	3	BL	F40PH-3C	3000	1997
3104-3105	2 — 5	BL	F40PH-3C	3000	2000

SAN JOAQUIN VALLEY RR SJVR Exeter CA

1751,1754-1755	3	GM	GP9	1750	1954-1956
1761,1763-1764	3	GM	GP9	1750	1980
1825-1826	2	GM	GP28	1800	1964
2035,2037-2038					
2041-2043	6	GM	GP20	2000	1962-1961
	14				

SAN LUIS CENTRAL RR SLC Monte Vista CO

70	1	GM	SW8	800	1952
71	1	GE	70-TON	600	1955
	2				

SAN MANUEL ARIZONA RR SMA San Manuel AZ

16-19	4	GM	GP38-2	2000	1974-1978
20-21	2	GM	GP40-2	3000	1972
	6				

SAN PEDRO & SOUTHWESTERN RR SWKR Benson AZ

23	1	GM	SW900	900	1951
1501	1	GM	SW1500M	1500	1964
2039,2044,2046	3	GM	GP20	2000	1961-1977
	5				

SANTA CRUZ BIG TREES & PACIFIC RY SCBG Felton CA

20	1	WHIT	4-TON	420	1943
2600,2641	2	GM	CF7	1500	1971
	3				

SANTA FE SOUTHERN RY SFS Santa Fe NM

92	1	GM	GP7	1500	1953
93	1	GM	GP16	1600	1974
	2				

SANTA MARIA VALLEY RR SMV Santa Maria CA

70,80	2	GE	70-TON	660	1948-1956
1801	1	GM	GP9	1750	1992
	3				

SAVANNAH PORT TERMINAL RR SSDK Savannah GA

1001-1002	2	GM	SW1001	1000	1977
8237	1	GM	GP7	1500	1951
	3				

SEASHORE TROLLEY MUSEUM-NEERHS Kennebunkport ME

D1-ME	1	DAV	10-TON	200	1946
52-AV	1	BRIL	ELECTRIC	35-TON	1909
100-ASL	1	LAC	ELECTRIC	30-TON	1906
300-OR	1	BALD	ELECTRIC	50-TON	1920
504-M&SC	1	OC	ELECTRIC	35-TON	1924
0514-BE	1	BE	ELECTRIC	50-TON	1914
648-C&LE	1	CCC	ELECTRIC	40-TON	1930
1280-RI	1	RI	ELECTRIC	30-TON	1912
	8				

SEMINOLE GULF RY SGLR Fort Myers FL

571-577	7	GM	GP9	1750	1956
578	1	GM	GP10	1850	1956
	8				

SEMO PORT RR SE Scott City MO

1823	1 GM	GP7	1500	1951

SEPTA-SOUTHEASTERN PENNSYLVANIA TRANSPORTATION AUTH SPTA

Philadelphia PA

CW6-CW7	2 GE	45-TON	300	1942-1941
50-52	3 GM	SW1200	1200	1987
60-61	2 REP	RL1000P	1000	1992
2301-2307	7 GM	ELECTRIC	7000	1987
2308	1 ABB	ELECTRIC **	7000	1996
	15	* AEM7 MODEL ** ALP44 MODEL		

SEQUATCHIE VALLEY RR South Pittsburg TN

706	1 GM	GP7	1500
960	1 GM	GP9	1750
1488,1688	2 GM	SW1200	1200
	4		

SHAWNEE TERMINAL RY Cairo IL

106	1 GM	SW1	600	1950

SIDNEY & LOWE RR Sidney NE

7-8	2 GM	GP10	1800	1979
6342	1 GM	GP35R	2500	1979
	3			

SIERRA RR Oakdale CA

40,42,44	3 BALD	S12	1200	1951-1955
46	1 GM	GP9	1750	
	4			

SIERRA RY CO OF CALIFORNIA-RAILTOWN 1897 SRYC Jamestown CA

2-HLC	1 LIMA	STEAM	3-TRUCK	1922
3-S	1 ROG	STEAM	4-6-0	1891
7-PLC	1 LIMA	STEAM	3-TRUCK	1923
28-S	1 BALD	STEAM	2-8-0	1922
34-S	1 BALD	STEAM	2-8-2	1925
45,59-USA	2 GE	80-TON	470	1953
546,613-USA	2 ALCO	MRS1	1600	1953
7417-USA	1 GE	45-TON	300	1942
	10			

SILVER CREEK & STEPHENSON RR Freeport IL

2	1 HEIS	STEAM	2-TRUCK	1912
3	1 PLYM	12-TON	60	1938
5	1 BRKV	14-TON	150	c1945
	3			

SISSETON MILBANK RR SMRR Milbank SD

627,651	2 GM	SW1200	1200	1954-1953

SMITHSONIAN INSTITUTION Washington DC

-C&A	1 STEP	STEAM	4-2-0	1831
-CV	1 WILM	STEAM	2-2-2T	1851
-PEP	1 HEIS	STEAM	0-4-0F	1938
3-WS	1 BALD	STEAM	0-4-2T	1883
3-SC *	1 BALD	STEAM	4-4-0	1876
13-DOT	1 ALCO	RS1	1000	1941
1401-SRY	1 ALCO	STEAM	4-6-2	1926
	7	* 3'GAUGE		

SMS RAIL SERVICE Bridgeport NJ

300	1 BLH	S12	1200	1952
552-554	3 BLH	AS616	1600	1951-1954
1293	1 BLW	DS44-10	1000	1947
	5			

SNOQUALMIE VALLEY RR Snoqualmie WA

1	1 FM	H12-44	1200	1951
201	1 ALCO	RSD4	1600	1951
7320	1 GE	45-TON	300	1940
	3			

SOMERSET RR SOM Binghamton NY

1 A	1 GE	50-TON	300	1950
2 B	1 GE	45-TON	300	1959
7 C	1 GE	144-TON	1100	1983
8 D	1 GE	95-TON	670	1993
9 E	1 GM	SW8M	800	1950
	5	A BINGHAMPTON B BAINBRIDGE		
		C LANSING D BARKER E DRESDEN		

SOO LINE (SEE CANADIAN PACIFIC ALSO ST LAWRENCE & HUDSON)

402-414	3 GM	GP9	1750	1954-1955
532,543	2 GM	SD10	1800	1952-1954
738-756	9 GM	SD40	3000	1969-1971
757-789	17 GM	SD40-2	3000	1972-1993
1203-1204	2 GM	SW1200	1200	1962-1965
1400-1401	2 GM	SW1500	1500	1966
1532-1563	32 GM	MP15AC	1500	1975
2008-2064	18 GM	GP40	3000	1966-1969
3013-3019	6 GM	GP38	2000	1971
4100-4106	6 GM	GP15CAT	1500	1990-1991
4200-4204	5 GM	GP9M	1750	1991
4300-4302	3 GM	GP30CAT	2000	1990
4400-4515	46 GM	GP38-2	2000	1974-1993
4598-4599	2 GM	GP39-2	2300	1978
4600-4648	4 GM	GP40	3000	1966-1993
6000-6020	21 GM	SD60	3800	1987
6021-6057	37 GM	SD60	3800	1989
6058-6062	5 GM	SD60M	3800	1989
6240-6241	2 GM	SD39	2300	1968
6450	1 GM	SD40B	3000	1971
6601-6623 A	22 GM	SD40-2	3000	1979-1984
8500-8580 B	81 GE	AC4400CW	4400	1998
	326			

NOTES

A EXCEPT 6605,6608

B ALL PRINTED CANADIAN PACIFIC RY

SOUTH BRANCH VALLEY RR SBVR Moorefield WV

45	1	GE	45-TON	300	1943
2001,6135,6240					
6352,6447,6506					
6600,6604	8	GM	GP9	1750	1955-1957
7172	1	GM	BL2	1500	1948
	10				

SOUTH BROOKLYN RY Brooklyn NY

N1-N2	2	GE	65-TON	300	1974

SOUTH BUFFALO RY SB Lackawanna NY

1	1	GM	SLUG	0	1985
4-7	4	GM	SW1500	1500	1967-1972
19-20	2	GM	MP15	1500	1975
21	1	GM	NW2	1200	1941
30-33,38	5	GM	SW1200	1200	1964-1965
34-37,39	5	GM	SW9	1200	1952-1955
50-53	4	GM	SW1200	1200	1950-1951
72	1	GM	SW7	1200	1950
	22	EXCLUDES SLUG			

SOUTH CAROLINA CENTRAL RR SCRF Hartsville SC

8	1	GM	NW2	1200	1984
75,77,8383	3	GM	GP10	1850	1974-1975
2027	1	GM	GP16	1750	1979
2053,2207	2	GM	GP7	1500	1979-1980
6187,6555	2	GM	GP9	1750	1954-1957
	9				

SOUTH CAROLINA PUBLIC RYS SCPS Charleston SC

	1	GM	GP9	1750	1957

SOUTH CENTRAL FLORIDA EXPRESS SCFE Clewiston FL

9011-9012,9018	3	GM	GP7	1500	1952
9013-9015,9019-					
9020	5	ICG	GP8	1600	1978
9016-9017	2	GM	GP16	1600	1978
9021-9022	2	GM	GP18	1800	1980
9023-9026	4	GM	GP11	1750	1980
	16				

SOUTH CENTRAL TENNESSEE RR SCTR Centerville TN

103	1	GM	GP7	1750	
121	1	GM	SW1200	1200	1956
152	1	GM	GP7	1500	1950
738-739	2	GM	GP38	2000	
	5				

SOUTHEASTERN RY MUSEUM NRHS Duluth GA

DAYTON-NCR	1	LIMA	STEAM	0-4-0F	1913
MAUD-SRY	1	BALD	STEAM	0-4-4T	1876
2,5-HRR	2	GE	44-TON	3000	1950-1941
3-70 ARM	1	B-W	BOXCAB	300	1929
9-CL	1	HEIS	STEAM	2-TRUCK	1924
21-CVR	1	BALD	STEAM	2-8-0	1924

NRHS Cont

97-GPC	1	PORT	STEAM	0-6-0	1943
203-GM	1	BALD	STEAM	2-10-0	1928
290-A&WP	1	LIMA	STEAM	4-6-2	1926
750-S&A	1	ALCO	STEAM	4-6-2	1910
2594-SRY	1	GM	GP30	2250	1962
6901-SRY	1	GM	E8A	2250	1950
8202-SRY	1	GM	SW7	1200	1950
	14				

SOUTHERN ALABAMA RR Troy AL

9	1	GM	SW1	600	
7013	1	GM	SW9	1200	
9424	1	GM	GP18	1800	1962
	3				

SOUTHERN CALIFORNIA CHAPTER-R&LHS Pomona CA

2-OHT	1	SCH	STEAM	0-6-0	1887
3-FGS	1	CLIM	STEAM	3-TRUCK	1909
3-USP *	1	BALD	STEAM	2-8-0	1903
3450-ATSF	1	BALD	STEAM	4-6-4	1927
4014-UP	1	ALCO	STEAM	4-8-8-4	1941
5021-SP	1	ALCO	STEAM	4-10-2	1926
6915-UP	1	GM	DDA40X	6600	1969
9000-UP	1	ALCO	STEAM	4-12-2	1926
	8	* 3'GAUGE			

SOUTHERN CALIFORNIA REGIONAL RAIL AUTH (METROLINK)

Los Angeles CA

851-869	19	GM	F59PH	3000	1992
870-873	4	GM	F59PH	3000	1993
874-881	8	GM	F59PHI	3000	1995
882-883	2	GM	F59PHI	3000	1996
	33				

SOUTHERN FREIGHT RR Oak Ridge TN

39-5308,39-5310	2	ALCO	RS3	1600	1951

SOUTHERN INDIANA RY SIND Sellersburg IN

100-101	2	GE	65-TON	400	1947-1946
102	1	GE	80-TON	500	1962
	3				

SOUTHERN ONTARIO RY Hamilton ON

1200	1	GM	SW1200B	1200	1998
1201,1285,1359 1367	4	GM	SW1200	1200	1957-1960
1752,4205	2	GM	GP9	1750	1954-1956
3502,3508,3585	3	BBD	HR412	2000	1973,1981
5005	1	GM	GP35	2250	1964
	11				

SOUTHERN PACIFIC - SEE UNION PACIFIC SYSTEM

SOUTHERN RR CO OF NEW JERSEY SRNJ Winslow NJ

59	1 ALCO	RS1	1000	1948
100	1 GM	GP9	1750	1956
102	1 GM	GP10	1850	1978
410,412	2 GE	44-TON	360-400	1953
414	1 ALCO	C420	2000	1964
727-728-B&LE	2 GM	F7A	1500	1953
	8	EXPECTING WIDE CAB ALCO UNIT		

SOUTHERN RY OF BRITISH COLUMBIA SRY New Westminster BC

122,124,129	3 GM	GP9	1750	1957-1968
151-153	3 GM	MP15DC	1500	1975
381	1 GM	SD38AC	2000	1971
382-384	3 GM	SD38-2	2000	1972-1974
900-909	10 GM	SW900	900	1955-1958
910-911	2 GM	SW1000	1000	1967-1969
	22			

SOUTHERN SAN LUIS VALLEY RR SSLV Alamosa CO

D500	1 SSLV		210	1954

SOUTHERN SWITCHING LONE STAR RR SSC Abilene TX

1865-1866	2 GM	NW2	1000	

SOUTH KANSAS & OKLAHOMA RR SKOL Coffeyville KS

103	1 GM	GP7	1500	
789,797	2 GM	GP35L	2500	
1001	1 GM	CF7	1500	
1274	1 GM	SW10	1000	
1505,1601,1722	3 GM	GP16	1750	
2184,2188,2191	3 GM	GP7	1500	
2211,2240,3002				
3005,3030-3031				
3040,3046,3052	9 GM	GP30	2250	
4101,4103,4111-				
4112,4114,4117	6 GM	GP30	2250	
4153	1 GM	GP20E	1800	
4259	1 GM	GP30	2250	
6606,6628-6629	3 GM	GP35	2500	
	31			

SOUTH ORIENT RR SO San Angelo TX

101-109	9 GM	GP7	1500	1994-1996

SOUTH PLAINS LAMESA RR SLAL Slaton TX

1555	1 GM	GP7	1500	1952
1958	1 GM	GP9	1750	1954
	2			

SOUTH SIMCOE RY SSR Tottenham ON

10-PG	1 R&H	28-TON	250	1950
22-CP	1 CLC	DIESEL-HYD	500	1960
136-CP	1 ROG	STEAM	4-4-0	1883
1057-CP	1 MLW	STEAM	4-6-0	1912
	4			

SOUTHWESTERN RR SW Hurley NM/Ogden UT

25,27-30	5	GM	GP30	2500	1979
2163-2164,2182					
4291-4292	5	GM	GP7	1500	1979
6798	1	GM	GP40	3000	1979
	11				

SOUTHWEST PENNSYLVANIA RR Verona PA

1706	1	GM	GP16	1600	1982
7576	1	GM	GP10	1850	1980
	2				

SPIRIT OF WASHINGTON DINNER TRAIN SWDT Renton WA

82,84	2	GM	F9A	1750	1954-1956
100-102	2	GM	F7A	1500	
	4				

ST CROIX VALLEY RR Hinckley MN

104	1	GM	GP7	1500	
189	1	GM	GP18	1800	
	2				

STEAMTOWN NATIONAL HISTORIC SITE SUSA Scranton PA

1-BSC	1	BALD	STEAM	2-6-2	1914
1-MRL	1	LIMA	STEAM	2-TRUCK	1910
2-BC	1	PORT	STEAM	0-4-0T	1937
3-EJLS	1	ALCO	STEAM	0-6-0T	1927
7-GPC	1	VULC	STEAM	2-4-2T	1911
8-SC	1	BALD	STEAM	0-6-0	1923
15-RV	1	BALD	STEAM	2-8-0	1916
26-BALD	1	BALD	STEAM	0-6-0	1929
43-NHTR	1	VULC	STEAM	0-4-0T	1919
44-NKP	1	ALCO	STEAM	4-6-0	1905
47-CNR	1	MLW	STEAM	4-6-4T	1914
210-N&SL	1	ALCO	STEAM	2-6-0	1923
514-NKP	1	GM	GP9	1750	1958
519-MC	1	ALCO	STEAM	2-8-0	1913
565-DL&W	1	ALCO	STEAM	2-6-0	1908
759-NKP	1	LIMA	STEAM	2-8-4	1944
790-ICRR	1	ALCO	STEAM	2-8-0	1903
1923-L&BR	1	ALCO	STEAM	2-8-0	1920
2124-RDG	1	B-R	STEAM	4-8-4	1947
2317-CPR	1	MLW	STEAM	4-6-2	1923
2816-CPR	1	MLW	STEAM	4-6-4	1930
2929-CPR	1	CLC	STEAM	4-4-4	1938
3254-CNR	1	CLC	STEAM	2-8-2	1917
3377-CNR	1	CLC	STEAM	2-8-2	1919
3713-B&M	1	LIMA	STEAM	4-6-2	1934
4012-UP	1	ALCO	STEAM	4-8-8-4	1941
5288-CNR	1	MLW	STEAM	4-6-2	1919
6039-GTW	1	BALD	STEAM	4-8-2	1925
6816-PSEG	1	PORT	STEAM	0-6-0F	1923

STEELTON & HIGHSPIRE RR SH Steelton PA

11	1		SLUG	0	1975
70,73-75,78-79	6	GM	SW9	1200	1965-1980
71	1	GM	SW7	1200	1981
77	1	GM	SW1200	1200	1989
	8		EXCLUDES SLUG		

STEWARTSTOWN RR STRT Stewartstown PA

9	1	PLYM	35-TON	200	1943
10	1	GE	44-TON	380	1946
	2				

STILLWATER CENTRAL RR Stillwater OK

2178	1	GM	GP7	1500	
3046	1	GM	GP35	2500	
4103	1	GM	GP30	2250	
	3				

ST LAWRENCE & ATLANTIC RR SLR Auburn ME

50,52,58,60					
62,64,68	7	GM	GP9	1750	1954-1956
3000,3702,3717					
3733	4	GM	GP40 *	3000	1978
3501,3505,3512					
3516-3517,3519					
3562,3569,3573					
3578-3579	11	MLW	M420	2000	
8748-8749	2	GM	GP16	1850	
	24		* 3000 IS LLPX 3702 IS GSCX		

ST LAWRENCE & HUDSON RY (SEE CANADIAN PACIFIC ALSO SOO LINE)

1000-1117	21	GM	SLUG	0	1984-1997
1201	1	GM	SW9	1200	1958-1960
1213-1273	8	GM	SW1200RS	1200	1958-1960
1502-1697	43	GM	GP9R	1500	1980-1988
3034-3111	7	GM	GP38-2	2000	1983-1986
4650-4657	8	GM	GP40	3000	1966-1967
5415-5499	14	GM	SD40	3000	1971
5507-5563	20	GM	SD40	3000	1966-1967
5565-6069	138	GM	SD40-2	3000	1972-1983
7303-7312	10	GM	GP38-2	2000	1972
8132-8176	13	GM	SW1200RS	1200	1958-1960
	262		EXCLUDES SLUGS AND 12 UNITS LEASED TO		
			AMT MONTREAL INCL AMTRAK 319 - F40PH		

ST LOUIS IRON MOUNTAIN & SOUTHERN RY SLIM Jackson MO

5	1	PORT	STEAM	2-4-2	1946
300	1	ALCO	STEAM	2-6-0	1925
911	1	BLH	30-TON	180	1951
5898	1	GM	E8A	2250	1951
	4				

ST MARIES RIVER RR STMA St Maries ID

101-103	3	GM	GP9	1750	1980
501-502	2	GM	SW1200	1200	1981
	5				

ST MARYS RR SM St Marys GA

503	1	GM	SW1500	1500	1998
504-505	2	GM	MP15	1500	1988-1976
	3				

STOCKTON TERMINAL & EASTERN RR STE Stockton CA

505,507	2	ALCO	S1	660	1942
557,560	2	ALCO	S2	1000	1943-1950
564	1	ALCO	S4	1000	1951
9319	1	GM	SW1200	1200	1963
	6				

STONE MOUNTAIN SCENIC RR Stone Mountain GA

60,104	2	BALD	STEAM	4-4-0	1922,1919
110	1	VULC	STEAM	2-6-2	1927
6143,6147	2	GM	FP7A	1500	1950
5896	1	GM	GP7	1500	1953
6661	1	GM	GP9	1750	1956
	7				

STOURBRIDGE RR SBRR Honesdale PA

54	1	GM	BL2	1500	1949
430	1	GM	SW7	1200	1950
	2				

STRASBURG RR SRC Strasburg PA

1-SRR	1	PLYM	20-TON	GAS	1926
2-PW&P	1	PLYM	10-TON	GAS	1930
4-RDG *	1	BURN	STEAM	0-4-0C	1903
31-CNR	1	BALD	STEAM	0-6-0	1908
33-PRR	1	GE	44-TON	380	1948
89-CNR	1	CLC	STEAM	2-6-0	1910
90-GWR	1	BALD	STEAM	2-10-0	1924
475-N&W	1	BALD	STEAM	4-8-0	1906
972-CP	1	MLW	STEAM	4-6-0	1912
2233-L&BC	1	GM	GP30	2250	1963
	10	* LOANED TO RR MUSEUM OF PENNSYLVANIA			

SUMPTER VALLEY RR (3'Gauge) Sumpter Valley OR

1	1	PLYM	20-TON	128	c1927
3	1	HEIS	STEAM	2-TRUCK	1915
19-20	2	ALCO	STEAM	2-8-2	1920
1021	1	PLYM	10-TON	B	1920
	5				

SWEETWATER CENTRAL SWITCHING Sweetwater TX

9525	1	GM	GP38	2000	1969

TACOMA EASTERN RY TE Tacoma WA

439	1	GM	SD9R	1750	1980
684 *	1	ALCO	C415	1500	1968
	2	NOT OWNED BY TACOMA EASTERN			

TACOMA RAIL TMBL Tacoma WA

1202-1204	3	GM	SW1200	1200	1951-1965
2000-2003	4	NRE	GP20	2000	1985-1989
3000	1	GM	SD40	3000	
	8				

TALLEYRAND TERMINAL RR Jacksonville FL

154	1	GM	GP7	1500	1952
266	1	GM	SW10	1000	1981
278	1	GM	SW1200	1200	1962
	3				

TENNESSEE CENTRAL RY MUSEUM Brentwood TN

52-USA	1	GM	SW8	800	1954
1061-USA	1	PLYM	10-TON	150	
4068,4080-NYC					
5764-PRR,6902 *	4	GM	E8A	2250	1951
	6	* 6902 BROADWAY DINNER TRAIN			

TENNESSEE SOUTHERN RR Mt Pleasant TN

201,2506	2	GM	CF7	1500	1973
523,2558.2593	3	GM	GP30	2250	1962-1963
514,1726,1782					
6173,6583	5	GM	GP9	1750	1956-1958
5981	1	GM	GP7M	1750	1958
	11				

TENNESSEE VALLEY RR MUSEUM TVRM Chattanooga TN

27-SCT,36	2	BALD	VO1000	1000	1942
349-COFG	1	BALD	STEAM	4-4-0	1891
509-L&A	1	BALD	STEAM	4-6-0	1913
610-611-USA	2	BALD	STEAM	2-8-0	1951
630-SRY	1	ALCO	STEAM	2-8-0	1903
1616-L&N	1	GE	U25B	2500	1963
1824,1829,1832	3	GM	GP7L	1500	1951
4501-SRY	1	BALD	STEAM	2-8-2	1911
6910-K&T	1	BALD	STEAM	2-8-2	1920
6914-SRY	1	GM	E8A	2250	1953
8014-8669-USAF	6	ALCO	RSD1	1000	1942-1944
	20				

TENNKEN RR TKEN Dyersburg TN

9433-9435	3	GM	GP28	1750	1964-1965

TERMINAL RR ASSN OF ST LOUIS TRRA St Louis MO

17	1	GM	SD7M	1750	1999
560	1	GM	SLUG	0	1977
1229-1243	10	GM	SW1200	1200	1964-1965
1501-1517 *	16	GM	SW1500	1500	1967-1971
	27	EXCLUDES SLUG * EXCEPT 1514			

TERMINAL RY ALABAMA STATE DOCKS TASD Mobile AL

761,771-772					
801-802	5	GM	MP15	1500	1976-1980
803	1	GM	MP15AC	1500	1980
821-822	2	GM	MP15	1500	1982
	8				

TEXAS & NEW MEXICO RR TNMR Hobbs NM

173	1	GM	GP9	1750	1980
2078	1	GM	GP16	1850	1979
3808	1	GM	GP38	2000	
	3				

TEXAS & NORTHERN RY TN Lone Star TX

1-2	2	ALGM	SLUGS	0	1976-1983
24,45,53-56	6	ALCO	S3M	600	1976-1980
992-995	4	GM	CF7M	1250	1977
996	1	GM	GP10	1850	
997	1	GM	GP7M	1250	1950
998-999	2	GM	MP15	1500	1975
	14	EXCLUDES SLUGS			

TEXAS CITY TERMINAL RY TCT Texas City TX

35-37	3	GM	MP15	1500	1982

TEXAS GONZALES & NORTHERN RY TXGN Gonzales TX

92	1	GM	SW1200	1200	1965
2584	1	GM	SW1500	1500	
	2				

TEXAS MEXICAN RY TM Laredo TX

852	1	GM	GP7	1500	1998
853	1	GM	GP9	1750	1998
854	1	GM	GP18	1800	1963-1998
868	1	GM	GP35	2500	1998
	4				

TEXAS NORTHEASTERN RR TNER Sherman TX

2166	1	GM	GP16	1850	1990
2219	1	GM	GP7	1500	1979
3802-3806 LLPX	2	GM	GP38-3	2000	1969
3860,3862-3863	3	GM	GP38	2000	1969
	7				

TEXAS NORTH ORIENT RY Sweetwater TX

203-204	2	GM	GP9	1750	1957

TEXAS NORTH WESTERN RY TXNW Sunray TX

88-89	2	GM	SW7	1200	1951

TEXAS OKLAHOMA & EASTERN RR TOE

D12-D14,D24	4	GM	GP40	3000	1967-1972
D15-D16,D20,D23					
D25	5	GM	GP40-2	3000	1967-1974
	9				

TEXAS ROCK CRUSHER RY Brownwood TX

305,307	2	GM	CF7	1500	

TEXAS SOUTH-EASTERN RR TSE Diboll TX

301	1	BALD	S8	800	1950
1007	1	BALD	VO1000	1000	1944
	2				

TEXAS STATE RR TSRR Rusk TX

1-TSE	1	GE	45-TON	350	1944
7-PC&N	1	ALCO	RS2	1500	1947
8-USN	1	ALCO	MRS3	1600	1953
22	1	GE	70-TON	600	1956
201-T&P	1	COOK	STEAM	4-6-0	1901
300-USA	1	BALD	STEAM	2-8-0	1917

TSRR Cont

400-T&G	1	BALD	STEAM	2-8-2	1917
500-ATSF	1	BALD	STEAM	4-6-2	1911
610-T&P	1	LIMA	STEAM	2-10-4	1927
	9				

TEXAS TRANSPORTATION MUSEUM TTM San Antonio TX

1-UGIC	1	BALD	STEAM	0-4-0T	1925
4-USAF	1	GE	45-TON	300	1942
6-MCSA	1	BALD	STEAM	2-8-0	1911
4035-USA	1	BLH	RS4TC	600	1954
7071-USAF	1	GE	44-TON	300	1942
	5				

THERMAL BELT RY Bostic NC

1	1	JRS	SW-CUMM	600	1976

TIMBERROCK RR DeRidder LA

2009	1	GM	GP20	2000	
7021	1	GM	GP7	1500	
	2				

TIOGA CENTRAL RR Wellsboro PA

14-BCRR	1	ALCO	S2	1000	1947
47,62-WTRR	2	ALCO	RS1	1000	1945-1950
240-NYS&W	1	ALCO	RS1	1000	1951
506-D&H	1	BL	RS3U	2000	1975
	5				

TIOGA SCENIC RY Owego NY

1811,1816	2	MLW	RS18	1800	1980

TOLEDO LAKE ERIE & WESTERN RY MUSEUM TLEW Waterville OH

1-AARR	1	WHIT	44-TON	360	1941
15-BEDT	1	PORT	STEAM	0-6-0	1908
112-USS	1	ALCO	S2	1000	1946
202-DE	1	BALD	STEAM	0-6-0	1920
5109-C&O,9752-NYC	2	ALCO	S4	1000	1948
	6				

TOLEDO PEORIA & WESTERN RY TPW East Peoria IL

1500	1	GM	F7A	1500	1952
1601-1602	2	GM	GP8	1600	1982
2001-2019	9	GM	GP20	2000	1977-1984
2050-2066	9	GM	GP20M	2300	1997-1998
	21				

TOMAHAWK RY MTW Tomahawk WI

80	1	GM	SW12	1200	1980
83,1587	2	GM	SW1500	1500	1970-1966
	3				

TOPPENISH SIMCOE & WESTERN RR TSWR Toppenish WA

12	1	GE	65-TON	470	1941
2070	1	ALCO	MRS1	1600	1953
	2				

TORONTO TRANSIT COMMISSION (4'-10 1/4) Toronto ON

RT7	1	P-A	50-TON	475	1997
RT12	1	NIPP	50-TON	192	1968
RT18	1	ANBL	50-TON	700	1977
	3				

TOWANDA-MONROETON SHIPPERS LIFELINE TMSS Monroeton PA

26	1	GM	SW1	600	1939

TRANSISCO RAIL

3 NREX	1	GM	SW900	900	

TRANSKENTUCKY TRANSPORTATION RR TTIS Paris KY

242-261	8	GE	U28B	2800	1966
361,5727,5735					
5758,5763,5788					
5791,5793,5797	9	GE	U36B	3600	1970-1972
	17				

TRANSPORTACION FERROVIARIA MEXICANA TFM Monterrey MEXICO

1020-1034	15	BL	SW1504	1500	1994
1035-1045	11	BL	MP15AC	1500	1994
1100-1149	50	GM	GP38-2	2000	1994
1200	1	GM	SD45	3600	1987
1300-1313	14	GM	SD40	3000	1987
1314-1321	8	GM	SDP40	3000	1987-1988
1322-1351	30	GM	SD40	3000	1987-1988
1401-1439	39	GM	SD40-2	3000	1986-1988
1600-1674	75	GM	SD70MAC	4000	1999
2100-2106	7	GE	B23-7	2250	1981
2200-2267	68	GE	C30-7	3000	1981-1989
2300-2322	23	GE	C30-SUPER7R	3000	1992
2323-2392	69	GE	C30-SUPER7N	3000	1990-1991
2393-2405	13	GE	C30-SUPER7MP	3000	1994
2600-2649	50	GE	AC4400CW	4400	1998
2650-2674	25	GE	AC4400CW	4400	1999
	498				

RENTALS

1150-1155 HELM	6	GM	GP38	2000	
1156 HELM	1	GM	GP38AC	2000	
1157-1160 HELM	4	GM	GP40	3000	
1500-1504 HELM	5	BL	SD40-3	3000	
1505-1515 HELM	11	GM	SD40-2	3000	
1516-1521 HELM	6	GM	SD40	3000	
1522-1526 HELM	5	GM	SD45-2M	3000	
	38				

TRAVEL TOWN RR MUSEUM EQUIPMENT Los Angeles CA

1-CONRK	1	ALCO	STEAM	0-6-0T	1925
1-ST&E	1	NORR	STEAM	4-4-0	1864
1-TT	1	GM	MODEL 40	300	1942
2-CPLT	1	LIMA	STEAM	3-TRUCK	1922
2-PL	1	HEIS	STEAM	3-TRUCK	1918
7-S&F	1	ALCO	STEAM	2-6-2	1902

TT Cont

20-SP	1	BALD	STEAM	0-4-0T	c1880
26-WP	1	ALCO	STEAM	2-8-0	1909
31-LA	1	DAV	STEAM	0-4-0T	1921
32-LA	1	ALCO	STEAM	0-4-0T	1914
56-CWR	1	BALD	RS12	1200	1955
664-ATSF	1	BALD	STEAM	2-8-0	1899
1000-SMV	1	ALCO	STEAM	2-8-2	1920
1273-SP	1	SP	STEAM	0-6-0	1921
1544-PE	1	NSRR	ELECTRIC	500	1902
3025-SP	1	ALCO	STEAM	4-4-2	1904
4439-UP	1	BALD	STEAM	0-6-0	1918
	17				

TRI-RAIL - TRI-COUNTY COMMUTER RAIL Ft Lauderdale FL

801-805	5	BL	F40PHL-2	3200	1995-1997
807-809	3	BL	F40PHC-2C	3000	1999
810-811	2	BL	F40PHR	3000	1998
	10				

TRONA RY TRC Trona CA

2000	1	GM	SW1200	1200	1965
2001	1	GM	SD9	1750	1976
3001-3006	6	ALST	SD40-2M	3000	1992
	8				

TUCSON CORNELIA & GILA BEND RR TCG Ajo AZ

52	1	GM	NW2	1000	1947
53	1	GM	SW7	1200	1951
	2				

TULSA-SAPULPA UNION RY TSU Sapulpa OK

101-103	3	GM	SW1	600	1940-1947
104	1	GM	SW9	1200	1952
107	1	GM	SW7	1200	1949
	5				

TURTLE CREEK INDUSTRIAL RR TCKR Export PA

462	1	GM	SW1	600	1949
550	1	GM	SW7	1200	1949
	2				

TURTLE CREEK VALLEY RY Lebanon OH

55	1	GM	GP7	1500	1953

TUSCOLA & SAGINAW BAY RY TSBY Owosso MI

385-394,2648	9	GM	GP35	2500	1964
1977	1	GM	NW2	1000	1977
2126	1	GE	25-TON	150	1955
	11				

TWEETSIE RR TRR (3'Gauge) Blowing Rock NC

12-ET&WNC	1	BALD	STEAM	4-6-0	1917
190-WP&Y	1	BALD	STEAM	2-8-2	1943
	2				

TWIN CITIES & WESTERN RR TCW Glencoe MN

201,302,9830		3 GM	SLUGS	0		
2001-2005,3515		6 GEN2	GEN2-CAT	2000		1982
		6	EXCEPT SLUGS			

TYBURN RR TYBR Penndel PA

390-USS		1 GE	45-TON	300		R1980
400-HSRR		1 GE	44-TON	380		1947
		2				

UNION COUNTY INDUSTRIAL RR UCIR Milton PA

1500		1 GM	SW8	800		1953

UNION PACIFIC RR CONSOLIDATED ROSTER BY HERITAGE + RENTALS
HERITAGE LINES UP,SP,SSW,D&RGW,C&NW,MP,MKT,WP,P&LE

5-8	UP	4 GM	FUEL TNDR	0		1996
9-31	MP	23 GM	SLUG	0		1978-1981
96	UP	1 GM	SW1000M	1200		1982
100-378	SP	274 GE	AC4400CW	4390	A	1995
100-129	MP	29 GE	B23-7	2250	B	1978
130-149	MP	19 GE	B23-7	2250	C	1979
150-166	MP	17 GE	B23-7	2250		1980
170-184	MP	15 GE	B23-7	2250		1981
200-229	MP	30 GE	B30-7A	3000		1981
230-254	MP	25 GE	B30-7A	3000		1982
257-259	MP	3 GE	B23-7M	3000		1980
262	SP	1 GE	B30-7	3000		1980
300	MKT	1 GM	SLUG	0		1982
301-303	UP	3 BL	SLUG	0		1991
313	SP	1 GE	SLUG	0		1981
318-319	SP	2 GE	SLUG	0		1982
396	SP	1 GE	B36-7B	3750		1984
400-414	UP	9 GE	C30-7	3000	D	1977
415-423	UP	5 GE	C30-7	3000	E	1978
437-447	UP	5 GE	C30-7	3000	F	1979
458-491	UP	12 GE	C30-7	3000	G	1980
495-531	UP	22 GE	C30-7	3000	H	1981
564-597	UP	25 BL	C36M	3600	I	1999
601-635	MP	21 GE	C36-7	3750	J	1985
638,648	UP	2 GM	GP40	3000		1965
639-647	MP	6 GE	C36-7	3750	K	1985
649,651	MP	2 GE	C36-7	3750		1985
652	UP	1 GM	GP40	3000		1965
653,659	MP	2 GE	C36-7	3750		1985
667-684	MKT	16 GM	GP40	3000	L	1968
689-698	UP	3 GM	GP40	3000	M	1965
744	UP	1 GM	GP40	3000		1971
844	UP	1 ALCO	STEAM	4-8-4		1944
901,913	UP	2 GM	GP50	3500		1980
906-914	WP	6 GM	GP40-2	3000	N	1980
949,951	UP	2 GM	E9A	2000		1983
954-957	UP	3 GM	GP40X	3500	O	1978

963-969	MP	4	GM	GP50	3500	P		1980
963	UP	1	VMV	E9B	2000			1993
970-988	MP	10	GM	GP50	3500	Q		1981
1000-1003	WP	4	GM	SW1500	1500			1974
1005-1031	WP	27	GM	SW1500L	1500			1974
1010-1013	SP	3	GM	SLUG	0	R		1979
1059	UP	1	GM	SW1500	1500			1968
1068-1979	SP	7	GM	SW1500	1500	S		1967
1085-1089	UP	5	GM	SW1500	1500			1968
1090-1100	SP	6	GM	SW1500	1500	T		1968
1102-1108	UP	5	GM	SW1500	1500	U		1969
1109-1135	SP	9	GM	SW1500	1500	V		1969
1137-1152	SP	6	GM	SW1500	1500			1970
1153	UP	1	GM	SW1500	1500			1970
1158-1179	UP	8	GM	SW1500	1500	W		1971
1181-1215	SP	18	GM	SW1500	1500	X		1972
1223-1229	SP	3	GM	SW1500	1500	Y		1973
1289-1290	UP	2	GM	MP15L	1500			1973
1296	SP	1	GM	MP15	1500			1975
1300-1309	PLE	10	GM	MP15	1500			1974
1302-1316	CNW	14	GM	MP15	1500	Z		1975
1310-1314	PLE	5	GM	MP15	1500			1975
1315-1317	WP	3	GM	SW1500	1500			1973
1324-1327	MKT	4	GM	SW1500L	1500			1968
1330-1334	MP	5	GM	MP15	1500			1974
1335-1344	MP	10	GM	MP15L	1500			1974
1345-1354	MP	10	GM	MP15	1500			1975
1356-1392	MP	37	GM	MP15	1500			1982
1393-1396	MKT	4	GM	MP15AC	1500			1980
1397-1428	MKT	32	GM	MP15AC	1500			1976
1429-1430	MKT	2	GM	MP15ACL	1500			1976
1432-1433	SP	2	GM	MP15AC	1500			1975
1488	MKT	1	GM	MP15AC	1500			1976
1534	SP	1	GM	SD7	1500			1953
1542-1544	MP	3	GM	GP15-1L	1500			1976
1545,1554	UP	2	GM	GP15-1	1500			1976
1555-1569	MP	15	GM	GP15-1L	1500			1976
1570-1589	MP	20	GM	GP15-1	1500			1976
1590-1614	MP	25	GM	GP15-1	1500			1977
1600-1609	SP	5	GE	SLUG	0	AA		1981
1612-1613	SP	2	GE	SLUG	0			1982
1615-1644	MP	30	GM	GP15-1	1500			1979
1645-1664	MP	20	GM	GP15-1	1500			1981
1665-1744	MP	80	GM	GP15-1	1500			1982
1783-1796	MKT	6	GM	GP38	2000	AB		1970
1800-1828	MKT	29	GM	GP38-2L	2000			1972
1830-1846	MP	17	GM	GP38-2L	2000			1973
1866	UP	1	GM	GP38-2L	2000			1979

1910-1970	UP	61	GM	GP38-2L	2000		1972
1971-1978	MP	4	GM	GP38-2L	2000	AC	1972
1980-1981	MKT	2	GM	GP38	2000		1969
1982,1984	UP	2	GM	GP38-2L	2000		1972
1983-1991	MKT	7	GM	GP38	2000	AD	1970
1992-1994	UP	3	GM	GP38-2L	2000		1972
1996	MP	1	GM	GP38-2L	2000		1972
1997-1999	MKT	3	GM	GP38	2000		1970
2000-2039	UP	39	GM	GP38-2	2000	AE	1974
2040-2059	UP	20	GM	GP38-2	2000		1975
2060-2063	MKT	4	GM	GP38-2	2000		1976
2064	SP	1	GM	GP38-2	1500		1980
2070	UP	1	GM	GP38-2L	2000		1979
2076,2078	MP	2	GM	GP38-2L	2000		1973
2083	SP	1	GM	GP38-2	2000		1980
2084-2110	MP	13	GM	GP38-2L	2000	AF	1973
2111-2120	MP	10	GM	GP38-2L	2000		1974
2121-2132	MP	12	GM	GP38-2	2000		1975
2133-2137	MP	5	GM	GP38-2	2000		1976
2138-2157	MP	20	GM	GP38-2	2000		1977
2158-2237	MP	79	GM	GP38-2	2000	AG	1980
2238-2289	MP	52	GM	GP38-2L	2000		1976
2290-2334	MP	45	GM	GP38-2	2000		1981
2335-2343	MKT	9	GM	GP38-2	2000		1973
2344	MKT	1	GM	GP38-2L	2000		1973
2345-2348	MKT	4	GM	GP38-2	2000		1974
2350-2358	MKT	9	GM	GP39-2	2300		1977
2359-2378	MKT	20	GM	GP39-2L	2300		1984
2381-2382	ALST	2	GM	GP38-2L	2000		1972
2383-2389	HELM	7	GM	GP38-2L	2000		1969
2390-2398	MP	9	GM	GP38-2L	2000		1972
2400-2417	MKT	18	GM	GP38-3L	2000		1983
2418-2419	HELM	2	GM	GP38-2L	2000		1970
2421-2422	UP	2	GE	C30-7	3000		1978
2425	MKT	1	GM	GP38-3L	2000		1983
2428-2429	UP	2	GE	C30-7	3000		1978
2430-2458	UP	11	GE	C30-7	3000	AH	1979
2451-2480	SP	12	GM	SW1500	1500	AI	1967
2474	UP	1	GE	C30-7B	3000		1980
2482	SSW	1	GM	SW1500	1500		1968
2496-2508	SP	6	GM	SW1500	1500	AJ	1968
2500-2526	MKT	27	GM	GP38-3L	2000		1983
2513-2519	SSW	4	GM	SW1500	1500	AK	1969
2524-2552	SP	17	GM	SW1500	1500	AL	1969
2527-2550	HELM	24	BL	GP38-2L	2000		1998
2551	MKT	1	GM	GP38-3L	2000		1983
2552-2561	HELM	10	BL	GP38-2L	2000		1998
2553-2571	SP	9	GM	SW1500	1500	AM	1970
2562	MKT	1	GM	GP38-3L	2000		1983

2563-2570 MKT	7 GM	GP38-2L	2000	AN	1969
2572-2580 HELM	9 GM	GP38-2L	2000		1966
2580-2581 SSW	2 GM	SW1500	1500		1970
2581-2588 HELM	8 GM	GP38-2L	2000		1968
2583-2589 SSW	4 GM	SW1500	1500	AO	1971
2588-2612 SP	11 GM	SW1500	1500	AP	1971
2609-2659 MP	15 GE	C36-7	3750	AQ	1985
2613-2679 SP	26 GM	SW1500	1500		1972
2680-2688 SP	6 GM	SW1500	1500	AR	1973
2690-2696 SP	6 GM	MP15	1500	AS	1974
2699-2701 SP	3 GM	MP15	1500		1975
2702-2759 SP	54 GM	MP15AC	1500	AT	1975
2729-2750 MKT	22 GM	GP39-2L	2300		1983
2800-2805 UP	6 GM	SD38-2	2000		1972
2806-2814 UP	7 GM	SD38-2	2000	AU	1975
2816,2819 MP	2 GM	SD38-2	2000		1978
2817-2818 MP	2 GM	SD38-2	2000		1979
2820,2823 MP	2 GM	SD38-2	2000		1974
2821-2822 MP	2 GM	SD38-2	2000		1978
2824 UP	1 GM	SD38-2	2000		1975
2825-2829 MP	5 GM	SD38-2	2000		1998
2830,2832 SP	2 GM	SD38-2	2000		1973
2836-2842 MP	7 GM	SD38-2	2000		1978
2843,2845 MP	2 GM	SD38-2	2000		1979
2950-2966 UP	14 GM	SD40-2	3000	AV	1973
2967-2999 UP	30 GM	SD40-2	3000	AW	1974
2972-2976 SP	4 GM	SD38-2	2000	AX	1973
3000-3001 MKT	2 GM	GP40	3000		1969
3002-3006 WP	5 GM	GP40-2	3000		1979
3007 WP	1 GM	GP40-2	3000		1980
3016-3055 UP	32 GM	SD40-2	3000	AY	1974
3054-3067 DRGW	4 GM	GP40	3000	AZ	1966
3056-3087 UP	29 GM	SD40-2	3000	BA	1975
3071-3080 DRGW	4 GM	GP40	3000	BB	1967
3082-3085 DRGW	3 GM	GP40	3000	BC	1969
3086 SP	1 GM	GP40	3000		1971
3087-3091 DRGW	3 GM	GP40	3000	BD	1971
3089-3096 UP	6 GM	SD40-2	3000	BE	1976
3094-3114 DRGW	15 GM	GP40-2	3000	BF	1972
3100,3102 UP	2 GM	SD40-2R	3000		1976
3101 UP	1 GM	SD40-2R	3000		1977
3116-3128 DRGW	10 GM	GP40-2	3000	BG	1974
3123-3202 UP	78 GM	SD40-2R	3000	BH	1972
3129-3130 DRGW	2 GM	GP40-2	3000		1983
3131-3151 DRGW	10 GM	GP40	3000	BI	1968
3154-3155 DRGW	2 GM	GP60	3800		1990
3203-3242 UP	40 GM	SD40-2R	3000		1973
3243-3287 UP	44 GM	SD40-2R	3000	BJ	1974
3288-3304 UP	17 GM	SD40-2R	3000		1975
3305-3307 UP	3 GM	SD40-2R	3000		1976

UP Cont

3308,3318 UP	2	GM	SD40-2	3000		1976
3310-3331 UP	19	GM	SD40-2R	3000	BK	1976
3332-3333 UP	2	GM	SD40-2	3000		1976
3334 UP	1	GM	SD40-2R	3000		1976
3335,3344 UP	2	GM	SD40-2	3000		1977
3337-3346 UP	8	GM	SD40-2R	3000	BL	1977
3347-3348 UP	2	GM	SD40-2	3000		1977
3349,3351 UP	2	GM	SD40-2R	3000		1977
3350,3352 UP	2	GM	SD40-2	3000		1977
3353,3355 UP	2	GM	SD40-2R	3000		1977
3356-3357 UP	2	GM	SD40-2	3000		1977
3358-3359 UP	2	GM	SD40-2R	3000		1977
3360-3361 UP	2	GM	SD40-2	3000		1977
3362,3364 UP	2	GM	SD40-2R	3000		1977
3363,3365 UP	2	GM	SD40-2	3000		1977
3366-3372 UP	7	GM	SD40-2R	3000		1977
3373 UP	1	GM	SD40-2	3000		1977
3374-3377 UP	4	GM	SD40-2R	3000		1977
3378-3379 UP	2	GM	SD40-2	3000		1977
3380 UP	1	GM	SD40-2R	3000		1977
3381 UP	1	GM	SD40-2	3000		1977
3382-3385 UP	4	GM	SD40-2R	3000		1977
3386-3389 UP	3	GM	SD40-2	3000	BM	1977
3390-3391 UP	2	GM	SD40-2R	3000		1977
3392 UP	1	GM	SD40-2	3000		1977
3393-3396 UP	4	GM	SD40-2R	3000		1977
3397-3398 UP	2	GM	SD40-2	3000		1977
3399,3401 UP	2	GM	SD40-2R	3000		1977
3400-3403 UP	3	GM	SD40-2	3000	BN	1977
3404,3409 UP	2	GM	SD40-2T	3000		1977
3405,3408 UP	2	GM	SD40-2	3000		1977
3406-3407 UP	2	GM	SD40-2R	3000		1977
3410-3412 UP	3	GM	SD40-2	3000		1978
3413,3416 UP	2	GM	SD40-2R	3000		1978
3414-3420 UP	4	GM	SD40-2	3000	BO	1978
3418-3419 UP	2	GM	SD40-2R	3000		1978
3420,3461 UP	2	GM	SD40-2B	3000		1978
3421-3422 UP	2	GM	SD40-2R	3000		1978
3423-3424 UP	2	GM	SD40-2	3000		1978
3425-3427 UP	3	GM	SD40-2R	3000		1978
3428-3429 UP	2	GM	SD40-2	3000		1978
3430,3432 UP	2	GM	SD40-2R	3000		1978
3433-3443 UP	11	GM	SD40-2	3000		1978
3444,3449 UP	2	GM	SD40-2R	3000		1978
3445-3454 UP	6	GM	SD40-2	3000	BP	1978
3451-3453 UP	7	GM	SD40-2R	3000	BQ	1978
3460-3462 UP	3	GM	SD40-2	3000		1978
3463-3465 UP	3	GM	SD40-2R	3000		1978
3466-3470 UP	5	GM	SD40-2	3000		1978
3471,3473 UP	2	GM	SD40-2R	3000		1978

3472,3474 UP	2	GM	SD40-2	3000		1978
3475,3477 UP	2	GM	SD40-2R	3000		1978
3476,3478 UP	2	GM	SD40-2	3000		1978
3479,3484 UP	2	GM	SD40-2R	3000		1978
3480-3488 UP	6	GM	SD40-2	3000	BR	1978
3489-3493 UP	5	GM	SD40-2R	3000		1979
3494 UP	1	GM	SD40-2	3000		1979
3496-3508 UP	12	GM	SD40-2	3000	BS	1979
3509-3516 UP	8	GM	SD40-2R	3000		1979
3517-3518 UP	2	GM	SD40-2	3000		1979
3519,3521 UP	2	GM	SD40-2R	3000		1979
3520-3522 UP	3	GM	SD40-2	3000		1979
3524,3536 UP	2	GM	SD40-2R	3000		1979
3525-3529 UP	5	GM	SD40-2	3000		1979
3530-3532 UP	3	GM	SD40-2R	3000		1979
3533,3535 UP	2	GM	SD40-2	3000	BT	1979
3534-3556 UP	3	GM	SD40-2B	3000	BU	1979
3537-3538 UP	2	GM	SD40-2R	3000		1979
3539-3540 UP	2	GM	SD40-2	3000		1979
3541-3542 UP	2	GM	SD40-2R	3000		1979
3543-3552 UP	9	GM	SD40-2	3000		1979
3553,3557 UP	2	GM	SD40-2R	3000		1979
3554-3564 UP	4	GM	SD40-2	3000	BV	1979
3559,3563 UP	2	GM	SD40-2R	3000		1979
3560-3562 UP	3	GM	SD40-2	3000		1979
3565,3568 UP	2	GM	SD40-2R	3000		1979
3566-3570 UP	4	GM	SD40-2	3000	BW	1979
3571-3572 UP	2	GM	SD40-2R	3000		1979
3573-3578 UP	6	GM	SD40-2	3000		1979
3579,3586 UP	2	GM	SD40-2R	3000		1979
3580-3582 UP	3	GM	SD40-2	3000		1979
3583-3584 UP	2	GM	SD40-2R	3000		1979
3585-3593 UP	7	GM	SD40-2	3000	BX	1979
3592,3594 UP	2	GM	SD40-2R	3000		1979
3595-3597 UP	3	GM	SD40-2	3000		1979
3596-3598 UP	2	GM	SD40-2R	3000		1979
3599 UP	1	GM	SD40-2	3000		1979
3600-3602 UP	3	GM	SD40-2R	3000		1979
3603-3608 UP	9	GM	SD40-2	3000		1979
3609-3611 UP	3	GM	SD40-2	3000		1980
3612,3615 UP	2	GM	SD40-2R	3000		1980
3613-3618 UP	3	GM	SD40-2	3000	BY	1980
3619-3620 UP	2	GM	SD40-2R	3000		1980
3621-3626 UP	6	GM	SD40-2	3000		1980
3627,3632 UP	2	GM	SD40-2R	3000		1980
3628-3639 UP	9	GM	SD40-2	3000	BZ	1980
3638,3647 UP	2	GM	SD40-2R	3000		1980
3640 UP	1	GM	SD40-2B	3000		1980
3641-3642 UP	2	GM	SD40-2R	3000		1980
3643-3651 UP	8	GM	SD40-2	3000	CA	1980

3652,3658 UP	2	GM	SD40-2R	3000		1980
3653-3660 UP	7	GM	SD40-2	3000	CB	1980
3661-3662 UP	2	GM	SD40-2R	3000		1980
3663-3665 UP	3	GM	SD40-2	3000		1980
3666-3667 UP	2	GM	SD40-2R	3000		1980
3668-3670 UP	3	GM	SD40-2	3000		1980
3671,3673 UP	2	GM	SD40-2R	3000		1980
3672-3676 UP	4	GM	SD40-2	3000	CC	1980
3677,3680 UP	2	GM	SD40-2R	3000		1980
3678-3681 UP	3	GM	SD40-2	3000	CD	1980
3682-3683 UP	2	GM	SD40-2R	3000		1980
3684-3686 UP	3	GM	SD40-2	3000		1980
3687,3691 UP	2	GM	SD40-2R	3000		1980
3688-3695 UP	7	GM	SD40-2	3000	CE	1980
3696 UP	1	GM	SD40-2R	3000		1980
3697-3706 UP	10	GM	SD40-2	3000		1980
3707-3708 UP	2	GM	SD40-2R	3000		1980
3709-3715 UP	7	GM	SD40-2	3000		1980
3716-3717 UP	2	GM	SD40-2R	3000		1980
3718-3722 UP	5	GM	SD40-2	3000		1980
3723,3725 UP	2	GM	SD40-2R	3000		1980
3724,3732 UP	7	GM	SD40-2	3000	CF	1980
3731,3733 UP	2	GM	SD40-2R	3000		1980
3734-3735 UP	2	GM	SD40-2	3000		1980
3736-3737 UP	2	GM	SD40-2R	3000		1980
3739-3740 UP	2	GM	SD40-2	3000		1980
3741,3744 UP	2	GM	SD40-2R	3000		1980
3742-3743 UP	2	GM	SD40-2	3000		1980
3745,3751 UP	2	GM	SD40-2	3000		1980
3746,3750 UP	2	GM	SD40-2R	3000		1980
3747-3749 UP	3	GM	SD40-2	3000		1980
3752,3755 UP	2	GM	SD40-2R	3000		1980
3753-3757 UP	4	GM	SD40-2	3000	CG	1980
3758-3759 UP	2	GM	SD40-2R	3000		1980
3760-3768 UP	7	GM	SD40-2	3000	CH	1980
3761-3762 UP	2	GM	SD40-2R	3000		1980
3769-3773 UP	5	GM	SD40-2	3000		1981
3774 UP	1	GM	SD40-2R	3000		1981
3775-3782 UP	8	GM	SD40-2	3000		1981
3783 UP	1	GM	SD40-2B	3000		1981
3784,3791 UP	2	GM	SD40-2R	3000		1981
3785-3786 UP	2	GM	SD40-2	3000		1981
3787-3789 UP	3	GM	SD40-2R	3000		1981
3790 UP	1	GM	SD40-2	3000		1981
3792-3795 UP	4	GM	SD40-2	3000		1981
3796,3799 UP	2	GM	SD40-2R	3000		1981
3798-3805 UP	7	GM	SD40-2	3000	CI	1981
3806 UP	1	GM	SD40-2R	3000		1981
3807-3808 UP	2	GM	SD40-2	3000		1981
3809-3819 MKT	11	GM	SD40-2	3000		1978

3820-3826	MKT	7	GM	SD40-2	3000		1979
3827-3835	MKT	9	GM	SD40-2	3000		1980
3836-3843	MKT	7	GM	SD40-2	3000		1981
3905-3919	MP	15	GM	SD40-2	3000		1976
3920-3953	MP	34	GM	SD40-2	3000		1979
3954-3973	MP	20	GM	SD40-2	3000		1980
3985	UP	1	ALCO	STEAM	4-6-6-4		1944
4000-4274	UP	275	GM	SD70M	4000		2000
4001,4004	UP	2	GM	SD40T-2	3000		1974
4018-4019	UP	2	GM	SD40T-2	3000		1978
4035	UP	1	GM	SD40T-2	3000		1974
4046-4056	UP	5	GM	SD40T-2	3000	CJ	1975
4059-4066	UP	4	GM	SD40T-2	3000	CK	1977
4115,4119	MP	2	GM	SD40-2	3000		1973
4116-4118	MP	3	GM	SD40-2B	3000		1973
4120,4190	CNW	2	GM	GP7	1500		1952
4121-4163	MP	13	GM	SD40-2B	3000	CL	1974
4123-4161	MP	25	GM	SD40-2	3000	CM	1974
4202-4215	MP	12	GM	SD40-2	3000	CN	1975
4207	MP	1	GM	SD40-2B	3000		1975
4216-4265	MP	27	GM	SD40-2B	3000	CO	1978
4220-4264	MP	13	GM	SD40-2	3000	CP	1978
4266-4311	MP	13	GM	SD40-2	3000		1979
4267-4311	MP	25	GM	SD40-2B	3000	CQ	1979
4275-4499	UP	225	GM	SD70M	4000		2001
4307,4324	CNW	2	GM	GP7	1500		1957-1955
4312-4320	MP	5	GM	SD40-2	3000		1980
4313-4321	MP	5	GM	SD40-2B	3000	CR	1980
4369-4371	SP	3	GM	SD40T-2	3000		1974
4379,4383	SP	2	GM	SD40T-2	3000		1978
4389,4397	SP	2	GM	SD40T-2	3000		1979,1974
4400-4409	CNW	8	GM	GP15-1	1500	CS	1976
4403-4455	SP	13	GM	SD40T-2	3000	CT	1978
4462-4502	SP	16	GM	SD40T-2	3000	CU	1979
4500-4749	UP	250	GM	SD70M	4000		2002
4522-4559	SP	10	GM	SD40T-2	3000	CV	1980
4560	SP	1	GM	SD40T-2	3000		1974
4570,4572	SP	2	GM	SD40T-2	3000		1979
4586-4596	SP	6	GM	SD40T-2	3000	CW	1980
4600-4634	CNW	34	GM	GP38-2L	2000	CX	1979
4634,4703	SP	2	GM	SD40-2	3000		1969
4702-4703	CNW	2	GM	GP38-2L	2000		1979
4704	CNW	1	GM	GP38-2L	2000		1970
4705-4709	CNW	5	GM	GP38-2L	2000		1967
4710-4711	CNW	2	GM	GP38-2L	2000		1974-1973
4733-4763	UP	31	VMV	SD40-2	3000		1999
4750-4999	UP	250	GM	SD70M	4000		2003
4794-4831	SP	37	GM	SD40T-2	3000	CY	1973
4801-4844	SP	42	GM	GP38-2	2000	CZ	1980
4846-4873	SP	18	GM	GP38-2	2000	DA	1972

4890,4912	SP	2	GM	SD45T-2	3200		1973,1975
4923	UP	1	GM	SD40T-2	3000		1975
4945	SP	1	GM	SD40T-2	3000		1972
4965,4972	UP	2	GM	SD45T-2	3200		1975
5000,5004	MP	2	GM	SD50	3600		1984
5001,5005	MP	2	GM	SD50M	3500		1984
5006,5008	MP	2	GM	SD50	3600		1984
5007,5013	MP	4	GM	SD50M	3500	DB	1984
5014	MP	1	GM	SD50	3600		1984
5015-5017	MP	3	GM	SD50M	3500		1984
5018-5025	MP	8	GM	SD50	3600		1984
5026	MP	1	GM	SD50M	3500		1984
5028-5030	MP	3	GM	SD50	3600		1984
5031-5033	MP	3	GM	SD50M	3500		1984
5034,5036	MP	2	GM	SD50	3600		1984
5035-5040	MP	5	GM	SD50M	3500	DC	1984
5041,5043	MP	2	GM	SD50	3600		1984
5042,5044	MP	2	GM	SD50M	3500		1984
5045,5047	MP	2	GM	SD50	3600		1984
5046-5052	MP	6	GM	SD50M	3500	DD	1984
5053	MP	1	GM	SD50	3600		1984
5054-5057	MP	4	GM	SD50M	3500		1984
5058-5059	MP	2	GM	SD50	3600		1984
5060-5092	UP	31	GM	SD50M	3500	DE	1985
5093	UP	1	GM	SD50	3600		1985
5094	UP	1	GM	SD50M	3500		1985
5104-5110	UP	3	GM	SD50M	3500		1984
5100-5114	SP	15	GE	B23-7	2250		1980
5217,5236	SP	2	GM	GP40-2	3000		1984
5245,5247	UP	2	GM	GP40-2	3000		1974
5254-5265	UP	4	GM	GP40-2	3000		1972
5283	UP	1	GM	GP40-2	3000		1978
5309-5310	UP	2	GM	GP40-2	3000		1979
5318	WP	1	GM	GP40-2	3000		1980
5324,5338	SP	2	GM	GP40-2	3000		1980
5342-5355	DRGW	9	GM	SD40T-2	3000		1974
5347	UP	1	GM	GP40-2	3000		1972
5353,5371	SP	2	GM	GP40-2	3000		1980.1969
5350,5352	SP	2	GM	SD40T-2	3000		1974
5356-5373	DRGW	11	GM	SD40T-2	3000	DF	1975
5368	WP	1	GM	GP40-2	3000		1975,1977
5375-5385	DRGW	6	GM	SD40T-2	3000	DG	1977
5386-5392	DRGW	56	GM	SD40T-2	3000	DH	1978
5387-5397	SP	5	GM	SD40T-2	3000	DI	1978
5398-5413	DRGW	12	GM	SD40T-2	3000	DJ	1980
5399,5412	SP	2	GM	SD40T-2	3000		1980
5504-5505	UP	2	GM	GP40X	3500		1978
5500-5522	CNW	15	GM	GP40	3000	DK	1965
5501-5509	DRGW	8	GM	SD50M	3500	DL	1984
5504-5517	SP	5	GM	SD50M	3500	DM	1984

5510-5557	UP	45	GM	GP50	3500	DN	1980
5515	DRGW	1	GM	SD50M	3500		1984
5525-5537	CNW	10	GM	GP40	3000	DO	1966
5558-5566	MP	5	GM	GP50	3500	DP	1980
5571-5587	MP	10	GM	GP50	3500	DQ	1981
5609-5648	SP	23	GE	DASH8-40B	3900	DR	1987
5649-5680	UP	23	GE	DASH8-40B	4000	DS	1988
5682-5699	UP	12	GE	DASH8-40B	4000	DT	1989
5702	UP	1	GM	GP60	3800		1990
5703-5735	SP	18	GM	GP60	3800	DU	1988
5739,5757	UP	2	GM	GP60	3800		1989
5778,5811	UP	2	GM	GP60	3800		1990
5816-5867	SP	21	GM	GP60	3800	DV	1991
5869-5880	SP	8	GM	GP60	3800	DW	1993
5884-5891	SP	3	GM	GP60	3800	DX	1994
5945-5999	UP	51	GM	GP60	3800	DY	1986
6000-6059	UP	59	GM	SD60	3800	DZ	1986
6060-6084	UP	25	GM	SD60	3800		1987
6085-6109	UP	25	GM	SD60M	3800		1988
6110-6215	UP	105	GM	SD60M	3800	EA	1989
6216-6268	UP	52	GM	SD60M	3800	EF	1990
6269-6315	UP	47	GM	SD60M	3800		1991
6316-6365	UP	50	GM	SD60M	3800		1992
6500,6534	SP	2	GE	AC4400CW	4390		1995
6550-6699	UP	150	GE	AC4400CW	4390		1997
6656-6659	CNW	3	GM	SD38-2	2000	EG	1975
6701-6736	UP	3	GE	AC4400CW	4380	EH	1994
6738-6837	UP	100	GE	AC4400CW	4390		1996
6793-6828	SP	21	GM	SD45T-2	3200	EI	1972
6811	CNW	1	GM	SD40-2	3000		1973
6819-6890	CNW	14	GM	SD40-2	3000	EJ	1974
6838-6887	UP	50	GE	AC4400CW	4390		1995
6869-6882	SSW	9	GM	SD45T-2	3200		1975
6885	SSW	1	GM	SD45T-2	3200		1973
6886	SSW	1	GM	SD45T-2	3600		1975
6888-6892	SSW	3	GM	SD45T-2	3200	EK	1972
6898-6925	CNW	5	GM	SD40-2	3000		1975
6895	SP	1	GE	AC4400CW	4390		1995
6930-6935	CNW	4	GM	SD40-2	3000	EL	1976
6936	UP	1	GM	DDA40X	6600		1971
7000-7001	UP	2	GE	AC6000CW	6000		1996
7002	UP	1	GE	AC4400CW	4390		1997
7003	UP	1	GE	AC4400CW	6000		1996
7004-7009	UP	6	GE	AC4400CW	4390		1997
7005-7022	CNW	3	GM	SD50	3600	EM	1985
7010-7012	UP	3	GE	AC44/60CW	4390		1996
7013-7047	UP	35	GE	AC44/60CW	4390		1995
7048-7079	UP	32	GE	AC44/60CW	4390		1996
7080-7100	UP	21	GE	AC4400CW	4390		1997
7100-7119	SP	19	GM	GP40-2	3000	EN	1969

7101-7137	UP	37	GE	AC4400CW	4390		1998
7120-7138	SP	19	GM	GP40-2	3000		1969
7138-7297	UP	160	GE	AC4400CW	4390		1999
7231	SP	1	GM	GP40X	3500		1978
7240-7264	SP	9	GM	GP40-2	3000	EO	1984
7248-7273	SSW	21	GM	GP40-2	3000	EP	1984
7274-7275	SSW	2	GM	GP40-2	3000		1966
7276-7277	SSW	2	GM	GP40-2	3000		1968,1970
7278-7280	SSW	3	GM	GP40-2	3000		1971
7281-7282	SSW	2	GM	GP40-2	3000		1969,1966
7283-7287	SSW	5	GM	GP40-2	3000		1971,1966
7288-7289	SSW	2	GM	GP40-2	3000		1970,1966
7290-7291	SSW	2	GM	GP40-2	3000		1970,1967
7292-7293	SSW	2	GM	GP40-2	3000		1971
7294-7299	SP	6	GM	GP40-2	3000		1969
7300-7385	SP	65	GM	SD40-2	3000	EQ	1966
7300-7335	UP	36	GE	AC44/60CW	4390		1998
7336-7435	UP	100	GE	AC44/60CW	4390		2000
7401-7415	SP	7	GM	SD45-2	3200	ER	1966
7417-7464	SP	22	GM	SD45-2	3200		1967
7465-7536	SP	32	GM	SD45-2	3200	ES	1968
7500-7509	UP	8	GE	AC6000CW	6000	ET	1996
7510-7554	UP	45	GE	AC6000CW	6000		1998
7555-7604	UP	50	GE	AC6000CW	6000		2000
7600-7602	SP	3	GM	GP40-2	3000		1974
7608-7626	SP	17	GM	GP40-2	3000	EU	1978
7628-7655	SSW	23	GM	GP40-2	3000	EV	1979
7644,7653	SP	2	GM	GP40-2	3000		1979
7658-7677	SP	19	GM	GP40-2	3000	EW	1980
7754-7764	SP	7	GE	B36-7B	3750	EX	1984
7774-7799	SP	23	GE	B30-7	3000	EY	1980
7786,7797	SSW	2	GE	B30-7	3000		1980
7801-7802	SP	2	GE	B30-7	3000		1977
7803	SP	1	GE	B30-7B	3000		1977
7804,7807	SP	2	GE	B30-7	3000		1978
7805,7806	SP	2	GE	B30-7B	3000		1978
7808,7812	SP	2	GE	B30-7B	3000		1978
7811	SP	1	GE	B30-7	3000		1978
7813-7815	SP	3	GE	B30-7	3000		1978
7816	SP	1	GE	B30-7B	3000		1978
7817-7818	SP	2	GE	B30-7	3000		1978
7819-7820	SP	2	GE	B30-7B	3000		1978
7822-7823	SP	2	GE	B30-7	3000		1978
7824-7827	SP	4	GE	B30-7	3000		1979
7828-7831	SP	4	GE	B30-7B	3000		1979
7832-7834	SP	3	GE	B30-7	3000		1979
7835,7837	SP	2	GE	B30-7B	3000		1979
7836,7838	SP	2	GE	B30-7	3000		1979
7841-7844	SP	3	GE	B30-7B	3000	EZ	1979
7842-7855	SP	10	GE	B30-7	3000	FA	1979

7856-7858	SP	3	GE	B30-7B	3000		1979
7859-7867	SP	9	GE	B30-7	3000		1979
7869-7870	SP	2	GE	B30-7B	3000		1979
7871-7873	SP	3	GE	B30-7	3000		1979
7874-7880	SP	3	GE	B30-7B	3000	FB	1979
7882-7883	SP	2	GE	B30-7	3000		1979
7940-7959	SP	17	GE	GP40-2	3000	FC	1980
7960-7966	SSW	4	GM	GP40-2	3000	FD	1966
7963-7965	SP	3	GE	GP40-2	3000		1966
8000-8024	UP	25	GM	SD90/43MAC	4300		1995
8002-8039	SP	19	GE	DASH8-40B	3900	FE	1987
8002-8052	CNW	5	GM	SD60	3800	FF	1984
8025-8074	UP	50	GM	SD90/43MAC	4300		1996
8041-8074	SSW	10	GE	DASH8-40B	4000	FG	1989
8075-8178	UP	104	GM	SD90/43MAC	4300		1997
8077-8090	SSW	5	GE	DASH8-40B	4000	FH	1989
8179-8308	UP	130	GM	SD90/43MAC	4300		1998
8101-8200	SP	96	GE	DASH9-4400CW	4380	FI	1994
8230-8299	SP	51	GM	SD40T-2	3000	FJ	1980
8300,8306	SP	2	GM	SD40T-2	3000		1974
8327	SP	1	GM	SD40T-2	3000		1979
8307-8328	SP	15	GM	SD40T-2	3000	FK	1978
8324-8374	SSW	5	GM	SD40T-2	3000	FL	1978
8329-8341	SP	6	GM	SD40T-2	3000	FM	1979
8350-8356	SP	6	GM	SD40T-2	3000	FN	1974
8357-8370	SP	11	GM	SD40T-2	3000	FO	1978
8377-8391	SP	9	GM	SD40T-2	3000	FP	1979
8489-8533	SP	37	GM	SD40T-2	3000		1978
8501-8521	UP	21	GM	SD90MAC	6000		1998
8501-8530	CNW	24	GE	DASH8-40C	4000	FQ	1989
8522-8561	UP	40	GM	SD90MAC	6000		1999-2000
8534-8573	SP	32	GM	SD40T-2	3000		1979
8543-8577	CNW	17	GE	DASH8-41C	4135	FR	1991
8574-8706	SP	129	GM	SD40-2	3000	FS	1969
8601-8635	CNW	21	GE	DASH9-44CW	4380	FT	1993
8636-8730	CNW	86	GE	DASH9-44CW	4380	FU	1994
8801-8835	CNW	33	GE	AC4400CW	4380	FV	1994
9000-9029	MP	10	GE	C36-7	3750	FW	1985
9031,9033	UP	2	GE	DASH8-40C	4000		1989
9036	MP	1	GE	C36-7	3750		1985
9040,9044	UP	2	GE	DASH8-40C	4000		1989
9048-9049	MP	2	GE	C36-7	3750		1985
9050-9051	UP	2	GE	DASH8-40C	4000		1989
9053-9064	UP	12	GE	DASH8-40C	4000		1990
9065-9099	UP	18	GE	DASH8-41C	4135	FX	1991
9100-9174	UP	73	GE	DASH8-40C	4000	FY	1987
9175-9249	UP	74	GE	DASH8-40C	4000	FZ	1988
9195	SP	1	GM	SD45T-2B	3600		1972
9197,9201	SP	2	GM	SD45T-2	3200		1972
9207	SP	1	GM	SD45T-2B	3200		1972

UP Cont

Number	Owner	Qty	Builder	Model	HP	Notes	Year
9226-9259	SP	8	GM	SD45T-2	3200	HA	1972
9250-9355	UP	105	GE	DASH8-40C	4000	HB	1989
9259	SP	1	GM	SD45T-2	3200		1972
9262	SSW	1	GM	SD45T-2	3200		1973
9263-9270	SSW	3	GM	SD45T-2B	3200	HC	1973
9276	SSW	3	GM	SD45T-2	3200		1973
9288-9313	SP	5	GM	SD45T-2	3200	HD	1973
9291-9299	SSW	4	GM	SD45T-2	3200	HE	1973
9315,9325	SP	2	GM	SD45T-2B	3200		1974
9318	SP	1	GM	SD45T-2	3200		1974
9327	SP	1	GM	SD45T-2B	3200		1974
9329-9337	SP	3	GM	SD45T-2	3200		1974
9342-9343	SP	2	GM	SD45T-2	3200		1974
9344,9346	SP	2	GM	SD45T-2	3200		1975
9349	SP	1	GM	SD45T-2	3400		1975
9358-9365	SP	3	GM	SD45T-2	3200		1975
9356-9395	UP	40	GE	DASH8-40CW	4000		1990
9366	SP	1	GM	SD45T-2B	3200		1975
9368-9388	SP	3	GM	SD45T-2	3200		1975
9371-9404	SSW	11	GM	SD45T-2	3200	HF	1975
9396-9405	UP	10	GE	DASH8-41CW	4135		1990
9406-9455	UP	50	GE	DASH8-41CW	4135		1991
9456-9480	UP	25	GE	DASH8-41CW	4135		1992
9481-9559	UP	79	GE	DASH8-41CW	4135		1993
9564-9581	SP	3	GE	DASH9-44CW	4380	HG	1994
9596	UP	1	GE	DASH9-44CW	4380		1993
9632,9634	SP	2	GE	DASH9-44CW	4380		1994
9605-9617	SP	6	GM	GP60	3800		1988
9622-9634	SSW	9	GM	GP60	3800		1988
9635-9672	SSW	36	GM	GP60	3800		1989
9659,9668	UP	2	GE	DASH9-44CW	4380		1994
9670-9697	UP	12	GE	DASH9-44CW	4380	HH	1993
9673-9714	SSW	38	GM	GP60	3800		1990
9700-9739	UP	39	GE	DASH9-44CW	4380		1994
9715-9769	SP	32	GM	GP60	3800		1991
9760-9831	UP	8	GE	DASH9-44CW	4380		1994
9771-9784	SP	7	GM	GP60	3800		1993
9786-9794	SP	7	GM	GP60	3800		1994
9800-9824	SP	25	GM	SD70M	4000		1994
9997,9999		2	GE	AC4400CW	4380		1994
		8,139					

EXCLUDED SLUGS/TENDERS INCLUDES 1000 NEW SD70M UNITS FOR DELIVERY 2000-2003

RENTALS DURING YEAR

Number	Owner	Qty	Builder	Model	HP	Year
60-64	HBT	5	GM	MP15	1500	
GM90-GM91	LLPX	2	GM	SD90MAC	6000	1997-1998
151-154	GATX	4	GM	SW1500	1500	
155-158	LLPX	4	GM	MP15DC	1500	
505	HATX	1	GM	GP40-2	3000	
529-562	HLGX	18	GE	C30-7	3000	
580-594	GECX	12	GE	C30-7	3000	

UP RENTALS Cont

700-714	LMS	15	GE	DASH8-40CW	4000
750-751	HATX	2	GM	SD40-2/3	3000
3875-3878	HLCX	4	GM	GP38-3	2000
3593	HLCX	1	GM	GP39-2	2300
5057	HLCX	1	GM	SD40-3	3000
6072-6502	HLCX	8	GM	SD40-2/3	3000
6202-6401	HLCX	21	GM	SD40-2/3	3000
6061-6504	HLCX	14	GM	SD40-3	3000
7000-7024	EMDX	25	GM	SD70	4000
7349-7378	GSCX	15	GM	SD40-2	3000
7359-7373	GSCX	20	GM	SD40-2	3000
9001-9020	MKCX	17	GM	SD40-2	3000
9020-9042	MPI	14	GM	SD40-2	3000
9030-9047	MKCX	11	GM	SD40-2	3000
		214			

NOTES

A	EXCEPT	145,221,224,256,279 B EXCEPT 128 C EXCEPT 136
D	EXCEPT	401,403-404,406,412-413 E EXCEPT 416,419,421-422
F	ACTUAL	437-438,444-445,447
G	ACTUAL	458,462,464,468,470,472,474,476-477,480,490-491
H	EXCEPT	497,500,502-503,505-507,513,516,519 -520,526,528-530
I	EXCEPT	579,582-583,587,590-593,595
J	EXCEPT	602,604-605,609,611-612,614-615,620-621,626,629,631-632
K	ACTUAL	629,633-634,645-647 L EXCEPT 668,673
M	ACTUAL	689,691,698 N EXCEPT 909,913 O EXCEPT 956
P	EXCEPT	966-968 Q EXCEPT 973,975-976,979-981,983,985-986
R	EXCEPT	1011 S EXCEPT 1070,1073,1075-1076,1078
T	EXCEPT	1092,1094,1096-1098 U EXCEPT 1103-1104
V	ACTUAL	1109,1112,1114,1117-1118,1128,1132-1133,1135
W	ACTUAL	1158,1162-1163,1165-1166,1174-1175,1179
X	EXCEPT	1184,1186-1188,1191-1192,1197,1200,1202-1203,1207-1209
		1213 *1204-1205,1212, SW1000M BUILT 1980 1200 HP
Y	ACTUAL	1223,1227,1229 *1223 SW1000M BUILT 1980 1200 HP
Z	EXCEPT	1313 AA EXCEPT 1602-1605,1607
AB	ACTUAL	1783,1785,1792-1794,1796
AC	ACTUAL	1971,1973,1977-1978 AD EXCEPT 1984,1990
AE	EXCEPT	2026 AF EXCEPT 2085-2086,2091 AG EXCEPT 2185
AH	ACTUAL	2430-2431,2433-2435,2438,2443-2444,2451,2454,2457-2458
AI	ACTUAL	2451,2453-2454,2457-2460,2464,2467,2469,2475,2480
AJ	ACTUAL	2496,2498-2500,2503,2508 AK ACTUAL 2513-2514,2516,2519
AL	ACTUAL	2524-2525,2530-2531,2534-2540,2542,2545-2547,2550,2552
AM	ACTUAL	2553,2558,2562-2563,2565-2566,2568,2570-2571
AN	EXCEPT	2566 AO EXCEPT 2585,2587-2588
AP	ACTUAL	2588,2593,2599-2603,2607-2610,2612
AQ	ACTUAL	2609,2615,2621,2631-2632,2637-2638,2640-2642,2645
		2652-2653,2656,2658-2659 AR EXCEPT 2682,2684-2685

```
AS EXCEPT  2692 AT EXCEPT 2703-2704,2723,2757  AU EXCEPT 2812-2813
AV EXCEPT  2958,2960,2964  AW EXCEPT 2968,2988,2990  AX EXCEPT 2973
AY EXCEPT  3028,3031-3032,3036,3038,3042-3043,3049
AZ ACTUAL  3054,3056,3060,3067  BA EXCEPT 3063,3065,3077
BB ACTUAL  3071-3072,3075,3080  BC EXCEPT 3083  BD EXCEPT 3089-3090
BE EXCEPT  3093-3094  BF EXCEPT 3095,3099,3102,3106,3108,3112
BG EXCEPT  3122,3124-3125  BH EXCEPT 3146,3178
BI ACTUAL  3131-3133,3136,3141-3142,3145,3149-3151  BJ EXCEPT 3282
BK EXCEPT  3316,3318,3325  BL EXCEPT 3334  BM EXCEPT 3388
BN EXCEPT  3401  BO EXCEPT 3416  BP EXCEPT 3449,3451-3453
BQ EXCEPT  3454-3455  BR EXCEPT 3484  BS EXCEPT 3502  BT EXCEPT 3534
BU ACTUAL  3534,3550,3556  BV EXCEPT 3556-3557,3559-3563
BW EXCEPT  3568  BX EXCEPT 3658  3592  BY EXCEPT 3615-3617
BZ EXCEPT  3632,3636,3638  CA EXCEPT 3647  CB EXCEPT 3658
CC EXCEPT  3623  CD EXCEPT 3680  CE EXCEPT 3691  CF EXCEPT 3725,3731
CG EXCEPT  3750  CH EXCEPT 3761-3762  CI EXCEPT 3799
CJ ACTUAL  4046-4047,4049,4053,4056  CK ACTUAL 4059,4063-4066
CL EXCEPT  4123,4126,4129-4132,4135,4137-4141,4143,4146-4162
CM EXCEPT  4124-4125,4127-4128,4130,4132-4134,4136,4141-4142
           4144-4145,4159  CN EXCEPT 4207,4211
CO EXCEPT  4218,4220,4224,4227-4228,4233-4234,4237-4238,4240,4242-
           4243,4245,4246,4248-4249,4252,4255-4258,4261,4264
CP ACTUAL  4220,  EXCEPT 4224,4228,4233-4234,4237-4238,4242-4243
                  4245-4246,4248-4249,4256,4258,4264
CQ EXCEPT  4269-4270,4273,4275-4276,4278,4280,4283,4285-4286
           4288-4289,4292-4293,4302,4306-4310
CR EXCEPT  4314,4318-4320  CS EXCEPT 4403,4407
CT EXCEPT  4406,4408-4416,4418,4420-4424,4426,4428,4430-4431
           4433-4440,4442,4444-4452
CU ACTUAL  4462-4464,4467,4471-4472,4474,4476,4478-4479,4483
           4490,4494,4497-4498,4501-4502
CV ACTUAL  4522,4528,4546,4548,4550-4555,4559
CW EXCEPT  4587-4588,4590-4591,4595  CX EXCEPT 4601
CY EXCEPT  4819  CZ EXCEPT 4808,4820
DA EXCEPT  4847,4851-4852,4856,4858,4866-4868,4870,4872
           *4873 BUILT 1971  DB EXCEPT 5010-5011
DC EXCEPT  5036  DD EXCEPT 5047  DE EXCEPT 5065,5069
DF EXCEPT  5358-5359,5362,5366,5368-5370
DG EXCEPT  5378-5381,5383  DH EXCEPT 5387-5388
DI EXCEPT  5389-5392,5395-5396  DJ EXCEPT 5399,5402,5408,5412
DK EXCEPT  5504-5507,5511,5513-5514,5519  DL EXCEPT 5504
DM ACTUAL  5504,5511,5513-5514,5519  DN EXCEPT 5511,5523,5530
DO EXCEPT  5530,5532,5536  DP EXCEPT 5561-5563,5565
DQ EXCEPT  5572,5575-5576,5580,5582,5585-5586
DR EXCEPT  5611,5613,5619-5622,5625-5626,5628,5631,5633
           5637-5639,5641,5644
DS EXCEPT  5650,5653,5656,5664,5666-5668,5670,5675
DT EXCEPT  5684-5686,5694,5696
DU ACTUAL  5703-5707,5711,5713-5716,5718,5721-5723,5726
           5728,5731,5735
```

```
DV   ACTUAL   5816-5817,5819,5823-5824,5828-5829,5835-5836,5838,5840
               5842-5843,5846,5852,5856,5859,5862,5865-5876
DW   EXCEPT   5870,5874,5877,5879   DX ACTUAL 5884,5887,5891
DY   EXCEPT   5967,5970,5981,5995   DZ EXCEPT 6014   EA EXCEPT 6143
EF   EXCEPT   6244   EG EXCEPT 6658   EH ACTUAL 6701,6724,6736
EI   ACTUAL   6793,6795,6797,6799-6801,6803,6806-6811,6813,6815
               6817,6819,6821-6823,6828
EJ   ACTUAL   6819,6836,6847,6856,6858,6866-6867,6871,6873,6877-6878
               6880-6888   EK EXCEPT 6889-6890
EL   EXCEPT   6932-6933   EM ACTUAL 7005,7009,7022   EN EXCEPT 7101
EO   ACTUAL   7240-7246,7255,7264   EP EXCEPT 7255,7258,7264,7267-7268
EQ   EXCEPT   7303,7315,7317-7318,7329-7330,7340-7342,7344,7347
               7351,7353,7355,7361,7369,7372-7373,7381-7382,7384
ER   ACTUAL   7401,7406,7411-7415   ES ACTUAL 7465,7468,7465-7478
               7481-7482,7484,7488,7489-7498   EXCEPT 7503,7505,7507
               7509,7511,7515-7516,7518-7522,7524,7528-7529,7534
ET   ACTUAL   7500,7502,7504-7509   EU EXCEPT 7612,7618
EV   EXCEPT   7643-7644,7646,7650,7653   EW EXCEPT 7673
EX   EXCEPT   7755,7760-7762   EY EXCEPT 7776,7786,7797
EZ   EXCEPT   7842   FA EXCEPT 7846,7854   FB EXCEPT 7875-7878
FC   EXCEPT   7941,7955,7957   FD ACTUAL 7960-7962,7966
FE   ACTUAL   8002,8010-8014,8016-8017,8019,8022-8024,8028-8230,8032
               8035,8038-8039   FF ACTUAL 8002,8040,8045,8051-8052
FG   ACTUAL   8041,8044,8047,8057,8059-8061,8063,8068,8074
FH   ACTUAL   8077-8079,8088,8090   FI EXCEPT 8111,8117,8168,8170
FJ   EXCEPT   8243,8252-8253,8260,8264,8273-8274,8278,8280,8282
               8284-8286,8289-8291,8294,8298
FK   ACTUAL   8307-8316,8318,8320-8322,8328
FL   ACTUAL   8324,8326,8372-8374   FM ACTUAL 8329,8331,8335-8337,8341
FN   EXCEPT   8353   FO EXCEPT 8364,8366,8369
FP   ACTUAL   8307-8316,8318,8320-8322,8328
FQ   EXCEPT   8502,8507,8509,8511,8525
FR   ACTUAL   8543,8555-85566,8558,8561,8563-8565,8567-8572,8574-8575
               8577   FS EXCEPT 8608,8617,8651,8677
FT   ACTUAL   8601-8605,8607-8608,8610,8613-8618,8621,8624,8628
               8629,8631-8632,8634-8635
FU   EXCEPT   8656,8658-8659,8673,8686,8690,8699,8712,8727
FV   EXCEPT   8822,8834   FW ACTUAL 9000,9002,9004-9005,9011-9012,9014
               9020,9026,9029   FX ACTUAL 9065-9066,9069,9071-9072,9074
               9078,9085,9088,9090,9092-9099   FY EXCEPT 9118,9154
FZ   EXCEPT   9186   HA ACTUAL 9226,9231,9234,9238-9239,9242,9256,9259
HB   EXCEPT   9274   HC EXCEPT 9265-9269
HD   ACTUAL   9288,9303,9310-9311,9313
HE   ACTUAL   9291,9295,9298-9299
HF   ACTUAL   9371-9372,9374,9378,9380-9381,9387,9393,9396,9403-9404
HG   ACTUAL   9564,9575,9581   HH ACTUAL 9670,9673,9675-9676
               9683-9684,9686-9687,9689-9690,9695,9697
```

UNION RR URR Hall PA

1-9	9	GM	SW1500	1500	1972-1973
10-33	24	GM	MP15DC	1500	1974-1977
565-573	6	GM	SW9	1200	1951-1953
	39				

UNITED RR HIST SOC NEW JERSEY Middletown NJ

16-17-RV	2	GE	70-TON	600	1951-1954
25-NYS&W	1	WHIT	25-TON	150	1942
26	1	FM	H12-44	1200	
206-NYS&W	1	ALCO	S2	1000	1942
412-B&O	1	BALD	VO1000	1000	1945
418,424-C&NW	2	GM	F7A	1500	1949
436,438-ERIE	2	GM	SW9	1200	1952
492-RDG	1	ALCO	RS3	1600	1952
576,578-LV	2	GM	F7A	1500	1949
834-835-ERIE	2	GM	E8A	2250	1953-1952
958-AMT	1	GE	E60CP	6000	1974
1523-1524-CNJ	2	GM	GP7	1500	1952
3372-NJDOT	1	GE	U34CH	3400	1971
4253,4326-PRR/B&O	2	GM	E8A	2250	1952-1953
4877,4879-PRR *	2	PRR	ELECTRIC	4620	1939
7000-PRR	1	GM	GP9	1750	1956
	24	* GG1 MODELS			

UPPER MERION & PLYMOUTH RR UMP Conshohocken PA

9007	1	GM	SW9	1200	1956
9009	1	GM	SW7	1200	1950
	2				

U S ARMY TRANSPORTATION MUSEUM Fort Eustis VA

607	1	LIMA	STEAM	2-8-0	1945
1811	1	GM	MRS1	1600	1955
V1923 *	1	VULC	STEAM	0-6-0	1946
	3	* NARROW GAUGE			

UTAH CENTRAL RY Ogden UT

82-83	2	GM	SW1500	1500	1974

UTAH RY UTAH Martin UT + RENTALS

2000-2009	10	GM	GP38	2000	
2959,3108	2	GM	SD35	2500	
9001-9011	11	BL	SD40-2	3000	1991
9012	1	BL	SD45-2	3600	1991
9013	1	BL	F45	3600	1983
	25				

RENTALS				
1010-1073 GWRX	7	GM	GP10	1850
2033,2040 NREX	2	GM	SD20	2000
	9			

UTAH STATE RR MUSEUM Ogden UT

26-UP	1 GE	GAS-TURBINE	8500	1958
223-D&RG	1 GRAN	STEAM	2-8-0	1881
1236-1237-USAF	2 GE	44-TON	400	1953
1606-USAF	1 GE	80-TON	480	1953
3769-SP	1 GM	GP9E	1750	1957
6916-UP	1 GM	DDA40X	6600	1969
7277-USAF	1 ALCO	S1	660	1941
	8			

VALDOSTA RY VR Valdosta GA

184	1 GM	GP7	1500	1950
1284	1 GM	GP10	1850	1957
	2			

VALLEY RR VALE Essex CT

40	1 ALCO	STEAM	2-8-2	1920
97	1 ALCO	STEAM	2-8-0	1926
103	1 BALD	STEAM	2-6-2	1925
0900-0901,7145	3 GE	80-TON	500	1947-1935
1246	1 MLW	STEAM	4-6-2	1946
	7	DIVERSE OWNERS AT ESSEX, OLD SAYBROOK RHODE ISLAND ETC.		

VANCOUVER WHARVES RY Vancouver BC

820-821,823	3 ALST	SW1500	1500	1995-1996
822	1 GM	SW1200	1200	1966
	4			

VANDALIA RR VRRC Vandalia IL

104	1 GM	SW9	1200	1950

VENTURA COUNTY RY VCY Oxnard CA

7,9,11	3 ALCO	S6	1000	1956
100	1 GM	GP9	1750	1980
1200	1 GM	SW1200	1200	1985
	5			

VERDE CANYON RR Clarksdale AZ

1510,1512	2 GM	FP7A	1500	1953

VERMONT NORTHERN RY

511-515	5 GM	GP35R	2000	

VERMONT RY VTR Rutland VT

201-202	2 GM	GP38-2	2000	1972-1974
301	1 GM	GP40	3000	1966
801	1 GM	GP18 *	1800	1961
	4	* REMOTE CONTROL		

VIA RAIL CANADA VIA

202,204	2 GM	SW1000	1000	1966-1967
6300,6302,6304				
6307,6308,6311				
6313	7 ALST	FP9A	1800	1984
6400-6458 *	57 GM	F40PH-2	3000	1986-1989
6902,6905,6907				
6914,6917,6919				
6921	7 BBD	LRC	2750	1980-1984
	73	* EXCEPT 6447		

VIRGINIA & TRUCKEE RR VTRR Virginia City NV

8 *	1	BALD	STEAM	2-6-2	1907
29	1	BALD	STEAM	2-8-0	1916
30	1	SP	STEAM	0-6-0	1919
	3	* FEATHER RIVER SHORT LINE-OWNER			

VIRGINIA MUSEUM OF TRANSPORTATION VMT Roanoke VA

-BRS	1	WHIT	35-TON	340	1940
1-CEL	1	PORT	STEAM	0-4-0F	1944
D3-W&LE	1	GM	NW2	1000	1941
3-VC	1	PORT	DIESEL	B-B	1944
4-VGN	1	BALD	STEAM	0-8-0	1910
6-N&W	1	BALD	STEAM	2-8-0	1897
10-CW	1	ALCO	T6	1000	1959
34-EJL	1	BALD	STEAM	0-6-0T	1923
135-V	1	GE	ELECTRIC	3300	1956
197-COFG	1	GM	SD7	1500	1951
200-MEAD	1	PLYM	DIE-MECH-CAT	70	1935
300-N&W	1	ALCO	RS3	1600	1955
521N&W,532-NKP	2	GM	GP9	1750	1958-1959
611-N&W	1	N&W	STEAM	4-8-4	1950
686-PCZ	1	GE	42-TON	PANA-MULE	1914
763-NKP	1	LIMA	STEAM	2-8-4	1944
1002-RF&P	1	GM	E8A	2250	1949
1009-WAB	1	GM	E8A	2250	1951
1135-N&W	1	ALCO	C630	3000	1967
1776-N&W	1	GM	SD45	3600	1970
2289-SEA	1	GM	SW7	1200	1951
4919-PRR	1	PRR	ELECTRIC	4620	1942
5828-C&O	1	GM	GP7	1500	1952
6670-EL	1	GM	SDP45	3600	1969
9914-N&W	1	FM	SLUG H24	0	1976
	25	EXCLUDES SLUG			

VIRGINIA RY EXPRESS - NORTHERN VIRGINIA TRANSPORTATION COMM

				NVTC	Arlington VA
V01-V10	10	BL	GP35-2C	2300	1991-1992
V20-V21	2	BL	GP40-2C	3000	1993
V22-V23	2	ALST	GP40PH2	3000	1995
	14				

VIRGINIA SOUTHERN RR VSRR Keysville VA

174,900	2	GM	GP9	1750	1954-1963
2185	1	GM	GP7	1500	1979
	3				

WABASH CENTRAL RR Bluffton IN

3	1	GM	GP20	2000	
6	1	GM	GP10	1850	
	2				

WABUSH LAKE RY Wabush LABRADOR CANADA

903,907-911	6	MLW	RS18	1800	1964

WALKERSVILLE SOUTHERN RR WS Walkersville MD

1	1 PLYM	JLB-18	160	1942
2	1 DAV	25-TON	175	1939
3	1 WHIT	45-TON	300	1942

3

WALKING HORSE & EASTERN RR Shelbyville TN

806	1 GM	FP7A	1500	1951
1585	1 GM	NW2	1000	1948

2

WANAMAKER KEMPTON & SOUTHERN RR WKS Kempton PA

2	1 PORT	STEAM	0-4-0T	1920
65	1 PORT	STEAM	0-6-0T	1930
602	1 WHIT	70-TON	650	1944
7250	1 GE	45-TON	300	1942

4

WARREN & SALINE RIVER RR WSR Warren AR

538	1 GM	SW1200	1200	1980
539	1 GM	SW1	600	1949

2

WARREN & TRUMBULL RR Warren OH

52	1 GM	SW9	1200	1953

WATERLOO-ST JACOBS RY Waterloo ON

6305-6306	2 ALST	FP9A	1800	1983

WCTU RY WCTR White City OR

5117,5119	2 GE	70-TON	600	1951-1955

WELLSBORO & CORNING RR WCOR Wellsboro PA

800	1 GM	SW800	800	1950

WEST CHESTER RR West Chester PA

9	1 GE	65-TON	350	1940
3	1 ALCO	S2	1000	1949
99	1 GM	GP9	1750	1957
1803	1 MLW	RS18U	1800	1958

4

WEST COAST EXPRESS BCTS Vancouver BC

901-905	5 GM	F59PHI	3200	1995

WEST COAST RY HERITAGE PK Squamish BC

2-PGE	1 BALD	STEAM	2-6-2T	1910
16-CL	1 BALD	STEAM	2-8-2	1929
74-CN	1 GE	80-TON	500	1947
183-GN	1 ALCO	RS1	1000	1951
551-PGE	1 GE	65-TON	500	1948
561-PGE	1 MLW	RSC3	1000	1951
941-BCER	1 GE	70-TON	600	1949
960-BCER	1 A-GE	ELECTRIC		1912
4069-CP	1 GM	FP7A	1500	1952
4097-D&H	1 ALCO	RS3	1600	1952
4459-CP	1 GM	F7B	1500	1953
6503-CP	1 MLW	S3	660	1951
8019-CN	1 MLW	S4	1000	1952

13

WESTERN KENTUCKY RY Clay KY

1338,1342.1347	3	GM	GP18	1800	1960-1961
3419	1	GM	GP10	1750	1976
	4				

WESTERN MARYLAND SCENIC RR WMSR Cumberland MD

734-WM	1	BALD	STEAM	2-8-0	1916
2131,2175	2	GM	GP30	2250	1963
	3				

WESTERN RAIL ROAD WRRC New Braunfels TX

534,1007	2	GM	SW1	600	1943-1942
9617	1	GM	SW1200	1200	1955
	3				

WESTERN RAIL SWITCHING Richmond CA

201-202	2	GM	SW1200	1200	1980

WESTERN RY MUSEUM WRM Suisun City CA

L.2-NASM	1	PORT	44-TON	300	1942
2-SCLC	1	WHIT	25-TON	150	1926
30-CCT	1	GE	70-TON	600	1947
78-SPCC	1	PORT	STEAM	0-4-0T	1906
94-WP	1	ALCO	STEAM	4-6-0	1909
334-WP	1	ALCO	STEAM	2-8-2	1929
407-KCC	1	GE	ELECTRIC	1500	1947
502-VE	1	GE	44-TON	380	1945
612,614-USN	2	ALCO	MRS1	1600	1953
652,654-SN	2	A-GE	ELECTRIC	1000	1928-1930
700-UCC	1	GE	ELECTRIC	1000	1926
712-SN	1	GM	GP7	1500	1953
771-KMC	1	GE	ELECTRIC	1500	1955
917D-WP	1	GM	F7A	1500	1950
1001-STL	1	OT	ELECTRIC	260	1910
2978-RDL	1	LIMA	STEAM	2-TRUCK	1918
	18				

WESTERN VANCOUVER ISLAND INDUSTRIAL HERITAGE SOCIETY
Port Alberni BC

1-WIW	1	BUDA	14-TON	140	1928
2-WL	1	LIMA	STEAM	2-TRUCK	1912
7-CL	1	BALD	STEAM	2-8-2T	1929
11-AP&P	1	GE	45-TON	300	1942
107-AP	1	PLYM	8-TON	100	1927
8427-CP	1	MLW	RS3	1600	1948
	6				

WEST ISLE LINE Alpaugh CA

3399	1	GM	GP9E	1750	1971

WEST MICHIGAN RR WJ Paw Paw MI

203	1	ALCO	RS3	1200	1952

WEST TENNESSEE RR WTNN Trenton TN

1852-1853,2054	3	ALCO	RSD12	1500	1956
3510,3560,3576	3	MLW	M420	2000	1973-1976
	6				

WEST TEXAS & LUBBOCK RR WTLR Lubbock TX

91,105,113,118	4 GM	GP7M		1750	

WEST VIRGINIA NORTHERN RR WVN Kingwood WV

50,52	2 GM	SW1200	1200	1955-1960	

INCLUDES KINGWOOD NORTHERN

WHEELING & LAKE ERIE RY WE Brewster OH

1301	1 GM	GP35	2500	1965	
2645,2650-2655					
2600-2662,2664					
2666,2679,2691					
2695,2699,2703					
2705-2706,2708-					
2709,2712-2713					
3045	24 GM	GP35	2500	1965	
3016,3034,3046					
3048-3049,3067-					
3068,3073,3102					
4001,4003,4016					
4018,4025	14 GM	SD40	3000	1966-1971	
1203	1 GM	SW1200	1200	1979	
1501-1502	2 GM	SW1500	1500	1971	
	42				

WHETSTONE VALLEY EXPRESS Milbank SD

992	1 GE	44-TON	300	1942	

WHITE MOUNTAIN CENTRAL RR WMCR Lincoln NH

1	1 PORT STEAM		0-4-0	1930	
4	1 HEIS STEAM		2-TRUCK	1929	
5	1 LIMA STEAM		2-TRUCK	1919	
5	1 BALD STEAM		2-4-2	1906	
6	1 CLIM STEAM		2-TRUCK	1921	
	5				

WHITE PASS & YUKON WPY (3'Gauge) Skagway AK

DUCHESS *	1 BALD STEAM		0-6-0T		1878
73	1 BALD STEAM		2-8-2	1947	
90-97	8 GE	EXP/80-TON	890	1954-1963	
96	1 BALD STEAM		2-8-0		
98-100	3 GE	EXP/80-TON	990	1966	
101,103-104					
106-107	5 MLW	DL535E	1200	1969-1999	
108-110	3 MLW	DL535E	1200	1971	
114	1 MLW	DL535E	1200	1982	
	23	* DISPLAY NOT OWNED BY WP&Y			

WHITE RIVER RY Flippin AR

2089-USA	1 ALCO	RSX4	1600	1953	

WHITEWATER VALLEY RR WVRR Connersville IN

6-EBT	1 BALD STEAM		0-6-0	1907	
8-M&W	1 GE	70-TON	600	1946	
11-SWPC	1 VULC STEAM		0-4-0T	1924	
25-CUT	1 LH	SW7.5	750	1951	

WVRR Cont

100-FSM	1	BALD	STEAM	2-6-2	1919
210-C&HC	1	GE	70-TON	600	1946
320-B&O	1	GM	SW12	1200	1950
709-ARMC	1	LH	SW10	1000	1950
2561-JJ	1	PLYM	32-TON	GAS	1931
9339-NYC	1	ALCO	S1	660	1948
	10				

WICHITA TILLMAN & JACKSON RY WTJR Wichita Falls TX

2058,2086,4364					
4367,4370,4443					
4451,4454	8	GM	GP7	1500	1954-1973

WILLAMETTE & PACIFIC RR WPRR Albany OR

101-102	2	GMNW	SLUGS	0	1986-1988
1201-1204	4	GM	SW1200M	1200	1953
1501	1	GM	SD7	1500	1952
1551	1	GM	SW1500	1500	1969
1801-1803	3	GM	GP9	1800	1956-1959
1851-1855	5	GM	SD9	1800	1953-1955
2301-2317	17	GM	GP39-2	2300	1974
3001-3002	2	GM	GP40P-2U	3000	1969
	33	EXCLUDES SLUGS			
		INCLUDES PORTLAND & WESTERN			

RENTALS

4364,4433 LLWX	2	GM	SD9	1800	1953-1955

WILLAMETTE VALLEY RY WVR Independence OR

3859	1	GM	GP9	1750	1978
2501-2503	3	GM	GP35	2500	1979
	4				

WILMINGTON & WESTERN RY WWRC/WILM Wilmington DE

37	1	ALCO	STEAM	2-8-2T	1924
58	1	BALD	STEAM	0-6-0	1907
92	1	CLC	STEAM	2-6-0	1910
98	1	ALCO	STEAM	4-4-0	1909
114,8404	2	GM	SW1	600	1942
	6				

WILMINGTON TERMINAL RR WTRY Wilmington NC

1201-1202	2	GM	SW1200	1200	1966
1801	1	FM	H16-44	1600	
	3				

WINAMAC SOUTHERN RY WSRY Kokomo IN

1754	1	GM	GP9	1750	1959

WINCHESTER & WESTERN RR - NEW JERSEY DIVISION WW

Bridgeton NJ

120	1	ALCO	SLUG	0	1979
459,475,517,520	4	GM	GP9	1750	1956-1958
575,752	2	BL	GP10	1800	1978
732,811	2	GM	GP9	1750	1956-1959
	8	EXCLUDES SLUG			

WINCHESTER & WESTERN RR - VIRGINIA DIVISION WW Gore VA

107	1 ALCO	SLUG	0	
403,445	2 GM	GP10	1850	1979
498,709	2 GM	GP9	1750	1955
	4 EXCLUDES SLUG			

WINDSOR & HANTSPORT RY WHRC Hantsport NS

8019,8026-8027				
8034,8036-8038				
8041,8042,8046	10 MLW	RS23	1000	1959-1961

WINIFREDE RR WNFR Winifrede WV

13	1 GM	SW1500	1500	1966

WINNIPESAUKEE SCENIC RR Meridith NH

2	1 GE	44-TON	360	1942
302	1 GM	GP7	1500	1950
1008	1 ALCO	S1	660	1949
	3			

WIREGRASS CENTRAL RR WGCR Enterprise AL

2876	1 GM	GP9	1750	
2881-2883,2886	4 GM	GP38	2000	1966
	5			

WISCASSET WATERVILLE & FARMINGTON RY MUSEUM (2'Gauge) Alna ME

9	1 PORT	STEAM	0-4-4T	1891
10	1 VULC	DIESEL-HY	12-TON	1904
51	1 BRKV	BSA-2-TON	25	1946
52	1 PLYM	15-TON	DIES-HYD	1977
	4			

WISCONSIN & SOUTHERN RR WSOR Horicon WI

10A,10C	2 GM	E9A	2400	1955-1956
701,751-752				
2002	4 GM	GP7R	1500	1981-1973
1201-1202	2 GM	SW1200	1200	1954
2001-2003,4118	4 GM	GP20	2000	1962
2008-2009,2012-				
2016	6 GM	SD20R	2000	1978
3501,6547,6552				
6579,6595,6604				
6620,6668	8 GM	GP35	2500	1964
4326	1 GM	GP7	1500	1972
4490-4494	4 GM	GP9R	1750	1978
4493	1 GM	GP18	1800	1978
4513,4533,4535	3 GM	GP10	1850	
6622-6646	5 GM	SD18	1800	
	40			

WISCONSIN CENTRAL WC Rosemont IL - RENTALS

1	1 GM	SW1	600	
582-590	9 GM	SDL39	2300	1969
700,703,711				
713	4 GM	GP30	2250	1963
719	1 GM	GP30	2250	1963
726	1 GM	GP35	2500	1964

WC Cont

1231-1237	7	GM	SW1200	1200	1965-1966
1550-1571	22	GM	SW1500	1500	1968-1970
1702	1	GM	GP9	1750	1956
2052-2060	5	GM	GP35M	2000	1964
2500	1	GM	SD35	2500	1965
2551-2558	7	GM	GP35	2500	1964
3002-3024	15	GM	GP40	3000	1970
4002-4013	6	GM	GP35M	2000	1964
4501,4505,4508	3	GM	GP9	1750	1956-1957
6497-6556,7495-					
7589,9501-9539	111	GM	SD45 *	3600	1967-1971
6650-6656	7	GM	FP45	3600	1982-1983
	201		* 9511 IS SDP45		

INCLUDES FOX VALLEY & WESTERN

WMATA-WASHINGTON METROPOLITAN AREA TRANSIT AUTHORITY WMAT
Washington DC

L001-L002	2	GE	44-TON	440 *	1943-1953
L011-L012	2	GE	45-TON	440	1944
L021	1	DAV	44-TON	440	1953
	5		* L002 IS 400HP		

WYOMING-COLORADO RR WTCO Laramie WY/Vale OR

6083	1	GM	SD7	1500	

YADKIN VALLEY RR YVRR Rural Hall NC

204,206	2	GM	GP9	1750	1957
2881-2883,2886					
3614	5	GM	GP38	2000	1966
	7				

YOLO SHORTLINE RR YSLR Woodland CA

50	1	GE	50-TON	360	1939
101	1	ALCO	S1	660	1942
131-133	3	GM	GP9R	2000	1958-1959
1233	1	BALD	STEAM	0-6-0	1918
	6				

YORKRAIL YKR York PA

1600,1602,1604					
1606	4	GM	GP16	1600	1981
1754	1	GM	GP9	1750	1956
	5				

YOSEMITE MOUNTAIN SUGAR PINE RR (3'Gauge) Fish Camp CA

5	1	VULC	10-TON	200	1935
10,15-WL	2	LIMA	STEAM	3-TRUCK	1928-1913
	3				

YUMA VALLEY RY Yuma AZ

41	1	WHIT	30-TON	180	1941
52	1	DAV	44-TON	380	1952
	2				

Numbers	Owner	Qty	Builder	Model	HP	Year
700-739	LMS	40	GE	DASH8-40CW	4000	1994
1003-1018		4	CR	MT4	0	1957
1100-1128		29	CR	MT6	0	1978-1979
1600-1699		100	GM	GP15-1	1500	1979
1900-1966		56	GE	B23-7	2250	1978
1967-2023		50	GE	B23-7	2250	1979
2030-2040	MGA	11	GE	B23-7R	2250	1972
2557-2580		24	GM	SD70	4000	1998
2801-2816		11	GE	B23-7	2250	1977
3275-3279	RDG	5	GM	GP40-2	3000	1973
3280-3312		31	GM	GP40-2	3000	1977
3313-3345		31	GM	GP40-2	3000	1978
3346-3385		40	GM	GP40-2	3000	1979
3386-3403		17	GM	GP40-2	3000	1980
4020-4022		3	GM	E8A	2250	1951
4100-4127		28	GM	SD80MAC	5000	1996
4128-4129	EMD	2	GM	SD80MAC	5000	1997
4130-4144		15	GM	SD70MAC	4000	1998
5000-5059		55	GE	B36-7	3750	1983
5060-5089		30	GE	DASH8-40B	4000	1988
5500-5574		75	GM	SD60M	3800	1993
5575-5578		4	GM	SD60I	3800	1994
5579-5654		76	GM	SD60I	3800	1995
6000-6021		22	GE	DASH8-39C	3900	1986
6025-6049		25	GE	DASH8-40C	4000	1989
6050-6099		50	GE	DASH8-40CW	4000	1990
6100-6149		50	GE	DASH8-40CW	4000	1991
6150-6229		80	GE	DASH8-40CW	4000	1993
6230-6285		56	GE	DASH8-40CW	4000	1994
6358-6440		81	GM	SD40-2	3000	1977
6441-6482		42	GM	SD40-2	3000	1978
6483-6524		42	GM	SD40-2	3000	1979
6550-6599		50	GE	C30-7A	3100	1984
6610-6619		10	GE	DASH8-32C	3200	1984
6620-6644		25	GE	C36-7	3750	1985
6654-6666	EL	11	GM	SD45-2	3600	1972
6700-6739		40	GM	SD50	3500	1983
6740-6779		40	GM	SD50	3500	1984
6780-6804		25	GM	SD50	3600	1985
6805-6834		30	GM	SD50	3600	1986
6840-6842		3	GM	SD60	3800	1985
6843-6867		25	GM	SD60	3800	1989
6925-6959	PC	34	GM	SD38	2000	1970

6960-6999		40	JUN	SD40-2	3000	1966-1971
7600,7604	CSX	2	GM	GP38	2000	1967
7656-7659	LV	4	GM	GP38	2000	1971
7670-7746	PC	66	GM	GP38	2000	1970-1969
7868-7939	PC	63	GM	GP38	2000	1971
8040-8162	PC	120	GM	GP38-2	2000	1973
8163-8180		17	GM	GP38-2	2000	1977
8181-8255		74	GM	GP38-2	2000	1978
8256-8281		24	GM	GP38-2	2000	1979
9400-9422	RDG	21	GM	SW1001	1000	1973
9503-9507	PC	5	GM	SW1500	1500	1971
9510-9559	PC	30	GM	SW1500	1500	1972
9560-9583	PC	19	GM	SW1500	1500	1973
9584-9588	PC	3	GM	SW1500	1500	1970
9589-9599	RDG	9	GM	SW1500	1500	1966
9606,9607	IU	2	GM	SW1500	1500	1966,1969
9609-9610	IU	2	GM	SW1500	1500	1972
9611-9620	RDG	5	GM	SW1500	1500	1969

1,951   EXCEPT   SLUGS